LUNACY
The Best of the Cornell Lunatic

Edited by Joey Green

Lunatic Press
Los Angeles

The officers, staff, and alumni of the *Cornell Lunatic* have generously granted permission to reprint in this book the copyrighted works cited on pages 208-212.

Nothing in this book necessarily reflects any of the opinions, ideas, hopes, dreams, or delusions of the staff of the *Cornell Lunatic*, the only award-winning humor magazine at Cornell University. Any similarities to real or imagined people and places are either coincidental or intentional. Offended readers be forewarned: financial constraints preclude our capacity to monetarily reciprocate any damages claimed. In other words, lighten up already. This book will self-destruct in ten seconds. Happiness is buying a copy of this book for a friend, or two copies for yourself. Requests for advertising or subscription information, submissions, letters to the editor, junk mail, undergarments, speaker wire, or breaded pork should be sent to: Cornell Lunatic, Box 56, Willard Straight Hall, Cornell University, Ithaca, NY 14853.

Published by Lunatic Press, Los Angeles
www.lunaticpress.com

Cover illustration © 1983, 2008 by B.K. Taylor.

Book design by Joey Green

Distributed by Independent Publishers Group
PRINTED IN THE UNITED STATES OF AMERICA

Library of Congress Control Number: 2007906748

ISBN: 0-9772590-3-X
ISBN-13: 978-0-9772590-38

10 9 8 7 6 5 4 3 2 1

For Jerry Buttwater

CORNELL LUNATIC

CAMPUS HUMOR MAGAZINE

Cornell Lunatic founded 1978
Owned and Published by the Cornell Lunatic at Cornell University

CoNTenTS

Suicidal Duck in "Duck Season"

Sweet Days of Lunacy

At the mention of the *Cornell Lunatic*, this withered old man's ears perk up. Yes, I remember every moment I spent with that naughty, naughty rag. We were a stylish bunch, we were. They said we made Cornell laugh—its students, its teachers, even the useless administrators. I'd say we made Cornell live.

Now here I lie with a diseased liver, dictating to my young personal assistant, Bunni. I will tell you about the *Lunatic*, yes.

The night I joined the *Lunatic* was the night of the Joanhart Ball, a quite lovely event. I was sipping port when I overheard a rowdy, yet smashingly dressed group of sophisticates. They were speaking in jest about a lady in attendance who simply was dressed wretchedly. Joining in the conversation, I quipped, "She seems of the type who would purchase eighteen-button gloves, then storm back into the store later, demanding the missing fifteen buttons," to which there was a response of uproarious laughter. "It appears that her tailor's mind is twisted, probably from the use of lower-class pharmaceutical products—if she even has a tailor," I added. We all had a jolly good laugh. Then a young man named Maurice, who was whiter than the shoes I wear after Memorial Day, asked me if I would be interested in writing for the *Cornell Lunatic*. I replied that I would, if he would first tie a piece of asparagus in a Windsor knot around his neck, whilst singing "Polly Wolly Doodle." Maurice complied, to which we cheered and then toasted to the future of the *Lunatic*.

O, the humor we wrote. Scandalous. Scathing. We mocked everything respected about the institution of Cornell. In a hilarious series of caricatures, we depicted the president of Cornell as an aged Russian peasant woman, wearing nothing but a babushka over her head. Maurice penned an extremely witty story about the Dean, who wore a white bow tie to a black tie affair. After attempting to dye the tie with Cabernet Sauvignon, the president's wife believed that he was bleeding and then swiftly fainted, face-first into a platter of assorted international cheeses. Just thinking about that story makes me emit a hearty guffaw.

And our pranks—they were the pièce de résistance to a grand meal. When it was icy on Buffalo street, we would pitch pennies into the street, then watch the students who could not afford luxurious off-campus housing scramble for them. They would inevitably slip and take tumbles down the hill, sometimes being caught under the wheels of Hansom carriages. It was all delightful fun, I'd say. On another occasion, we stole the chime masters' sheet music and replaced them with some absolutely miserable pieces by Schönberg; all day long, ladies held their mink stoles over their ears while we were amused by the pained reactions to the awful discord of the chimes.

The *Cornell Lunatic* is celebrating its 120th anniversary this year, and the quality of its humor today is just plain execrable. Deplorable. I have seen a daguerreotype of the current staff, and they are a ragtag gang, completely lacking in style and fashion sense. I wish to go now, as it is time for Bunni to make my pain go away.

What Is This Lunatic Crap?

BY JERRY C. BUTTWATER

You, dear friend, are a lunatic. You heard what I said. You're a lunatic. Oh, don't get all bent out of shape. Why is it that every time Jerry Buttwater opens his mouth, people get offended (and I get hospitalized)?

"Nice tits, babe." *Smack!*

"Can I buy you a drink, or do you just want the money?" *Pow!*

Do we live in a society so puritanical that it's impossible for me to pay someone a compliment without losing the right to come within one hundred yards of them? That's right—by calling you a "lunatic," Jerry Buttwater was trying to pay you a compliment.

"But how could you possibly be paying me a compliment?" you ask, "*The New Illustrated Webster's Dictionary of the English Language* says that this **lu•na•tic** (loó-nə-tik) you speak of is a noun that means 'insane person.' I know because I looked it up. I am not an insane person! And I'm not certain what a noun is, but I'm pretty sure I'm not one of those either!"

Yes, some might say that a lunatic is an insane person. These are probably the same individuals who conspire to create an environment where chicks are uncomfortable with their true feelings toward Jerry Buttwater. Instead of succumbing to my irresistible charms as they obviously long to do, they are forced to bottle up their raw animal lust. It's just like that book named after that Van Halen album.

My point is this: don't believe everything you read—whether it's a reference book or the liner notes to *Diver Down*. Of course, you may say, "Well, I'm reading *this*. Why should I believe you?" To this, I say shut up, smart-ass.

To be a lunatic is to be a free spirit—someone who is not afraid to operate outside the boundaries of what society deems "normal." Contrary to what Mr. Webster and his hired goons would like you to believe, this is not a bad thing. Let me give you an example. I seem to remember hearing about a bunch of guys up in Massachusetts who didn't like the way they were being treated by the British. They dressed up like Indians and threw a bunch of tea into the ocean. Lunatics? Most definitely. But were they insane? Hardly! Barry, Tom, Sib, Bradley, and Fran would go on to form Boston—arguably one of the finest rock quintets of 1978.

If you think about it, weren't all the great men (and chicks) of history lunatics? Just look at that guy who flew to Europe for the first time. You know who I'm talking about. His name sounds like that smelly cheese. Or that broad who discovered radium. Or Charleton Heston. Or all those people who pissed off the church.

Then, of course, there's good ol' Jerry B. himself. I refuse to be bound by the restraints of society. If Jerry Buttwater wants to grab a chick's breast then, by gosh, he grabs it. You'd think that such a lucky female would enjoy the refreshing straightforwardness and simplicity of my action. But, invariably, she is an avid reader of *Webster's*. Jerry B. barely has time to say, "Oh, I'm sorry, I thought that was a braille nametag," before he is pummeled into unconsciousness. But every lunatic pays a price for greatness at sometime. At least I'm not the radium chick.

Lastly, let's not forget the name of this fine publication you hold in your hands. (It's called the *Lunatic*. If you haven't figured that out by now, I take back everything I've said. You're a moron.) If you thought being a lunatic was such a terrible thing, then why did you lay down your hard-earned cash for this book? You could have put that money toward the new issue of *D-Cup* (good issue, by the way). I'll tell you why you bought this book. Because deep down, somewhere below your recesses and to the left of your cockles, you already *knew* what it means to be a lunatic. And by supporting Jerry Buttwater and his talented colleagues, you are being a lunatic—a free spirit—in your own way. Just keep away from my chicks—too many free spirits can kill the mood. Catch my drift?

So when Jerry Buttwater says, "You, dear friend, are a lunatic," you should be flattered by my use of the term "lunatic." It is a compliment. The word "dear," however, is meant as a scathing attack on your manhood, sissyboy.

THE TIMBERTOES

Winter was here. It was cold inside the Timbertoes' house. "What should we do to warm up?"

"Let's build a fire!"   "But we have no firewood left." "We already burned the kitchen table."

Father and Mother thought. Tommy thought too. But Tommy did not think fast enough.

Father unscrewed Tommy's arms. Mother made kindling from Tommy's hair. "What do we burn next?"

Chapter 1

Grow Up Already

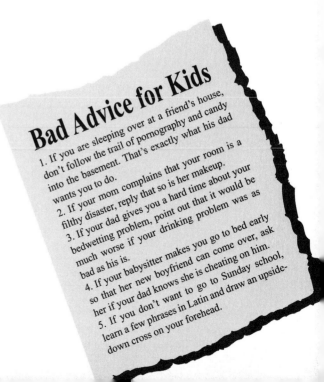

Bad Advice for Kids

1. If you are sleeping over at a friend's house, don't follow the trail of pornography and candy into the basement. That's exactly what his dad wants you to do.

2. If your mom complains that your room is a filthy disaster, reply that so is her makeup.

3. If your dad gives you a hard time about your bedwetting problem, point out that it would be much worse if your drinking problem was as bad as his is.

4. If your babysitter makes you go to bed early so that her new boyfriend can come over, ask her if your dad knows she is cheating on him.

5. If you don't want to go to Sunday school, learn a few phrases in Latin and draw an upside-down cross on your forehead.

emember the good old days, when you could walk into your local convenience store, slap a nickel on the counter, and receive not only a massive chunk of gum but some damn fine humor to boot? Well, I recently coughed up a nickel for a piece of gum (actually, I took five pennies out of the "Take-a-Penny, Give-a-Penny" box), little suspecting that what lay in store would chill me to the core.

While chomping away on the gum, I leisurely perused the comic portion of my treat to find the same recycled humor that I'd been enjoying since childhood. But the "fortune" beneath the comic read: "Don't accept rides from three-legged camels." At first glance, this might appear like an average, enigmatic, off-the-cuff quip. But, since I have the rest of the page to fill, let's take a closer look.

Why would Bazooka Joe urge us to refuse rides from three-legged camels? Camels are neither indigenous to the United States nor even a minor mode of transportation. And camels don't drive cars. So, if transportation safety isn't the issue here, then what is?

Why does the fortune specify three-legged camels rather than four-legged camels? That's right! Because they're fundamentally different from the norm. So, is Bazooka Joe telling us to reject three-legged camels just because they're a minority? Apparently so.

In the hands of the average child, this "fortune" has far-reaching consequences. Kids don't stop to think when they read Bazooka Joe—but the insidious seed has been planted. If kids are told to reject "minority camels," what's to stop them from discriminating against other out-groups?

In essence, Bazooka Joe is fostering intolerance among today's youth. Do we really want our children to read this trash? Bazooka Joe should be promoting equality, not prejudice. Where will it end? Let's put an end to this insanity. The penny candy counter should not be a forum for mind control.

JACK AND THE BEAN STALK

The genre of the fairy tale is one of the best known and, unfortunately, one of the most insipid. As a tool of education, the fairy tale, because of its inherent simplicity, has limitless possibilities. If the instructive value of the fairy tale could be expressed in a more intelligent and comprehensive style, its didactic nature could further educate an already captive audience.

Many famous authors have told fairy tales in their own unique style. We researched such authors, and, unable to single out one example from our findings, compiled the following version of "Jack and the Bean Stalk."

CATCHER IN THE BEAN STALK

In the style of J.D. Salinger

I must have told you about this guy, Jack. I probably mentioned him before, I'm sure of it. He lived with his mother. I realize that's not the greatest living situation in the world. I know I could never do it. I'm really glad to be at school and to be independent and all. If there's one thing I hate, it's having to live with my mother. She never lets me do half the things I do now, like sitting around shooting the bull.

Anyway, I was telling you about Jack and his old lady. They lived in this tumble-down shack because they were poor. And I mean poor. Sometimes they wouldn't even get to eat. You know when you're broke you can always borrow money from someone in the dorm. I know I do. And you can always get something to eat. At least you can order a pizza or something, for Chrissake.

Jack and his mom didn't have any cash. All they had was this cow. At least they owned something aside from their tumble-down shack. I don't know why it had to be a cow. Can you imagine owning a cow? Or drinking milk from it? You wouldn't even know where it's been. I know I wouldn't drink it. What I like is soda or some kind of juice. You can keep your cow milk. I won't have anything that's not out of a bottle.

But Jack couldn't get enough of the stuff, being a growing boy and all. He drank it night and day. And the cow couldn't give Jack enough milk. I mean, cows can only make so much milk for a guy. Why Jack wanted to drink so much milk sure beats the hell out of me. All I can tell you is I'm glad as hell I don't have to drink cow's milk and live with my mother in the poorhouse like Jack.

BEANS AND TIME
In the style of Martin Heidegger

It therefore became the imperative project of the old woman (Mother-as-such) to begin a process that would lead to the acquisition of substance requisite to the organic maintenance of Jack (Being-the-son-of). Thus, the man (Dasein, Being there) was forced to make the non-phenomenal decision toward the cow (Moo-sein, Being-in-the-barn) consequent to its disposition. Mother-as-such possessed nothing of sensitivity or futurity, and presented the possibility of Steaks-for-a-week-as-such. But within the perceived ontical environment of Being-the-son-of, the death (or, more accurately, the finite process, demising) of Being-in-the-barn would create a schism of certain hermeneutical bonds, demanding a temporary state of anxiety. Whereupon the essential question of a remunerative evaluation (although relativistic in nature) of Being-in-the-barn replaces the a priori opposition (Not-Being-into).

THE HAPPY HOOFER
In the style of Xavier Hollander

It was foolish to argue. As his mother was explaining how he should sell the cow, Jack could not ignore the sensitive movements of her full, red lips or the sensual heaving of her still ample breasts. Memories of his childhood flashed in his mind, of the days when his loving and ravenous tongue had caressed those soft nipples, and the soft gasps she would emit when the pleasure became too great.

He was tying a rope around the neck of the cow when he first felt a strange tingling in that delicate spot below his belly, and began to worry that his mother might notice the ever-increasing bulge that now distended his torn yet form-fitting jeans. She had noticed, and could hardly keep her eyes off it. As Jack led the cow away, his mother's gaze was drawn to his firm behind as it danced and swayed beneath his tight pants.

And the cow noticed too. As drops of fresh milk began to glisten at the ends of her firm, young utters, she thought of the way his warm hands had felt that morning, gently teasing and urging the last drops of fluid from her longing body.

They didn't get one hundred feet down the road before Jack, in the heat of passion, wrapped his body around the cow and lay her softly in a pile of leaves at the side of the road . . .

"Cigarette?" Jack offered, a teasing smile still visible on his lips.

BHAGAVAD BEAN STALK
In the style of the Bhagavad Gita

And so it was that Jack came from the house of his mother into the city of man to sell the sacred cow that he had brought with him.

On a street of the city he saw an old man. His face revealed that he was of great age and wisdom; his body bore the scars of renunciation of the ways of society: three skin diseases, running sores, and a violent cough. But in his serene gaze Jack marked well the bliss of a holy man.

"O, blessed saint, is there a place in the city of man where young boys named Jack go to sell cows that they have brought from the house of their mother?"

"Ah, my son who knows so little, but what does it mean to sell, or indeed, to transfer? For has it not been written that over all the things of earth, Shiva is master? We can no sooner sell that which is of Shiva than we can extinguish the flame of righteous guidance, that burns on the mountain of everlasting hygiene, overlooking sea of the expanding waistband."

"Well spoken, holy man! For the first time I have truly grasped the meaning of the ancient scriptures, not to mention several George Harrison songs. But, lo, I am still hungry. How could this be?"

But what is this thing, hunger? Is it no more than a manifestation of mankind's inability to transcend the bounds of time, space, and unsightly bulges? Can we not thus see the illusory nature of hunger?"

The holy man had spoken truly, but unfortunately young Jack couldn't keep up with the double negatives and fell into depression. Seeing this, the holy man comforted the boy with a gift of twelve magic but poisonous beans, from which it is said strange things would grow, and further showed his wisdom and grace by absconding with the cow that had been the source of such sadness for Jack.

HOW JACK BROUGHT THE BEANS TO HIS MOTHER AND WHAT HAPPENED AFTERWARDS
In the style of Voltaire

After Jack left the city with the beans, he decided to make his way home, pondering all the while the strange things that occurred in the world around him. When Jack reached his home, he saw his mother standing near the house, staring off into the distance.

"It is you," exclaimed his mother, "you must come inside and eat and tell me what has become of the cow."

"But first," replied Jack, "you must tell me what has happened to our house, for I notice that there is little left of it but a few bricks, and it appears that some terrible woe has befallen you, for I notice that you are bleeding from the cheeks and that your right leg has been torn asunder from your body. Tell me then, mother, what has passed?"

His mother went on to tell him the story of how the Bulgars and the Turks had come to the village, disemboweled all of the men with their sharp swords, raped all of the women, and destroyed all of the houses.

"But now things are for the best, as they are gone, and though I am in pain and near death, I am alive and happy. Now eat, and tell me what has become of the cow."

Jack was confused and pondered a while the strange events of the world, wondering how his mother could be so happy when it appeared that the utmost woe had befallen her. He then ate the delicious roast dog his mother had prepared, and told her the story of the city, the cow, and the magical beans. Hearing this, his mother flew into a violent rage.

"How could you be so foolish, for now I have nothing to live for," she cried, upon which she immediately disemboweled herself with the carving knife.

"Oh, what sorrow there is in this strange world," thought Jack, finishing his drumstick of dog, "but all is for the best as I still have my beans and lots of delicious dog to eat."

Jack planted the beans and fell asleep, wondering if there was, somewhere, another land where people were good and happy. When he awoke, he found the beans had grown into a large stalk. Jack pondered the bean stalk and then climbed up to its top where he found another strange and different world.

"Perhaps in this unknown place all men are happy and everything is for the best," thought Jack.

STEAL THIS BEAN STALK
In the style of Abbie Hoffman

Now this part of the story may sound a little weird, but trust me, it's all real.

You see, at the top of this bean stalk is some other world or something, with fields of clouds, and all sorts of other crazy things you'd probably never believe. You'd probably say I was tripping or something, but I know I wasn't because this stuff was weirder than anything I've ever seen tripping. Especially this castle, it was really huge and sitting in the middle of the field. I know it was a really dumb thing to do, but I decided to check it out.

So I go inside the place, and wow, everything in there is really big, you know, like the sets for the TV show *Land of the Giants*—remember it? Anyway, the next thing I know, I hear this real loud noise and turn around to see this real, live giant! I'm not kidding, just like the ones in the fairy tales, a fucking-out-loud giant! Well, the first thing I do is get the hell out of there because this guy really gives me the creeps. I'm not usually a negative guy, but this dude was like a giant-size cop or something, and I was getting real bad vibes, because I was still a little stoned, and in no mood for dealing with thirty-foot heat. So I go into this closet and figure I'll lay back and smoke a joint and wait till the big guy takes off.

I was toking up and thinking what a weird day it had been, when I notice, over in a corner, this thing they call a harp (which is like an electric guitar, kind of, except there's more strings and no electricity), and it's got this chick's head stuck on it, and also there's this big, white duck. And then the chick on the guitar starts talking! And she's telling me how this giant guy is really a drag and how it's a pain in the ass to live up there in the clouds because it's hard to get good drugs, and all like that. Then she tells me that the big duck can lay these eggs made out of gold, and that I could have some if I help them escape. So I told her that I just scored a pound of this really fine gold and really didn't need any more, and I almost freaked when she said she meant real gold, you know, the metal stuff.

So right then I grabbed them both and made a run for it, because I figured I could use a new amp and maybe some "Yes" albums, some of their earlier stuff . . .

EXODUS, CHAPTER 31, VERSES 1–5
In the style of the Bible

1 And it came to pass, that Jack did run forth, and through the temple of the Giant, that he might bring salvation unto Goose and Harp.

2 But, lo, then did the Giant, with sharp ear and short wit, hear them, and even as unto a hammered thumb, did he pronounce great oaths, and did call upon false idols, among these, Elvis, that he should bring evil unto them.

3 And fee fi fo fum said he unto them, though he knew not what it meant, nor has anyone known before or since, not even God.

4 And then did Jack go forth amidst the furnishings that he might hide among them, and under them find shelter. And Goose and Harp they went forth also, they being carried by Jack.

5 And frightful noises did they make, as even unto disco, that they did harken the Giant, and yea, then did Jack bearing heavily upon Goose and Harp beat it from the dwelling, and unto the fields did he then run.

BLOOD OF ENGLISHMAN
In the style of e.e. cummings

jack crossed(with
in hand ; fowl creatrix of the root
of evil,also
singing strings,still
,unplucked,also)
the fields
of clouds'nwheat'nclouds

and yet behind:gianTrampling
fefifofumfefifofum,
resounding,and
him thinking:

i surely die carrying
what?(these in question?in
question)but a-
head:the head of that(the other)
 green giant: forgotten
stalk, no longer
stalk!escape!

:thinking that lie was,and
to take leave,taking
to those(the other)leaves,soon,
still sooner, de-
scend-
ing.

A MIDSUMMER'S NIGHT BEAN
In the style of William Shakespeare

FELLATIO: Speak, sir for thou young Jack hast seen;
And descending was he from such dreading air
That, methinks, his ugly squash'd doom
Be soon and nigh, and pretty quick at that!

For that large man with fo fum on his lips
Hast made some timbersome, conjunctive gains
While through the bean'd verdure ever-falling
And in his arms, regard, he still enfolds
That noisy lyre (no Apollo's voice!),
And ever yet that squealing, gilded layer
(With bacon, aye, the finest banker's breakfast!),
That, again, methinks him wasted quick.

OMELET: One damn cannot I give for what thee thinks!
For view, our Jack has just been safely grounded,
And runs he with such haste for sharpened axe
That, I fear, yon Giant sorely plopped.
And see him swing with sweaty, beaded brow
(Glad he use'd Dial that Jack must be!),
And see the vine a-tremble and a-sway
As mine own knees have done preceding love:
And witness further how that stalk of green
Doth from its sturdy pose decline and fall,
As has, engaged in love, mine member done.
How like that ended Giant is love then,
When passion softens even the biggest men.
[Exeunt.]

CONCLUSION
In the style of a college research paper

Finally, it can be seen that, having returned to his mother with the harp that sang and the goose that laid the golden eggs, Jack did fulfill all of his original objectives, and thus terminate his adventure. From the preceding texts it can be inferred that, given the nature of his turmoil and the subsequent abatement thereof, along with the immense financial augmentation incurred by his household in general, Jack indeed improved the quality of his life on practical, as well as aesthetic, levels. It is, therefore, with unqualified pleasure and justifiable emphasis that the author exclaims at the end of the work, "And they lived happily ever after!"

in "Do You Want Some Fries?"

Once there was a tree
and she hated this little boy.
Every day he would come
and climb all over her
and play
and generally annoy her.
So the tree would throw her apples
at the boy's head.
And she would shake very hard when
he climbed on her branches so that
he would fall out and break his legs.
But the boy never did fall.
And the tree was upset.

The Giving Grief Tree

by Snell Sliverstein

Then one day the boy came to the tree
and said, "I want to buy things and have fun.
I want a red sports car so girls
will like me
and I can get lucky.
I want some money.
Can you give me some money?"
"You are a *stupid* boy," said the tree. "Didn't they
teach you anything at that fancy college of yours?
I'm a *tree*. I live in the middle of the fricking *forest*.
Why would I have any money?"
"Couldn't you give me your apples so I could
sell them in the city?" asked the boy.
"Get a job, you lazy son of a bitch," said the tree.
So the boy left.
And the tree was happy.

But time went by.
And the boy grew older.
He went off to college
to study some silly major
like sociology.
He was too far away to annoy the tree.
And the tree was happy.

The boy stayed away for a long time . . . .
Then one day he came back
and the tree shook with anger.
"What the hell do you want now?" asked
the tree.
"I want a house," he said.
"I want a big mansion like the one
on *The Fresh Prince of Bel-Air*
with a swimming pool and a butler.
Can you give me a house?"
The tree laughed very hard because
the boy was shallow and dumb.
She hit him in the eye with one of
her apples and said, "Get out of
my face, chump!
I'm not giving you diddly squat."
So the boy left.

The tree was pretty sure that
the boy was gone for good this time.
But she was wrong because
one day he came back.
"You are a dense, pitiful schmuck,"
said the tree. "I already told you
that I'm not giving you any money."
"I have no use for money," said the boy.
"I am too old and wrinkled for girls
to find me attractive—
no matter how much money I have.
Besides, I can't even get it up anymore.
And I told you I won't give you
a house," said the tree.
"I don't want a house," said the boy.
"I am old and paranoid
and I would be afraid to live alone."
"So what is it you want, then?" asked the tree.
"Not that I'll give it to you."
"You ruined my life," said the boy.
"Because of you I never got lucky,
and I never had any friends.
So now I want revenge."
So the boy chopped down the tree.
But he didn't do it right
and the tree fell on him,
crushing him to death.
And the tree was happy.

THE END

Letter from Camp

Dear Roger,

Camp is great! We hardly do anything. We play softball and soccer, but mostly we just lay around the bunks doing nothing. The cabin is a real dump. The counselors are really wild. Once they took on the whole bunk and everybody got thrown around. Boy was that fun! Bruce, that's my counselor, picked me up over his head and tossed me fifteen feet. I almost landed in a sticker bush! I was lucky! Then, there are these bugs called needle bugs. They're gigantic and they live in the pine trees, and if they bite you, you get real sick and die. So we always kill them when we find them. But you can't squash them, because their smell attracts more. So you gotta burn them. We sometimes trap them in trash cans and spay them with Right Guard torches, or else we pile up toilet paper and pour Bruce's aftershave over it, and when we light it on fire, it goes *whoosh!*

The guys in this bunk are too much. One of them's so fat we call him Santa Claus. He never takes a shower, not one yet this summer, and he smells like vinegar. We even made up a song about him:

He's cuttin' a fart, sniffin' it twice,
Gonna find out if it smells real nice,
Santa Claus is coming to town.

The other night, after lights out, we stood in the middle of the bunk and sang it. Then the counselor O.D. ("On Duty") came over and said he'd brain the next guy who made a sound. Everyone was real quiet until he left the bunk porch. Then somebody hooted, and somebody else made a fart noise, and everybody laughed.

Yesterday, Bruce had these white cards from the directors and asked everybody if they took a shit or a shower this week. I wonder why they do that? Santa lied and said he'd taken a shower, but he hasn't. Even his bed smells like vinegar. We also call him "Vinny."

Really late one night, Bruce got in and made a lot of noise and woke everybody up. Then he lifted one leg and said, "Torpedoes, Los, Fire One!" And he farted! It was the funniest thing I ever saw! Now everybody's doing it, walking around saying, "Torpedoes, Los, Fire One!"

The counselors are really violent. They have so many kinds of tortures. Like the pshong, when they twist your arm in a special way, and punch you just lightly, but it really hurts. And the noogie. That's when they rap your head with a knuckle. A super noogie is with a graduation ring. A waffle belly is when they put a tennis racket on your bare belly and rub with a wire hair brush. When they take off the racket, your belly's all red, except for the white lines where the racket strings were.

They have others they talk about but haven't done yet (just threaten). The shitwave is when they stick your head in a shit-filled toilet bowl and flush. The double whammy is two tubes of toothpaste squirted up somebody's asshole. I learned to sleep with my mouth closed after Bruce filled it with sea salt. I almost choked.

Now I'm under my blankets with a flashlight writing this. We just came back from a raid on Girls 17.

And we got away with it. I just had to take a break from writing this letter. Rick and Reid, two guys in the bunk, planned the raid. We had every guy on Boys Hill make hundreds of water balloons, and we had a whole supply of shaving cream. Rick and Reid had even stolen sticky cereal and bug juice syrup from the dining hall. Reid sent five guys up the hill for a diversion, and Martin Miller, the director's slave, was busy chasing them when Rick turned out the big lights and about thirty guys went charging up Girls Hill at four a.m.

No girls' cabin was left untouched. Most were soaked with bug juice, shaving cream, maple syrup, Sugar Smacks, and other goodies. We dumped beds, emptied cubbies, and threw all the clothes on the line into the lake. But Marvin came roaring up Girls Hill in the Marvinmobile and rounded up just about everyone. But Rick, Reid, and me hid out under the pines. Soon the loudspeakers all over camp began to blast reveille, just like they did every morning at eight o'clock. But it was only some guy who had escaped Marvin and set the record going.

Rick, Reid, and me split up because his girlfriend wasn't in the same bunk as Janis. I crept through her door and she was awake, but all the others in the bunk were asleep. How could they sleep through our raid? Anyway, we snuck over to the Bigtop, which is a barn turned gymnasium. Up in the second floor in the old lofts is lots of space and old mattresses. We picked a mattress all the way at the far end. We laid down on the mattress and starting kissing with our tongues. Pretty soon I was rubbing her tits and I was hard and she was breathing really heavy. So we took off all our clothes, except our underwear, and wrapped up in the blanket she had brought.

So we were holding and squeezing and squirming around, and I started rubbing her legs and finally stuck my hand in her panties. She was hugging me really tight and kissing me really hard and I reached further and felt something wet. It was really wet, and I wasn't too sure what to do, so I just kept rubbing for a while, and she really liked that 'cause she started to wiggle and moan.

After a while I started poking my fingers, and then I was sort of poking my finger in and out. And she started pulling off my underpants, saying, "C'mon, c'mon, put it in there, hurry up!" I was kinda scared 'cause she'd never been like that before, but now she was panting like some kind of animal. So I got on top of her and sort of pushed a little, but I couldn't feel anything much.

She was all excited and finally helped me with her hand, and it felt wet and I pushed more, but I wasn't getting anywhere, and she said, "C'mon, you have to push harder." So I pushed harder and harder, and she pushed harder and harder, but no luck. So we pushed and pushed, and all of a sudden, I felt her fingernails buried in my ass. We pushed really hard and something gave, and I was in her and it was warm and mushy, and it felt so so so good, I just wanted to push in and out, in and out, but then I felt kinda weird, really weird. I was pushing like crazy and then everything exploded like a cherry bomb, and I was hugging Janis and pushing and crying and laughing. Then it was over and I was really tired. Janis wanted to do it more, but then there was a bright light and Marvin was screaming, "What the hell is going on here! Get your

Andy Warhol's Artwork as a Child

clothes on, both of you! Get back to your bunks!" Marvin was turning from white to red.

Janis and I ran back to our own bunks. But I stopped at the canteen where all the snacks are kept. The doors are always locked, but one of the walls didn't make it to the ceiling by six inches. So I grabbed a garbage can, turned it upside down, and climbed in. I took everything I could carry, then ate all I could until I was sick. I threw all the wrappers in the woods behind the canteen, which was

pretty stupid because Marvin came by to find me, and he found all the wrappers and really went crazy. He threatened to give me the shitwave, but all he's going to do is take the money out of my canteen fund. Big deal.

Your friend,
Al

P.S. Tomorrow Bruce is going to make Santa take a shower. Reid says he's going to piss on him from the rafters, and Rick is going to throw Vinny's clothes in the lake!

2008 Board Game

SPECIAL CHESS

Initially, the gaming committee doubted whether "special athletes" could handle a game traditionally played by intellectuals. Champion Ryan Brody proved them wrong. He captured and swallowed his opponent's king within the very first minute of the match. He got game indeed!

SPECIAL TRIVIA

Just because your eyes are too far apart doesn't mean you can't excel at Trivial Pursuit. For three years, Suzie Solsburg has trampled through her competition, answering questions about everything from geography to history. Suzie, what state does not border Nebraska? "I went potty in my pants." Judges? Yes, we'll accept that!

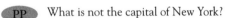

PP	What is not the capital of New York?
AE	What are eyes for?
HIS	Name something you once ate.
SN	Is a puppy a plant or an animal?
SL	What type of knob is found on a door?
WC	What game are we playing?

SPECIAL BOGGLE

Boggle can be a very challenging game . . . but not when there's an infinite number of possible permutations. Yes, this version of the popular game has numbers instead of letters. Special athlete Bartholomew Peterson instantly memorized all sixteen numbers exactly as they appeared in that grid and continues to recall them aloud to this day in an infinite sequence.

Special Olympics

SPECIAL CONNECT FOUR

Little Sikwili Puzambu of Uganda must have been practicing on a standard kid's Connect Four board. He slid in four chips before his opponent could even make a move! Yet, the judges were not impressed by his quick victory. Maybe in Uganda you're allowed to bludgeon your opponent to death with a large rock, but here in America that gets you a point deduction for poor sportsmanship.

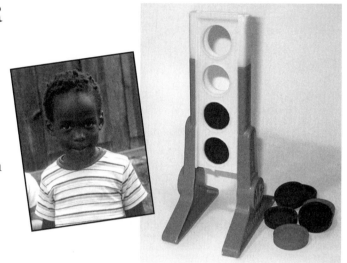

SPECIAL SCRABBLE

Because all of the pieces in Special Team Scrabble are blank, it's easy to get confused and start eating them. The winning team of Jake Quimby and Tiffany Horowitz were clearly not confused at all. The winning duo were able to put down all seven of their blank tiles in nearly every turn.

SPECIAL LIFE

In this Special Game of Life, winner Ronny Finkelton became a doctor, fathered four children, and bought a summer home in the Hamptons. He then cried for hours upon learning that in real life none of those things could ever happen to a special boy like him. As Mrs. Finkelton comforted her teary-eyed son, she wondered how to tell Ronny that he was responsible for his father's suicide.

Today's high school students represent a generation that grew up with television. Teachers are finding it increasingly difficult to deal with short attention spans. A need has arisen to teach upper-level subjects using the same mind-numbing mix of entertainment and learning that made *Sesame Street* and *Electric Company* so successful. Now, thanks to sizable grants and editorial assistance from Exxon and General Motors, the Children's Television Workshop proudly presents . . .

SPIRAL

Corporate Economics for Kids Who Grew Up on *Sesame Street*

A regular cast of peers teach basic lessons of microeconomics:

Dave: Hi, Mr. Dupont! You know, this six-pack you sold me is pretty flat. Could I return it and get my money back?

Mr. Dupont: I'm sorry, Dave, but I can't do that anymore. You see, I sold my store to Convenience Store Inc.

Dave: Well, gee, why does that matter?

Mr. Dupont: You see, Dave, this used to be a proprietorship. That means that I owned the store, and I had to take all the responsibility if something went wrong. Now I'm part of a corporation. One feature of a corporation is limited liability. That means that I can't be held responsible for the corporation's mistakes.

Dave: Can't you just return my money?

Mr. Dupont: I'm afraid you'll have to file your complaint with division headquarters.

Dave: Gosh, Mr. Dupont. I don't think you should have sold out like that. I liked your store better the old way.

Mr. Dupont: Now Dave, a lot of people like to be nostalgic about the so-called good old days of family-run, personal businesses, each with their own individual charm. But I sold the store for your benefit. You'll now have the security of knowing that when you go to my store, or any other owned by Convenience Store Inc., you can expect the same brands and the same bland quality. Remember, if it's good for the corporation, it's probably going to be good for you, too.

Dave: Yeah, I guess so. But I'd still like to return this beer.

Mr. Dupont: Dave, these are hard times. Economic solutions don't come easily. We all have to make sacrifices. Convenience Store Inc. has already tightened its belt by buying mediocre-quality merchandise. It's time for you to do your share.

Dave: You're right, Mr. Dupont. I'm ready to give up my consumer-oriented, hedonistic lifestyle. I'll sell my Japanese stereo and start buying Gallo instead of French wine. If mediocrity is good enough for big corporations, it's good enough for me. Heck, I bet I could learn to like flat beer.

John: We have a whole plate of cookies. How should we divide them up among the kids in the neighborhood?

Milty: That's easy. We sell them to whomever pays the most, according to market demand.

John: Well, I was thinking we could have Mayor Carter give them out equally, then charge the kids according to how much money they have.

Milty: That's socialism, John. Mayor Carter has enough to do without meddling in cookies.

John: But Milty, under your plan the poorer kids won't get any cookies at all.

Milty: Galbraith, don't be such an effete Cambridge bleeding-heart. Every time something goes wrong you want Mayor Carter to come running in to save the day. If those little snots would just go out and get a job . . . .

Cookie Monster: COOKIES!

John: Oh, well. Say, I saw a dynamite episode of your PBS show the other night.

Milty: I hear yours is doing all right, too. I'm working on this great plan to turn Yellowstone National Park over to private industry, and . . . . .

The EPA Grouch: Why don't you guys clean up this mess?

Oligopolis: Gosh, Big Oil, the EPA Grouch is really getting angry about all this garbage in Love Alley.

Big Oil: EPA's had his head in his can for too long, Oligopolis. If he did some basic present-worth analysis, he'd see why we can't clean up the alley.

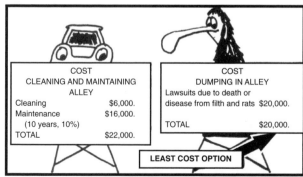

COST CLEANING AND MAINTAINING ALLEY	
Cleaning	$6,000.
Maintenance (10 years, 10%)	$16,000.
TOTAL	$22,000.

COST DUMPING IN ALLEY	
Lawsuits due to death or disease from filth and rats	$20,000.
TOTAL	$20,000.

LEAST COST OPTION

Oligopolis: What if EPA has Mayor Carter order us to clean up?

Big Oil: No problem. We just claim we didn't know that the garbage was dirty.

Make sure your students watch SPIRAL. It's in their best interest. . . as well as ours.

Collector's Guide to Beanie Babies

Chad, the rich brat beanie
My pants are from Tommy
my shirt's from the Gap
my car goes much faster
than your piece of crap

Bloody Squirrel, the roadkill beanie
You were drivin' too fast
down that Route 66
now I'm gonna be dinner
for some poor white-trash hicks

Brian, the acne-faced, post-pubescent beanie
My voice is a-changin'
my armpits are hairy
I get all excited
when I watch Drew Carey

Billy-Ray, the wife beatin' beanie
My truck has no engin'
my car has no tires
my shirt needs a mendin'
and my trailer's on fire

Stephanie, the annoying sorority girl beanie
I'm better than you
wanna come to my crush party?

Trichy, the tapeworm beanie
You ate some bad pork
in your stomach I'm restin'
'til I eat away
your whole large intestine

Whippy, the sado-masochistic beanie
I put on my hood
and my spiked panties too
I told you to stop talking—
that's a whippin' for you

Leppie, the leprosy beanie
My body is rotting
my arms both fell off
I lose a new limb
each time that I cough

THE HARDLY BOYS

An Exciting Camping Trip

"This is going to be an exciting camping trip." The speaker was blond, seventeen-year-old Joe Hardly.

"Perhaps we will find another mystery there," said Joe's tall, dark-haired, eighteen-year-old brother Frank.

"Let's call chunky Chet Morton, and ask him if he wants to go along," suggested lanky Biff Hooper.

"Good idea!" exclaimed bright-eyed Tony Prito.

As Biff reached for the phone, the boys heard Chet's bright yellow jalopy pull into the driveway.

"Up here, Tubs!" Frank called goodheartedly from the second-floor window of his Bayport house. The fat boy ran up the stairs puffing and joined his friends. As they talked, the boys were startled by a sudden, loud scream outside.

"Somebody just screamed!" Joe cried out. He and Frank dashed from the room and down the carpeted stairs. The other boys followed the Hardly boys through the kitchen and out onto the grassy lawn. Chet stayed behind to sneak a snack in the deserted kitchen.

Excitedly speculating on the incident, the Hardly boys and their two chums circled the house for an hour, searching for clues. They were about to give up when suddenly Joe made a discovery.

"It's Aunt Gertrude!" he exclaimed as they encountered a tall, angular woman hanging above the garage.

"Hello Aunt Gertrude." Frank and Joe greeted their father's sister who made her home with them.

"Somebody screamed. Did you see anybody?" Frank asked, questioningly.

Aunt Gertrude silently twisted in the light summer breeze.

"What are you doing up there?" Biff asked in astonishment.

"Something tells me she doesn't feel like talking," said the always observant Frank, noting the blood dripping from the many huge gashes on her head and body.

"I don't think she is breathing," bright-eyed Tony added glumly.

"Aunt Gertrude is dead!" exclaimed Joe, excitedly.

"But why would anybody want to hang Aunt Gertrude?" Tony asked, frowning.

"That is what I want to know," declared Mr. Hardly. The tall, well-built private investigator had suddenly appeared from behind a bush. "Get flashlights and look for clues. I'll call Chief Collige."

"She must have struggled," Frank commented, noticing the killer's skin under her fingernails. Fenton Hardly had taught his sons well, and there was no better teacher.

"Look at this neat knife!" Joe exclaimed, finding a hunting knife in Aunt Gertrude's back. "It's just like the one Dad has."

"This will be great for our camping trip," Frank said, slipping the knife into his pocket.

Black And Blue

Just then, a black and blue police car turned the corner, weaved along the street, and roared up the driveway. The car smashed into Chet's jalopy and came to a halt, its red roof light flashing brightly. Police Chief Collige stumbled out of his car.

"It's Police Chief Collige!" Joe said.

The chief and Mr. Hardly had worked closely on many cases in the past. They worked so closely that they usually kept bumping into each other and solved few mysteries.

"Got another mystery, boys?" the officer asked in a slurred voice. "Have you solved it yet?"

"Not a clue," responded Mr. Hardly, wiping some fresh, red blood off his hands with a rag. "Frankly, I'm baffled."

"This was probably some prankster's idea of fun. That's what happens when you let those greaseballs into the neighborhood," the chief said, looking at Tony. "Hey, how did you scratch your face?" Chief Collige pointed to five long scratches on Mr. Hardly's face.

Fenton Hardly looked up, shocked. "Ah . . . a b-branch," he quickly stuttered.

"You should put some iodine on that," the chief suggested, helpfully.

"Yes, I will, thank you," Mr. Hardly replied.

"I've got to use your john," the chief said. "We stopped in at O'Brien's wake. Those Micks really know how to go, don't they?" The chief winked at Mr. Hardly.

"Yes, I would have gone too," agreed Mr. Hardly, "But Gertrude always criticized my drinking."

"Ah, a motive," said the chief, jokingly.

"But don't you want to see the body?" the lanky Biff asked.

"What for?" the chief responded, walking off toward the house. "I know what she looks like."

A Gun

When the chief came from the house, he had Chet handcuffed and was waving a gun threateningly at the frightened fat boy.

"Well, I guess this solves the mystery! Caught this blimp prowling about the house. Tried to attack me with this dangerous weapon." The chief triumphantly held up a hard salami.

"Help me, Mr. Hardly!" pleaded the bloated Chet. "I was just fixing a snack."

"You just keep quiet, boy," the chief said, waving the gun in Chet's face.

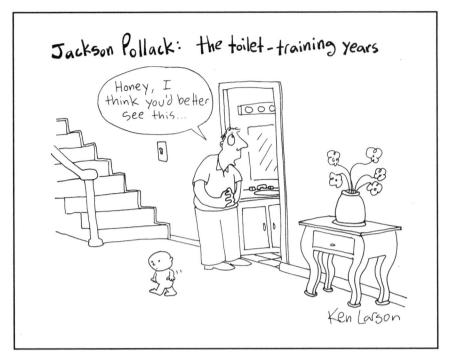

Jackson Pollack: the toilet-training years

Honey, I think you'd better see this...

Ken Larson

"That's just Chet Morton," Mr. Hardly said, laughing heartily.

"Well, you can't be too careful. The boy went through half a turkey and a dozen hardboiled eggs."

Chet shrugged, grinning.

They all chuckled as the embarrassed Chet bit into the salami and waddled back to the house to get some mustard.

"Why don't you come in for a drink, Chief?" Mr. Hardly asked.

"But what about Aunt Gertrude?" asked Frank.

"She won't say anything," Mr. Hardly replied.

"I mean the body," added Frank.

Just then, Chet, chewing on a drumstick, walked from the house to join his friends. "My jalopy!" he cried, "What happened to my jalopy?"

"You oaf!" replied the chief, now a bit more sober. "You're lucky I don't ticket you for reckless parking." The chief got into his car and roared off, the red roof light flashing brightly.

"We are lucky to have such a dedicated police chief," commented the older, dark-haired boy. The others nodded in agreement. Chet stared in disbelief at the twisted yellow metal, and unwrapped a candy bar.

The Next Morning

The next morning the Hardly boys rose early.

"I wish Aunt Gertrude was here to cook breakfast," Frank said.

"What for? Her comments were always so peppery and tart," Mr. Hardly quickly snapped. "You want breakfast? Here boys, eat this." The detective scraped a hearty meal of steak, potatoes, and gravy onto the boys' plates.

"Why would anyone kill Aunt Gertrude?" Frank asked.

"Well, don't look at me," chuckled Mr. Hardly. "Why don't you run out and check the mail, Joe?"

Joe left the breakfast table to check the morning mail.

"Can we still go on our camping trip, Dad?" asked Frank.

"Gee Willikers! When do you boys find time for schoolwork? Either you're out solving a mystery or on another camping trip. How are you two ever going to graduate?"

"But Dad, this is July. We're on summer vacation," Frank said.

"You two boys have been on summer vacation for the last forty volumes. Why don't you go out drinking or stealing hubcaps like normal teenagers?"

"We can't do that, Dad. We're the Hardly boys," Frank said. "We have an obligation to the community, to serve as character-building models."

Just then, Joe ran back into the house, holding a picture postcard and a full bottle of milk.

"Someone left this milk bottle on our front porch. I don't know what to make of it. Frankly, I'm baffled."

"It could be another prank," Frank declared. "Who is the postcard from?"

"I don't know, but this picture on the front may be a clue." The boys tried to figure out what the large green statue holding a torch could mean.

"I think it's from New York City," Joe cried, cleverly discovering the postmark and the New York City return address.

"You might be right," their father added. "Maybe this postcard is tied to Aunt Gertrude's murder. Hardly boys, you two will have to go to New York City to follow this lead."

"I guess this ends our plans for a camping trip," sulked Frank.

"Why no, boys!" said Mr. Hardly. "There are plenty of places to camp in the Big Apple, and there are lots of wild creatures, too."

"Can Chet come along?" Joe asked.

"Sure, take Biff also, but not that greaseball Tony Prito."

"Will you be coming, Dad?" dark-haired Frank asked.

"No, this could be dangerous," replied Mr. Hardly, who left the New York Police Department under circumstances never explained in any Hardly Boys book.

"When do we leave?" Joe asked, excitedly.

"You'll need the weekend to get ready."

"That long?" Frank looked dismayed.

"Yes, you see, Hardly boys, your pilot's licenses are for single engine planes, and you're going to need helicopter licenses for this trip."

The Trip

On Monday, tall, dark-haired Frank, blond, seventeen-year-old Joe, lanky Biff, and corpulent, good-natured Chet left for the Bayport International Airport to make the trip to New York City.

"Oh, it's the Hardly boys, Biff, and their fat friend Chet," said the young flight attendant as the boys entered the terminal building. "Off to solve another mystery on your summer vacation boys?"

"We really shouldn't talk about it," said Frank.

"We wouldn't want to put you in any

danger," Biff added.

"I understand. The pilot is holding the plane for you."

"Thank you!" cried Joe as they boarded the 707 jet for New York City.

When the boys landed, they went to the baggage claim. But their bags were not to be found.

"Where can our luggage be?" asked the bloated Chet, puffing.

"Somebody must have known we were coming. They probably pilfered our luggage, hoping to make us turn back," Frank figured.

Joe grimaced. "Holy mackerel!" he said. "You mean they would make us go without clean underwear!"

Undaunted, Frank urged the boys onward. "That's what we'll be up against from now on," he commented.

Without their bags, the four boys taxied to Central Park to set up camp. Biff and Frank pitched the tent while Joe searched for firewood.

A Strange Man

A strange man dressed in blue jeans and an old army jacket approached the boys. He had a wide-brimmed hat pulled down over his unshaven face.

"Obviously a good disguise," whispered Frank to the other boys.

"Got any smack?" asked the man. "Like, you cats wanna make it?"

"Make what?" asked Chet.

"Hey, far out! Like, make the scene."

"What's a scene?" asked Joe.

"Hey, you're pretty wild. Where'd you get those haircuts? They're out of sight!"

"What's going on? Is this a trick?" asked Biff, puzzled.

"Is he a communist?" asked Chet.

"Like, those Bermuda shorts and alligator shirts are too much, man. Really far-out threads!"

"What did you say?" asked Frank. "We are from Bayport."

"Like, got any bread?" replied the hippie.

"Whole wheat? Rye? Pumpernickel?" Chet asked.

"Pumpernickel!?! Whoa, you're really something else, baby. Do I want pumpernickel? Hey, that's heavy!"

"Heavy?" exclaimed Chet, a bit offended.

"Hey, what do you want?" Joe demanded.

The hippie grabbed Joe by his shirt. "Don't jive me, daddy-o. You'll attract the heat. Just don't be so uptight. Here, pop some of these." He offered the boys some barbiturates.

"No thank you, we already took our vitamins this morning," Frank replied.

"Vitamins? Like, wow. Hey, if you got the bread, Slim, we'll do up the town."

"Great!" exclaimed Frank, "we could use a guide. We just want to find this address." Frank handed the postcard to the hippie.

The guide took the postcard and the boys on a subway downtown to an apartment loft in Greenwich Village. A door opened into a large phosphorescent room filled with thick, blue smoke with a strange odor. Loud, uncoordinated music bounced off the walls, while people flowed in slow motion throughout, their bodies interwoven in peculiar postures.

"What's going on?" Chet asked.

Frank grabbed Joe and Chet, and pulled them to the street.

"Why did you pull us out like that?" Joe asked.

"You know the author's rules. No drugs or sex!" shouted Frank.

"Where is Biff?" Joe cried.

"He must be inside. We must rescue him, and fast!" Frank said. "There's no telling what they will do to him!"

When the boys went back, they found Biff floating on the ceiling, sucking on a cube of sugar.

"Biff, are you all right?" Frank asked.

"Hey, like wow, I see God," Biff said.

"You know sugar is bad for your teeth," Chet reminded Biff.

"It's too late," Frank said, solemnly. "We will have to go on without him."

A Fierce Growl

As the Hardly Boys walked back to Central Park, Chet's stomach gave a fierce growl.

"I'm hungry," cried Chet.

"We're in luck!" Frank declared. "New York has some of the best restaurants in the world." The dark-haired boy led the boys to a Horn & Hardart.

"We would like a hearty meal of steak, potatoes, and gravy," Joe said to the man behind the counter.

"Look, Jack," the scruffy chef said, without removing the cigarette dangling between his lips. "All we got is what's in them boxes!"

"No steak, potatoes, and gravy?" Chet asked, glumly.

The chef looked up, irritated. "Whatsamattah with you? I said no. You from Bayport or somethin'?" he replied, as his cigarette ashes dropped into the succotash.

Joe and Chet joined Frank at the coin-operated bank of food dispensers.

"What shall we have?" asked Chet, excitedly.

"There are so many choices," replied Joe. "Frankly, I'm baffled."

A line was beginning to form behind the chums.

"So you want a sandwich or a hot plate?" a cook asked.

"They both sound very good."

"How about the vegetable platter special?" suggested the cook.

"I hadn't thought of that," said Joe. "What is special about it?"

"It's less than a week old," sputtered the chef. "Make up your minds and get moving." The line behind the boys was growing.

"Let's see," began Chet, "Turkey sandwich, ham sandwich, roast beef sandwich, cheese sandwich, hot plate, vegetable platter . . ."

"Now that you've listed the menu, what will it be?" asked the cook.

"Oh, I wasn't listing the menu, sir," said Chet. "I was placing my order."

A Threatening Note

After a hearty meal, the sleuths returned to their Central Park campsite only to find a threatening note tacked to their tent.

"What does it say?" asked Joe.

Frank read the note aloud. "Leave New York City before you are killed!"

"Who is it from?" asked Chet, nervously. "A gang of villains?"

"No," Frank replied. "It is from the New York Tourist Advisory Board. Every visitor gets one."

It was getting dark. The boys crawled inside the tent to get ready for bed. Suddenly the tent became immersed in light.

"What is that light?" Chet whispered, sheepishly.

"I don't know," Frank admitted. "Maybe it is already morning," he said, consolingly.

The boys trembled in their sleeping bags as they heard a car door open. Foot steps approached their tent. The boys were silent.

"The police!" Joe exclaimed, relieved as an officer entered the tent holding a flashlight.

"What do you boys think you are doing camping in Central Park?" the policeman asked in a serious tone of voice.

"We are the Hardly boys. I am the dark-haired Frank Hardly, and the light-haired, seventeen-year-old is my brother Joe. The fat boy is our friend, Chet."

"So you are the famous Hardly Boys! I've read all your books. Come to police headquarters with me, boys. The lieutenant will be thrilled to meet the famous Hardly boys," the officer said.

They all started for the car.

"Wait a minute," the officer said. "The fat one will have to ride on the luggage rack." The police officer drove the Hardly boys downtown to police headquarters with Chet strapped good-naturedly to the rack.

A Postcard

At the door to police headquarters, they were greeted by the lieutenant.

"I have always wanted to meet the famous Hardly Boys," he said, extending his hand. "Hello boys, I'm glad you're here!"

The lieutenant brought the boys inside. "We found this hippie walking the streets with a postcard addressed to you. Perhaps it is the clue you were looking for," the lieutenant said. "Our lab has gone over it but they cannot make head or tail of its message."

"If I know my brother, tall dark-haired Frank, he will find the clue," said Joe, arrogantly.

Frank examined the postcard. "There is a picture of a green woman on this card!" he smiled. "The print is faded, I can barely make out the message. It looks like it has been through a washing machine. It was probably sent through the U.S. mail," he guessed, handing the postcard to Joe.

"You may be right about that," agreed Joe.

"But what does it mean?" asked the lieutenant.

Joe stared at the postcard. "Frankly, I'm baffled," he said, shaking his head. "Can we see the hippie?"

"Yes, they are questioning him now," the lieutenant replied. "But he is a tough one."

The boys entered the room where the hippie was leaning against a wall, urinating on the floor.

"Did he talk yet?" asked Chet.

"He refused to tell us anything," replied the guard. "He did confess to a parking violation and two overdue library books."

"Wait a minute!" cried Chet. "That man looks awfully familiar!"

"Yes," agreed Joe, "But where have we seen that unshaven face, wide brimmed hat, blue jeans, and old army jacket before?"

"Hardly Boys! Chet! Am I glad to see you!" cried the hippie as he took off his hat and wig.

"Why that's no hippie! That's our father, Fenton Hardly!" shouted Frank and Joe.

The boys told the Bayport detective what they had done in New York City, and about the hippie guide they had met.

"He was mighty suspicious," announced Frank.

"Golly!" chuckled Mr. Hardly. "I was the hippie guide! And you didn't even know! I was just trying to keep an eye on you boys and keep you out of trouble."

"Why did you take us to that apartment?" asked Joe.

"It was the return address of the postcard, boys."

"The postcard!" cried the lieutenant. "So that explains it! But why did you take the boys to the Village?"

"Huh?" gulped the Bayport detective.

"The return address on this post-card is from Grosset & Dunlap, a New York publishing house located in midtown Manhattan," said the Lieutenant.

"We must go there, then!" announced Frank. "Let's go, Dad!"

"No!" yelled Fenton Hardly. "Keep those boys away from me. I can't take it anymore. Every time I have a case, they solve it. They're always getting in the way."

"What's the matter, Dad?" asked Frank.

"Yes Father, please tell us. Have you discovered a clue?"

"Imbecilic plots! Moronic stories! Outdated adjectives! Goody-this, goody-that!" exulted Mr. Hardly.

"We must continue our sleuthing!" announced Frank.

"You boys are such fucking assholes!" barked Fenton Hardly.

A Mysterious Man

A mysterious man rushed into police headquarters, pointing at Fenton Hardly. "Arrest that man!" he yelled, "for the murder of children's literature."

"Who are you?" asked the confused lieutenant.

"I am Franklin W. Dixon," explained the man. "I write detective and mystery stories."

"What books do you write, Mr. Dixon?" Joe asked.

"Fucking asshole!" screamed Fenton Hardly.

"Mr. Hardly! No profanity, please, not in my books," Mr. Dixon corrected him severely.

"Those boys always have the clues staring them in the face," wept the Bayport detective, "and they still can't tell their heads from their asses."

"Hardly is the real villain," continued Dixon. "He tried to corrupt these boys. I sent them the postcard because I knew they were in terrible trouble."

"They're my boys, Dixon!" exclaimed Hardly. "They have to grow up and face reality. They can't live sheltered lives!"

"And that's why you killed Gertrude!" announced Mr. Dixon.

"What?!?" cried out the boys.

"Your father knew she wouldn't allow any hanky-panky."

"I can't believe it," Joe sobbed.

"Your father disguised himself as a hippie guide to trick you boys into becoming what he calls 'normal teenagers,'" added Mr. Dixon. "America would be lost without the wholesome Hardly boys."

"Let's go, Fenton Hardly." The Lieutenant handcuffed the Bayport detective and led him from the room.

"Now maybe we can get something to eat," suggested Chet. They all laughed heartily.

Make-a-Dysfunctional-Wish Foundation

There is nothing more tragic than a life taken before its time. It is even more heartbreaking when the simple wish of that young, terminally-ill child is denied by organizations with no vision. These kids need your help.

The Make-a-Dysfunctional-Wish Foundation was created in 1985 when a young child from Newark, New Jersey, was rejected from the Make-a-Wish Foundation.

His dying wish was to receive a lap dance from "a real, live stripper in a real, live strip joint." With the help of local donors like you, his full wish was granted and the first chapter of the Make-a-Dysfunctional-Wish Foundation was founded. Can we really deny the innocent dreams embedded in the hearts of these children? Can we really judge them for having the courage to go out with a bang? Of course not. Just listen to some of our children's wishes . . .

Mark Johnson, **eight-years-old, from Detroit, Michigan, has always been an action movie fan:** "I've always wanted to drive a Ferrari through a crowded city square. People would dodge all over the place. Maybe I'd even clip a few of the poor bastards. Then I'd load up the truck with extra tanks of gasoline and drive it off a cliff for a big explosion. That would be fuckin' awesome."

Johnny Capeli **from Brooklyn, New York, has just one thing on his mind:** "Hookers, baby. I want as many as money can buy—short ones, tall ones, thin ones, fat ones. No legs? No arms? I don't care, just bring 'em on."

Our 1000th wish was granted last year to *Megan Jones* **of Miami Beach, Florida, who wanted nothing except to get really, really high:** "I don't want any of that pot you give to the old ladies with cataracts, either. I want heroin, nothing but the best. I mean, I'm dying, right?"

Or *Francis Penty* **from Ithaca, New York:** "I want a lot of money so I can get my own harem of mail-order brides."

What about *Phillip Escobar* **of Fort Wayne, Indiana?** "I want to live in my own castle for a week. I'd be king and my servants would be other kids who are weaker and smaller than I am. Then, I could make them do stuff and I could beat them up whenever they pissed me off."

Despite all the good the Make-a-Dysfunctional-Wish Foundation has done, our job is far from over. There are so many children who deserve that one wish their twisted hearts desire most. Can you help these children realize their dreams? Here at the Make-a-Dysfunctional-Wish Foundation, we work tirelessly to make every wish a reality. However, with every demented smirk we put on the faces of these kids, we also have plenty of costs to cover. We take care of everything from the expense of realizing the wish to legal fees and bribes. If you care to make a donation, just contact your local chapter of the Make-a-Dysfunctional Wish Foundation. Any contribution of small, unmarked bills would mean the world to any of these kids.

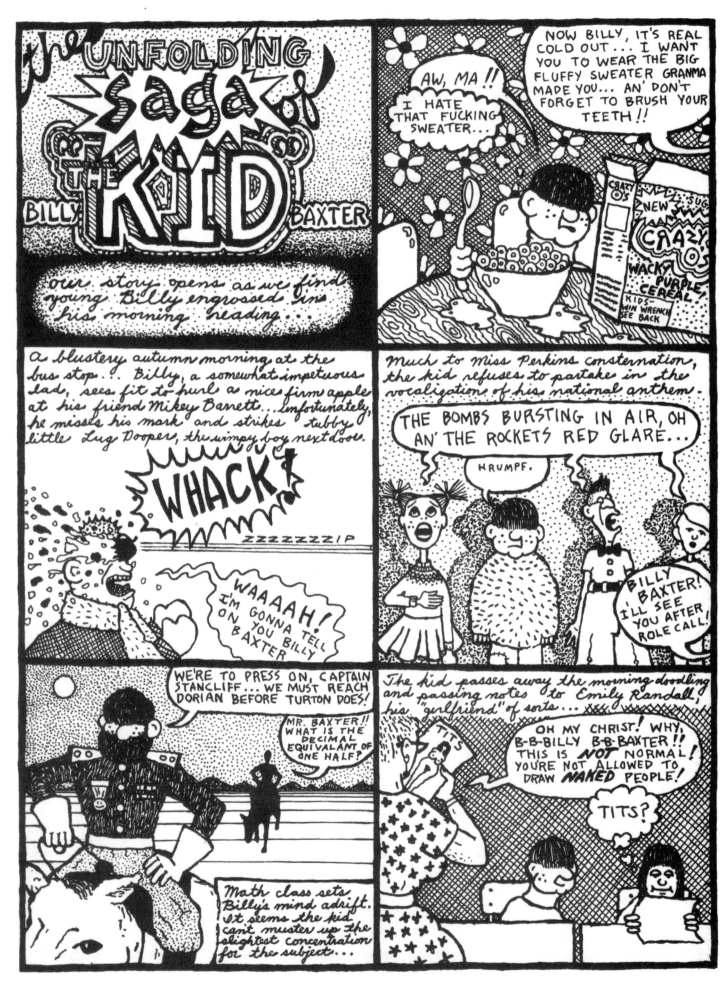

An Interview with Peter Pumpkin-Eater

"Peter, Peter, Pumpkin-Eater,
Had a wife and couldn't keep her,
He put her in a pumpkin shell
And there he kept her very well."

Every night, this rhyme is recited by millions of children who are unable to grasp its true implications as an anti-feminist text. However, members of Feminist Rights Expository Expatriates Bummed Over Nursery Rhymes (F.R.E.E.B.O.N.R) think Mr. Pumpkin-Eater is perpetuating the existence of a patriarchal society and the subjugation of women. His rhyme has become the subject of a major worldwide scandal and a major motion picture from the producers of *Showgirls.* Mr. Pumpkin-Eater, eager to confront these accusations and clear his good name, agreed to an interview in his living room, where he could remain close to his wife, who sat quietly in a pumpkin shell in the master bedroom.

Peter, how did your obsession with pumpkins begin?

Please address me by my formal surname.

Sorry, sir.

No, not sir. My name is Mr. Pumpkin-Eater.

So, Mr. Pumpkin-Eater, why do you keep your wife in a pumpkin shell?

I love her, but she is a promiscuous woman. I have to keep her in the shell. It's not so bad, really. She's got cable.

How often do you let your wife out of the shell?

A few times during the day to do the house chores and once or twice a night when I want to have sex.

Why not use a chastity belt or a muzzle to control your wife? Wouldn't that solve your problem?

No, because a chastity belt or a muzzle would not keep her away from men.

You say that you lock your wife in a pumpkin shell to curb her sex drive. Do you ever indulge and, if so, how do you justify it?

I never said I put her in the pumpkin shell to curb her sex drive. I said I put her in there to keep her from having sex with other men.

Sorry. Do you ever have affairs with other women?

I have affairs and it's okay. Men cannot get pregnant and are not restricted by social stigmas.

What do you think about countries where women are forced to wear covers or veils?

I think they are excellent. Those people really have the right idea, but, of course, it is best to lock them up. If women do have to move about, they should wear clothes that make them look ugly and scary.

Your poem is a nursery rhyme, but it sounds much more like an X-rated movie. Should little children be exposed to such vulgarity?

Most children are stupid. Anyway, they are exposed to so much vulgarity and profanity on television that they don't even notice the poem about me because its circulation isn't so high.

Don't you realize that if everyone had your attitude, the world would be a much uglier place for children?

It wasn't my choice to be the subject of a nursery rhyme. I can't help it if Mother Goose happened to find me irresistible.

Don't you believe in the equality of the sexes? Shouldn't women have the same rights as men?

Sure, sure. Listen, I'm expecting a honey in a couple of minutes. If you could wrap this little interview up, I'd appreciate it.

Fun Page

Magic!

I am The Great Magico!
I will teach you an amazing trick.
Hold your breath and count to
one hundred. Look! You are
turning blue like a smurf!

Farewell to My Arms

My arms fell off, and I can't put them back on
because I have no arms.
Can you help me put my arms back on?

Which One?

A   B

If "Doctor A" leaves Chicago on a train traveling at 50
m.p.h., and "Nurse B" leaves St. Louis on a train traveling at
75 m.p.h., from whom would you rather get a rectal exam?

Circle the Different One!

(**HINT:** He's the one with an erection.)

Ho Ho Ho!

Oh, no! Santa got himself drunk and
stuck in a chimney with a hooker
again. Quick, lube up Santa before
Mrs. Claus finds him, or little Jimmy
won't get his martini glasses.

Kiddie Riddle

Why was Six
afraid of Seven?
ANSWER: Because Seven
made harassing phone calls
to Six at odd hours of
the night.

Raving Savings

Unscramble the PIN number
to our Swiss bank account!
284334098734983

Fun with Science

Watch this E. Coli evolve.
Try not to breathe too much!

Chapter 2

Got Class?

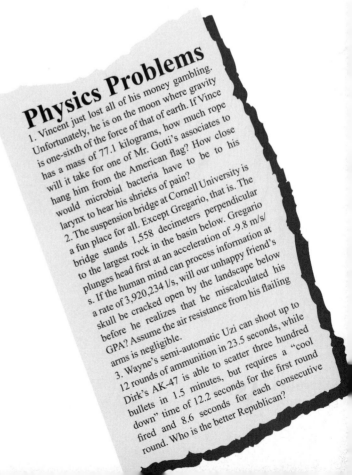

Physics Problems

1. Vincent just lost all of his money gambling. Unfortunately, he is on the moon where gravity is one-sixth of the force of that of earth. If Vince has a mass of 77.1 kilograms, how much rope will it take for one of Mr. Gotti's associates to hang him from the American flag? How close would microbial bacteria have to be to his larynx to hear his shrieks of pain?

2. The suspension bridge at Cornell University is a fun place for all. Except Gregario, that is. The bridge stands 1,558 decimeters perpendicular to the largest rock in the basin below. Gregario plunges head first at an acceleration of -9.8 m/s/s. If the human mind can process information at a rate of 3,920,234 l/s, will our unhappy friend's skull be cracked open by the landscape below before he realizes that he miscalculated his GPA? Assume the air resistance from his flailing arms is negligible.

3. Wayne's semi-automatic Uzi can shoot up to 12 rounds of ammunition in 23.5 seconds, while Dirk's AK-47 is able to scatter three hundred bullets in 1.5 minutes, but requires a "cool down" time of 12.2 seconds for the first round fired and 8.6 seconds for each consecutive round. Who is the better Republican?

s the hordes of new students descend upon our pristine campus, you will no doubt notice a strange feeling mounting in the pit of your stomach. You will be lost. You will be confused. You will see yourself for what you really are: alone, pathetic, and lost in a crowd of thousands of new students. And, you will find you need advice. You will need me. Why me? Because I am unique. I am rare. I am special. I am a *Cornell Daily Sun* senior editor. What does this mean? Worship me, for I am all-powerful and all-knowing.

You are nothing. You are a freshman, a mere three months out of high school, barely out of your blissful childhood existence, never having faced the cold reality of life away from the domestic wonderland of your mommy's house. Like that sentence? I know I do. That's what being in the fourth year of an English major does for you. Think you can write like this? Don't even try it, lest you find out what miserable failures you are. Yes, every one of you.

In the next few months, new experiences will abound. You will find yourself afloat in a sea of never-ending assignments, classes, and frat party invitations. And, you will find yourself drowning. For you are not me. Instead, you are you, a pathetic freshman, reading the *Cornell Daily Sun* in hopes of some semi-authentic pearl of wisdom that will save you from your disheartening fate. Isn't that the best sentence you've ever read? And I wrote it at four a.m.! Can you believe it? Oh, the joys of being me. I just love myself.

In conclusion, you should just quit now. Salvage the few bits of ego you have left and run back to your hometown, where you can nurse the burning pain of failure in relative oblivion. Isn't this the best sentence I've written yet? I know, I know, everyone wants to be me. But then in the end, isn't that the ultimate tragedy of existence? (Wow! I'm on such a roll!) Yes, there can only be one me, and unfortunately, it isn't you. Better luck next time.

College Applications Got You Down?
Tired of Saying You Were in Clubs That Never Existed?
Had It Up to Here With Talking To Your Lesbian Guidance Counselor?

The College Essay Service Can Help.

Just look at these sample applications from REAL customers:

"Briefly discuss a conflict you faced and how you resolved it."

SAM POLLANDER,
YALE APPLICATION

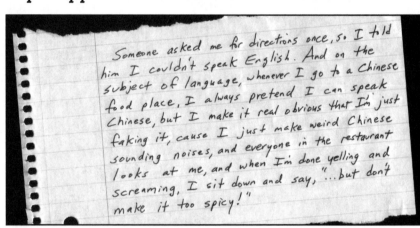

"Discuss a time in your life when you took a risk which later paid off."

BRYANT PORTLITTLE,
NYU APPLICATION

"Where do you see yourself after school?"

RUTEGER MAYNE,
COLGATE APPLICATION

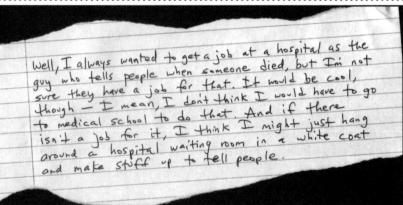

"Ask, then answer, an important question you would have liked us to ask."

FREDRICK HEINRICH WERSCISISER,
BOSTON COLLEGE, TRANSFER APPLICATION

HOTEL ADMINISTRATION 193: Cookies

Spring. 4 Credits.

We live in a mixed-up society that brainwashes people into thinking that Animal Crackers are crackers and Fig Newtons are fruit and cake. This controversial course defies convention by making a bold hypothesis: Both Fig Newtons and Animal Crackers are cookies! A large part of this course will attempt to deal with the startling implications of this theory (e.g., why it's wrong to serve Animal Crackers with cheese, and why it's inappropriate to eat Fig Newtons with a knife and fork).

PHILOSOPHY 201: Philosophies of Milk

Fall. 4 Credits.

Does milk have free will or do the forces of a fatalistic universe govern its actions? If milk goes sour, does it do so because it chooses to, or because it simply must? Furthermore, if we determine that milk goes sour because it chooses to, isn't it also reasonable for humans to hold a grudge against it? After all, what kind of dairy product would go out of its way to ruin my morning bowl of cereal!?! This course was created to justify the professor's indefatigable contempt for sour milk.

HISTORY 316: Book Burning

Fall. 3 Credits.

Throughout history various books have been burned because they were deemed too offensive. Were these books really vulgar or merely ahead of their time? As compelling as this debate is, this course will focus exclusively on the act of book burning itself. This course will encourage students to buy and burn over forty works of classic literature—all of which are available for purchase in the campus store. Buy, buy, buy! Burn, burn, burn! (Please note: burnt books are not returnable to the campus store.)

PSYCHOLOGY 113: How to Seduce a Professor

Fall. 3 Credits.

It's quite natural for female students to be wowed by their professor's charm and endless tirades against conservative America. Unfortunately, sometimes a professor's high ethical standards (and/or family) can pose an obstacle to an otherwise successful seduction. This course will teach you various mind games you'll need to play on your professor to get him into bed with you.

Such mind games include asking, "What do I need to do to get an A in this course?" and accepting his invitation to some "office after-hours." Grade for course largely based on enthusiasm, effort, and class participation.

AMERICANA 101: Welcome Exchange Students

Fall. 4 Credits.

So you just arrived in America, and now you not only want to interact with American students, you also want to find out what makes them tick. Have no fear! This no-holds-barred course will teach you what Americans are really thinking but are too polite to say when you're around. You'll learn what we really think about your country, the stereotypes we apply to your people, and what animal you most remind us of. After taking this course, you'll most likely want to deport yourself back to the motherland; but you'll have learned how to avoid letting the American pie hit your ass on the way out.

FOOD SCIENCE 401: The Future of Hot Dogs

Fall. 4 Credits.

In the future, when machines inevitably do the work of man, how will hot dogs be prepared for humans? Will the hot dogs be cooked and distributed by robotic hot dog vendors, or by futuristic vending machines that not only distribute food, but also cook it? Students will be urged to weigh the pros and cons of each possibility.

PHYS ED 205: The Running of the Bulls

Spring. 1 Credit.

Why let the citizens of Pamplona, Spain, have all the fun? Being chased by a bull isn't only the thrill of a lifetime, it's also a great workout! A bull charging at thirty miles-per-hour provides you with more motivation to run than a sweaty Richard Simmons ever could. The course will run from downtown, through the throngs of activists protesting against this class, up into the Veterinary School, and finally end in Schoellkopf Field, where the bulls will proceed to be slain by this year's meat science class. Course is pass/fail only. Requirements for passing include not being gored to death.

GEOGRAPHY 101: Finding Africa on the Map

Fall. 1 Credit.

Students will learn to find the continent of Africa on a standard map, and, if time permits, on a globe.

CORNELL
UNIVERSITY

ENGLISH 314: Poetry for Mathematicians

Fall. 2 Credits.

The course will study poetry from a mathematical perspective. Students will be expected to graph the quality of each poem based on such determinants as form, meaning, and lyricism. For a final project, students must select a Shakespearean sonnet and calculate its quality while rotating about the y axis.

LINGUISTICS 101: English for T.A.s

Fall. 4 Credits.

Covers useful phrases, such as "Ask the professor," "Hand in your homework, please," and "I was just an undergraduate last year; how the hell should I know?"

PSYCHOLOGY 270: Conservatives and Brain Disease

Spring. 4 Credits.

Study the correspondence between conservative Republicans and mind-debilitating brain aneurisms. Are they truly evil or merely a product of our society? Are idealistic liberal Democrats inherently stupid or does the world consistently fail to meet their unrealistic expectations?

GOVERNMENT 205: Anarchy in Society

Fall or Spring. ? Credits.

Taught wherever and whenever the instructor feels like it. Covers anything the professor wishes. Maybe you'll even firebomb a few Democrats for being too conservative. There is no preregistration or registration for this class.

LANGUAGE 100: English

Fall. 4 Credits.

Learning English is a great way to converse with people who speak English. How are you? I am fine. Of course you are, you're speaking English!

PHILOSOPHY 405: The Philosophy of Drinking

Fall. 4 Credits.

I drink, therefore I am drunk. This class deals with some of the age-old philosophical arguments surrounding drinking, such as: is puking fun? Does drinking lots of water make me an alcoholic? Just how much rum should be in a Rum and Coke for the drink to not be overpriced? Where the @$%##@ are my car keys? Students will contribute to the discussion by being drunk a lot.

PSYCHOLOGY 332: Talking to Fish

Spring. 5 Credits.

Do fish grow bigger or faster when they are consulted regularly about relevant social and political issues? Will talking to fish make them feel silly or self-conscious? What the hell is this? I'm not spending a semester talking to fish!

HISTORY 333: Understanding Sugar Cereal

Spring. 4 Credits.

The back of the cereal boxes in our archive serves as the text for this fascinating study of Sugar Cereal history. Just what kind of ship is Captain Crunch the captain of? Is he a nasty crunch pirate or a just benevolent crunch sailor? And just who or what are the Soggies? Learn what foul deeds proceeded Count Chocula, Frank 'n Berry, and Boo Berry's descent into the pastel cereal underworld, and the magic powers that enable Tony the Tiger to talk to humans. Students will be expected to sign a health form before taking this class because the sugar content in the cereals we will be sampling will be enough to plunge any diabetic into a life-threatening coma.

COMMUNICATIONS 101: Irresponsibility

Spring or Fall. 2 Credits.

Students are not obligated to familiarize themselves with the course syllabus. Attendance is neither required nor condoned, assignments are on file in the library, conveniently located near the photocopier, and the final exam is scheduled for the middle of July, making it unlikely, if not impossible, for students to show up. Students enrolled in the lab will spend two hours a week partaking in underage drinking, practicing unsafe sex, driving drunk, and making empty promises.

BIOLOGY 550: Cloning For Fun and Profit

Fall. 5 Credits.

With all the ethical questions being raised about cloning, it is natural to ask "Who cares?" This class will disregard any and all moral issues regarding cloning and do it just because we can. Just grab some cells and let the good times roll! Topics of study include: becoming immortal through cloning, using cloning to beat the casino, employing cloning in practical jokes, and selling clones into slavery. A lab fee of one hundred dollars and a DNA sample are required for all students wishing to enroll.

THEATER ARTS 334: Ducking
Spring. 4 Credits.

This class is dedicated solely to one of the most difficult of all theatrical techniques: ducking. Students will learn how to duck when they hear phrases like: "Hit the deck!" or "Look out!" or "Hey there, comin' in!" or "Whoa!" or "Duck!" or "Put your head down quickly, or I will strike it with something!"

MATHEMATICS 002: Change for a Dollar
Fall. 2 Credits.

Did you know that it's possible to have $1.19 in change and still not be able to give somebody change for a dollar? No, of course you didn't. Only math majors figure out that kind of nonsense. This class is devoted to the various ways to make change for a dollar. The class moves quickly, starting with "four quarters" and proceeding directly to more advanced topics like "a half dollar, four dimes, a nickel, and five pennies." Students will provide their own dollar bills.

COMMUNICATIONS 200: Talking To Others
Fall. 2 Credits.

This class is all about talking to other people. Students will be expected to talk with other people, and not with themselves. Any student caught intentionally talking to himself or herself will be considered in violation of the Campus Code of Academic Integrity. Various conversational techniques will be stressed, and the origins of modern phrases such as "Hey, what's up?" "Hey, how's it going?" "Hey," and "Hey there, buddy boy" are analyzed.

LINGUISTICS 444: Don King
Fallerastic. 4 Creditastic.

This class will be a splendifferific journey into the fantabulastic world of the most charismatastic fight promoter of all time. Learn the nuances and intricacies of this linguistifistic genius. Oooonly in America!

AMERICAN STUDIES 102: Value Meals
Fall. 6 Credits.

What is the significance of the "Number One" Value Meal? Is it less costly to get French fries even if you don't want them? In this course, students will tackle these and other important questions pertaining to the selection and acquisition of a value meal. The history of super sizing will be discussed, as will several relevant theories about the evolution of the term "Go Large." A supplementary lecture will be added for no additional cost.

(ACADEMIC DEPARTMENT) 110: Mad Libs
(Semester). (Number) Credits.

This class is dedicated to (noun). Students will be asked to (verb) papers on (adjective) topics including (sexual position), (place), and (member of the Monkees). Should they so choose, students can (adverb) (verb) to (verb) the (noun).

ECONOMICS 410: Socks for Jocks
Spring. 3 Credits.

Socks for Jocks is unique in that it is the only class that deals exclusively with the application and removal of everyday apparel. Techniques include learning to find clean socks by smelling the ones on the floor, finding socks that match, and recognizing when one foot has too many socks, the other not enough. Prerequisite: Sociology 96: Where Are My Pants?

ASTRONOMY 12: Clocks for Jocks
Spring. 3 Credits.

This introductory-level course is designed for those students who were admitted to the University solely based on athletic ability. For these students, who are often unable to budget their time effectively due to their inability to use clocks, college life can become a living hell of sports, parties, and casual sex. This class is geared toward those athletes who feel overwhelmed by a heavy academic course-load. There is only one textbook, and it is only four words long. This class is offered as part of the Courses for Jocks series, which also includes: Astronomy 100: Spock for Jocks; Gym 243: Jocks for Jocks; Geology 201: Rocks For Jocks; Urban Planning 322: Glocks For Jocks; Asian Studies 215: Woks For Jocks; and Business Administration 247: Stocks For Jocks.

CORNELL
UNIVERSITY

courses of study

SOCIOLOGY 400: Sidestepping 12-Step Programs
Fall. 12 Credits.

The perfect course for the substance abuser who, through legal or other means, has been forced to enter a 12-Step program to help end his/her addiction, yet who doesn't really want to give up the stuff. With a thorough understanding of brainwashing techniques and religious overtones unique to the program, students learn how to: lie without guilt about anything addiction-related; find exciting new methods to continue substance abuse without being caught or suspected; and claim to have put one's heart in God's hands whilst one has actually put half a bottle of Wild Turkey in one's stomach.

PHILOSOPHY 301: The Philosophy of Jell-O
Spring. 4 Credits.

A study of contemporary theories dealing with America's favorite gelatin desert. Is there really always room for Jell-O? And if so, why do we feel the need to stop eating it after say, one or two bowls? Why don't we just continue to ingest Jell-O until our insides have become one with its wiggly, squiggly goodness? And who chooses what flavor the Jell-O that eventually consumes us will be? Are we mere puppets, tied to the cruel strings of our gelatinous fate, or can we choose to stop eating Jell-O altogether and live as free men?

COMMUNICATIONS 401: Walking Up Stairs
Fall. 2 Credits.

In this introduction to the subtlety of walking up stairs, students will learn the difference between up and down. Recitation sections present role-playing scenarios: You lift your left foot, now what? Good. Okay, you step with the left foot, which comes next? No. If you step with the left foot again you will fall and subject yourself to injury. Upon completion of the course, students will find themselves exploring new worlds of second, even third floors. Students are encouraged to continue their trans-floor training by enrolling in Communications 402: Walking Down Stairs the following semester so they may return to the ground floor if need be.

SOCIOLOGY 34: Peer Pressure
Spring. 4 Credits.

Come on, why don't you just sign up for this class? Everybody else is doing it, what's a few more credits? Just sign up, man, it's going to be great. You're so lame. I don't know what your problem is. Are you some kind of loser? Just take the class—you won't regret it.

PSYCHOLOGY 393: Abnormal Bovine Psychology
Fall. 4 Credits.

It's not easy being a cow. Sometimes life gets too hectic, and the pressure becomes too much to bear—"Moooore milk! Moooore milk!" all the time, every day—it's enough to drive a cow crazy. This class will examine the underlying causes of bovine breakdown, including stress, anger, and udder frustration.

HOTEL ADMINISTRATION 13: Napkin Folding
Spring. 7 Credits.

This comprehensive seminar on the application of various folding techniques will give students valuable hands-on experience in the art of folding napkins, as well as the confidence they need to make those folds in a pressure situation. Various folds will be taught, including the corner-to-corner fold, the back-and-forth fold, and the Charles Barkley pointy-head fold. Students will be encouraged to work with various media, including traditional material such as cloth and paper, as well as newer experimental substances like tin foil, burlap, and wood. (Note: students will receive one napkin which they will use for the duration of the course.)

CHEMISTRY 302: Things That Go "Boom!"
Fall. 4 Credits.

This fascinating lecture explores the different ways in which things explode. Students will be exposed to numerous explosions of various intensity and destructiveness. Those who survive find Chemistry 302 to be a valuable, life-affirming experience. (Note: students must sign insurance waiver before they are allowed to participate in weekly lab.)

ART HISTORY 318: French Renaissance Art
Fall. 4 Credits.

You stupid, puritanical American swine, this course will cover the finest art the world has ever seen (not that you unsophisticated, hamburger-eating idiots would understand any of it). Americans will not be allowed to see any paintings.

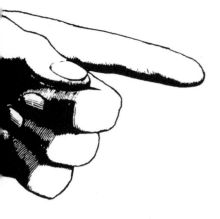

CONDENSED classics

Have you ever realized just minutes before class that you were unprepared? Never, right? You were supposed to read a long boring book. No time. Frantic pacing. You look at your watch. Not even enough time to read *Cliffs Notes*. But now there's help. You'll have to read all of these books before you graduate, so don't lose this list. Clip out this page, and glue it to your refrigerator!

● **ALICE'S ADVENTURES IN WONDERLAND—Lewis Carroll**
Carroll was fixated with chess and cocaine, and this book illustrates these obsessions.

● **ANNA KARENINA—Leo Tolstoy**
Warning! In the movie version, Anna lives.

● **ANIMAL FARM—George Orwell**
The pigs turn out to be just as bad as the previous owners, and it"s all a metaphor attacking the Soviet elite.

● **THE AUTOBIOGRAPHY OF MALCOLM X —Malcolm X**
The author didn't expect to live to read his book, and he didn't.

● **THE BIBLE—God**
Old Testament: God creates the world, makes a lot of laws, and the Jews break most of them. New Testament: Jesus gets nailed.

● **BILLY BUDD—Herman Melville**
Billy kills a man. He dies because of it, which reaffirms the existence of God.

● **BREAKFAST OF CHAMPIONS—Kurt Vonnegut**
Lots of crude drawings that have nothing to do with this story about Kilgore Trout.

● **CANDIDE—Voltaire**
Candide searches for the truth in the world, finds everything is for the best, and cultivates his own garden.

● **THE CANTERBURY TALES—Chaucer**
Pilgrims on the way to a shrine tell stories about medieval sex.

● **CATCH 22—Joseph Heller**
Yosarian runs the war his own way, discovers that everyone is crazy, and decides not to tell anyone.

● **THE CATCHER IN THE RYE—J.D. Salinger**
Holden Caulfield flunks out of prep school and we don't find out until the very end that he is writing from inside an asylum.

● **THE CRUCIBLE—Arthur Miller**
Joe McCarthy was too stupid to see that Arthur Miller was using the Salem witch hunts as an attack on his hearings.

● **DEATH OF A SALESMAN—Arthur Miller**
Willy Loman, the salesman, kills himself. His whole family is pretty fucked up, anyway.

● **A DOLL'S HOUSE—Henrik Ibsen**
Liza doesn't like being treated like a child.

● **DON QUIXOTE—Cervantes**
Don searches for truth and ends up battling it out with a windmill.

● **FINNEGAN'S WAKE—James Joyce**
Only three people in the entire world understand this senseless gibberish about God, man's fall from grace, and quarks.

● **GONE WITH THE WIND—Margaret Mitchell**
Scarlett gives a damn, but Rhett doesn't.

● **THE GRAPES OF WRATH—John Steinbeck**
The Joad family goes to California to find things are just as bad as in Oklahoma.

● **GRAVITY'S RAINBOW—Thomas Pynchon**
The "rainbow" refers to the trail a rocket makes. It takes place during World War II, and there is a lot of senseless violence.

● **HAMLET—William Shakespeare**
Hamlet has designs on his uncle who killed his father and married his mother. He feigns madness, and everyone is killed in the end in a crazed orgy of hate and lust.

● **JUDE THE OBSCURE—Thomas Hardy**
Jude is a saint in disguise, and he gets a symbolic job as a stonecutter.

● **JULIUS CAESAR—William Shakespeare**
Brutus falls on his sword when he realizes that killing Caesar only put Anthony and Octavius in power.

● **THE JUNGLE—Upton Sinclair**
Jergen goes to work in the stockyards, falls into a vat of pig entrails, and dies. Don't eat the bologna.

● **LADY CHATTERLY'S LOVER—D.H. Lawrence**
Lady Chatterly can't get it on with her crippled husband, so she has a passionate affair with her groundskeeper instead.

● **LES MISERABLES—Victor Hugo**
Great chase scenes in the sewers beneath Paris.

● **LITTLE WOMEN—Louisa May Alcott**
Four little girls act so good it makes you sick.

● **MACBETH—William Shakespeare**
The secret is: those who have had a Caesarian aren't of women born. Macbeth's head is stuck on a post, and Banquo climbs through a trap door.

● **THE MERCHANT OF VENICE—William Shakespeare**
Shylock the Jew is forced to give over half his property when he realizes that you can't take a pound of flesh without taking some blood also.

● **THE METAMORPHOSIS—Franz Kafka**
Gregory gets turned into a bug, dies, and his family is relieved.

● **MOBY DICK—Herman Melville**
A ship sinks, a whale dies, and Captain Ahab is dragged to his death. The story is an allegory of some sort.

● **1984—George Orwell**
Sex is unenjoyable, and is punishable by having rats eat your face out.

● **NO EXIT—Jean P. Sartre**
Three dead people get locked in a room, don't get along, and realize they're in hell.

● **THE ODYSSEY—Homer**
A bunch of guys get lost, find their way home, and a few live happily ever after.

● **OEDIPUS REX—Sophocles**
Oedipus ignores ominous oracles, marries his Mom, discovers what he has done, gouges out his eyes, and inspires Freud.

● **OLIVER TWIST—Charles Dickens**
Fagan and the Artful Dodger escape, Nancy dies, Bill gets killed, and Oliver gets a good home.

● **ON THE ROAD—Jack Kerouac**
Sal Paradise and Dean Morarity travel the country by hitching or driving in Dean's beat-up car. Dean ends up in New York and finally dumps Camille for Mary Lou.

● **OTHELLO—William Shakespeare**
Othello is jealous of everyone so he kills his wife Desdemona.

● **RETURN OF THE NATIVE—Thomas Hardy**
Almost everybody dies in the end in a freak Welsh storm.

● **ROMEO AND JULIET—William Shakespeare**
Boy meets girl. Boy loses girl. They both die, tragically.

● **ROSENCRANZ AND GUILDENSTERN ARE DEAD—Tom Stoppard**
Rosencranz and Guildenstem play question games before they take their own death sentence to England.

● **A SEPARATE PEACE—John Knowles**
Phineas falls to his death, but was really pushed by his best friend, who feels guilty about it afterwards.

● **SLAUGHTERHOUSE-FIVE—Kurt Vonnegut**
A man steals a teapot after the American Air Force bombs Dresden. Billy Pilgrim becomes unstuck in time and goes to Tralfamador where they watch him have sex. So it goes.

● **THE SOCIAL CONTRACT—Jean Jacques Rousseau**
Rousseau outlines his utopian government, but ruins the whole thing by declaring a need for a civil religion.

● **A STREETCAR NAMED DESIRE—Tennessee Williams**
Blanche DuBois gets committed. Stanley yells "Stella!" a lot.

● **THE TEMPEST—William Shakespeare**
Shakespeare's farewell play where he claims that "plays are like magic." This is the first and last play ever to take place on Bermuda, for whatever that's worth.

● **ULYSSES—James Joyce**
Stephen Dedalus grows up to discover that he hates Catholics and the Irish.

● **WAR AND PEACE—Leo Tolstoy**
People fight, then they make up—in 2,000 pages.

● **WOMEN IN LOVE—D.H. Lawrence**
The men learn that the only true love is love between males.

● **ZEN AND THE ART OF MOTORCYCLE MAINTENANCE—Robert Pirsig**
Phaedrus and his son ride a motorcycle to the West Coast and think they are profound.

Hot air, Ka-ka, and Jum-jum Beans

(*or* Writing Made Easy)

Every year, a new crop of freshman at the prestigious university where I teach ask me to tell them the secret of good writing—if it's the appearance of a semi-colon at the magical moment, spelling everything correctly, or what. Well, so finally, I thinks to myself, "Jason, ain't it about time you starts bleeding these people who been bleeding you all these years?" So I decides to put some of the techniques I've learned over my vast, girthful life, for good writing, in an article, and get paid for it.

To begin with, one of my favorite tricks for starting anything is an opening sentence. Have one. You'll be amazed at how it speeds things along. Don't worry too much over what's in it, whether it holds together syntactically, or even whether it has anything to do with what you're trying to write about, if indeed that's the case. I never put too much stock in opening sentences myself. I mean, for Chrissakes, you look at some of the famous ones, and they're just so much steamin' squigglies, as far as I'm concerned. And I should know, right? Take a look at *Moby Dick*, for example. "Call me Ishmael." What the hell is that? I'll tell you what it is: it's dookey, plain old ka-ka. Now what I would like to see here is a little humor, maybe something like, "Now you can call me Ishmael, or you can call me Ray, or you can call me Jay, or you can call me Ray Jay, but you doesn't haf to call me Ishmael."

Let's assume that you've gotten past the opening sentence by now. The next problem most students face is the all-important second sentence. I say, screw the second sentence; ignore it completely. Go straight into your third. You'll be much better off. For example, take a look at the first paragraph of my second novel, *The Dales of Wind*:

> "Maria, the farmer's niece, strode lovingly into the torpid, vorpal, mordant, cordial maelstrom of downtown Loudertown, leaned back on her still impeccable shoulders, sighed, burped, and lit up a joint. Then, he shot her."

Note how the reader begs for a second sentence. By not delivering, readers tend to read in their own second sentences here, making your job a hell of a lot easier. While I'm on the subject of my second novel, which by the way was a tense, fast-paced action novel, another question many students ask me is, "How can I write a tense, fast-paced action novel, you know, the kind that make a real lot of money and that any dog's left nut could write." Well, there's really no simple answer to your question. Some tit

on the cover sure helps, but the most important thing is probably the back-cover blurb, you know, the thing that determines whether you buy the book or not. I am in the habit of putting the same blurb on every one of my books, no matter what the subject matter. For example, here's the blurb from my twelfth novel, *Accept No Substitutes*:

> "Tinseltown—where there's lots of sex, and beauty fades as quickly as a young girl's dreams. Meet Julie, fresh off the farm (but that doesn't last for long, since she has lots of sex), who discovers that the casting couch can seat twelve. Meet Tony—big, strong, dumb, long—who discovers that a career in porn (lots of sex) can sometimes hurt one's political ambitions . . . "

This blurb alone made the bestseller list for twelve weeks. But that probably doesn't help you much. What may help you is knowing how to make the action points of your novel so tense and exciting that any would-be reader flipping through in the supermarket can't help but buy the shit. Probably the most important thing is to *keep your sentences short*. Sort of like this. And this. Really short now. Oooh. And fast. Super quick. My. Flaming. Hot. Hot. Very hot. Oh my. Oh yeah. Ouch. Get the idea?

"But what if I don't want to write a fast-paced action novel but let's say, a horror novel, you know, with movie rights?" I've got only one thing to say to you big boy, and that's: Same thing. Note how I set the mood in my thirty-third novel, *Cringe Drippings!*:

> "The small room dripped steamy ooze from its every pore. The doctor thought to himself, "Scalpel please, nurse," and then said it. With the first long incision came up a waft of bodsteam and the doctor leaned over so it would hit him in the face, like a hot fart. After a wave or two of pleasant nausea, the doctor plunged in, thinking, "Spleen, spleen. Christ, I'd like to squish this friggin' spleen. Hee-hee. I could do it, too. Hee-hee-hee. Go squishy." The doctor soon found himself getting an awkwardly angled hard-on. Throwing cleanliness to the breeze, he pulled his hands out of the patient, pulled up the sides of his smock, and thrust both hands down his pants in an insane effort to comfort his jaunty staff. The youthful head nurse giggled, "Oh my, doctor, now there's a piece that's

primed for a-jauntin' and a-juttin'." The doctor smiled and said, "You mayn't be commeuppin' so luvidly now, whens it starts its a-pressin' and a-ruttin' agin your barein me-bodikin by the first a-gleamin' o'th'moon, now will'ya, me fecklin' niiiassie?" The nurse was rightly speechless, and still the walls dripped ooze."

The astute reader will note here the use of a rare dialect called "Punkin' Me-Gaelic". This was not unintentional. The effect garnished is much greater than by gleaning any of the "Old Norse Bel-Climes," or even the "Cattish Dig-Krees."

Well then, you say, maybe I don't want to write a horror novel after all. I think I want to write one of those romance novels, you know, the kind with the interchangeable titles. Well, that's fine as long as you remember my simple rule: In an action novel, the reader wants to see action and sex; in a horror novel—horror and sex; in a historic novel—history and sex; and in a romance novel—sex and sex. Check out my ninety-third novel, *Love's Savage Passions*:

"Elana, the fabulously beautiful countess from the tiny country of Exotica, languished sighingly by her bedroom window, the breeze regularly cooling the heat rising between her slightly parted thighs—thighs that men fight wars over, die over, bend over—and, with one leg tucked magically under her, rocked ever so to and fro thinking all the while of the one man she could never keep, could never tame, and circles of tremorous pleasure radiated out from her undulating center, caromed palpitatingly off the inside of her skin (especially, she noted, her elbows and knees), and seemed to fly back home even faster, faster, ever faster, until she could take it no longer and screamed, 'Oh, I die,' and fainted dead away."

"Be that as it may, Professor," you say, with just a hint of malice in your eye, "say I want to write a detective novel." Well, just listen up. I am no stranger to the genre myself, you know, having written some 1,200 detective novels under forty different pseudonyms back when I was younger. For example, take my 683rd novel, *My Angry Rod Spits Hot Death*:

"To tell you the truth, I knew last Friday was gonna suck from the moment I woke up and accidentally discharged my .38 into Spay, my cat. To get me over the loss, I polished off a fifth of JD that I found under the bed and then drank it. To top things off, the whole Osmond family (including Jimmy) were doing a tap dance over my occipital lobes, and I wanted to know why. Then I knew. The phone—it was ringing. It was my girlfriend, Doll. No brains to spit on, but a mouth like a sump pump and a bottomless . . .

"'Mick, you gotta help, you just gotta. It's my brother. They worked him over pretty bad. And I'm out of . . . you know.'

"I didn't, so I hung up and tried to find my other bottle of JD. Reaching blindly under the bed, I found everything but: a .38, two .45s, six .30-odd-6's; three 9mm Uzis, the back half of Spay, and a subpeona. Needless to say, I went back to bed."

"But what if I'm tired of all this novel stuff? I want to make some real art; I want to write some poetry." Well, like everyone else who sold out, I used to write poetry. I had my "art" phase too, Goddamn it. Here's my personal favorite, *"Glitters, Jacking Off"* from the volume of the same name:

Like Whitman am I:
Plagiarizing, paraphrasing, proselytizing,
(Without:
        a:
shred, of, talent: am:
I: Good thing I fooled those:
MacArthur people)
Prose with words that sip, that sigh,
That spin around, that leap and fell, of curfews and
Refuse, and parting, oh hell.
Let us go then, we, to a land. and make wee-wee
For bucks, movies for kicks, watersports.
A thirst of ages then, it is:
A past of former time,
Spent only too quickly, and too soon.
A lover's dance, a dentist nitrous-oxized against a
Palimony suit. A trump of tyrants, a vaunt of jauntles.
A cult of willies, accountants from Philly.
My wife's but a wheelbarrow. two cats fighting in a paper bag.
sopping wet with dripping
Sweat. Gloomily gloomily merrily merrily my father
Doomed doomed doomed. And yet, I wake.

I trust all of this has been helpful to some of you out there. I certainly got paid for it. Oh, by the way, confidential to my three o'clock appointment tomorrow: I know that we're supposed to be discussing your thesis proposal. Nevertheless, why don't you drink a lot of fluids that day and, like, not go to the bathroom at all before our appointment. I think you'll find that I'll be much more receptive to this silly proposal thing. Be seeing ya.

Fellow destitute, you may not be well off financially, but you can still lead a full and enjoyable life at college. By cutting unnecessary expenses, you can easily save enough money for the real necessities: an iPod, U2 tickets, and beer. So here are some tips to help cut your living expenses:

LAUNDRY

To avoid those three-dollars-per-washload laundry expenses, hang around the laundry room and wait until a rich guy or gal fills a washing machine with clothes, pours in some laundry detergent, inserts a roll of quarters, and sets the wash a-launderin'. As soon as your mark leaves the room, remove the designer clothes from the machine and shove in your clothes. Remove your load just before the washing machine stops, and put the rich person's clothes back into the machine. He'll never notice (his clothes probably weren't dirty anyway, just a few brandy stains on his Benetton sweater), and you'll be saving yourself plenty of quarters and laundry detergent. You can use the same strategy for the dryers, but you'll have to work a lot faster, since most dryers on campus work for a maximum of five minutes (except for the ones that spin forever without producing any heat).

If you lack the courage to employ this surefire technique, make your clothes last. Underwear can be worn backwards, inside-out, or both—making a typical pair last for at least three or four days. The same goes for socks. Of course, you can avoid underwear and socks entirely by not wearing any. You really don't have to worry about shirts and pants, since they rarely get stained heavily. When they do, just toss some extra catsup or mustard on them and people will think you are wearing tie-dye. What about the smell? Buy a bottle of Old Spice and splash it on! No one will notice your real fragrance. And it's cheap! A bottle of Old Spice will last for an entire semester!

PERSONAL HYGIENE

You can cut down on the cost of shampooing your hair by, simply enough, not washing it. Instead, maintain your hair's appearance with the hair care program chosen by many Calculus Teaching Assistants: wash your hair only when you go home to visit your parents. If your friends

College on a Shoestring

question your hair care plan, just tell them that you believe in preserving America's lakes and rivers and that you love that "natural" look.

When and if you do wash, you need not buy soap. Just scrub yourself gently but firmly until you rub all the dirt off, or until your skin starts peeling off, whichever comes first.

As for oral hygiene, just rinse your mouth with salt water or soapy water (if you decide to buy the soap). This will get rid of most of the germs in your mouth. To eliminate all of the little buggers in your mouth, rinse your mouth with some of that Old Spice.

FOOD

Don't throw away old slices of pizza or bread just because they seem a little moldy. If they're white or green, just heat them up with a hair dryer and enjoy! Throw food away only if it seems to be moving by itself (an indication that it's not kosher). Second, save money by not buying dish detergents. Don't worry about the black-green crud at the bottom of your mug or bowl. It's probably just a population of harmless bacteria, which you can easily wipe out by pouring hot chocolate or tomato soup into the receptacle. If you really want to be on the safe side, sterilize your dishware with Old Spice.

ROOM

If you are planning to decorate your room with posters, you can save a lot of moolah by substituting costly poster putty with old chewing gum. Speaking of room decoration, you can stack empty Coke and Bud cans to form colorful sculptures. If your desk is wobbly, use pizza boxes to stabilize it (should you need to study from the Psychology textbooks that normally perform this function). Pizza boxes can also be very helpful with pest control. After a while, that one remaining pizza slice will ferment into cockroach poison.

SOCIAL LIFE

For women who would rather not spend too much money on jewelry, paper clips make excellent earrings.

Going steady with physics majors is great for your pocketbook since they are usually geeks and require little money for dates. Their idea of a good time is eating Kraft Macaroni & Cheese in front of a TV set, enabling you to reduce your weekly dating expenses to a mere eighty-nine cents (the cost of a box of macaroni and cheese). Also, if you whisper the formula $E=mc^2$ into a physics major's ear, he or she will become instantly aroused, which translates into more savings since you don't have to get him or her drunk to engage in sex. As for safe sex, there's no need to buy expensive condoms. Go to any biology lab and steal a rubber glove. Then cut off the fingers of the glove and *voila*: five custom-made condoms in five different sizes and shapes.

FINDING YOURSELF AT COLLEGE

Picking the right image for yourself when you get to college can be a scary thing. What is the displaced prom queen to do without her court? The class clown without his pre-algebra class? We understand what it means to be lost, without a prepackaged image to call your own. Luckily, though, college has a wide variety of stereotypes from which you can choose! Go ahead, be the first in your dormitory to associate yourself with a select group of homogeneous individuals!

"I'm dirty. And even if I'm really cute, you won't want to date me because even I am afraid to touch my own hair."

"Hi! I'm the surly graduate student who will be teaching your freshman writing seminar. You will never understand my pain. Never!"

"Oh my God! I, like, totally saw Lindsey wearing the same Kate Spade brown sling-back wedges with the Prada wool skirt! See you at Starbucks!"

"Holy smokes! According to these calculations I have a 10^{-23} chance of having a social life as an engineering student. Gee whiz."

"Oh, frat guy, you're fratastic!"

Do you fear individuality? Do you like beer? Do you have a penchant for stealing road signs? Do you really like beer?

"What the fuck are you looking at? Get used to my punk rock wrath as I serve you lunch at College Town Bagels."

"My briefcase is filled with child pornography."

Procrastination Made Easy

So you want to join the ranks of the irresponsible. Fine, but to become a world-class procrastinator you are going to have to give up some of the "morals" that you hold so dear. You must unlearn what you have learned. "Responsibility." "Work ethic." "Sense of pride." These banal phrases are signs of weakness, muttered only by those who have chosen to live in a world of starched shirt-collars and Kenny G. records. Not you. You are a free spirit. You scoff at those who reprimand you for not doing things their way. You laugh. You kick them in the shins. You do whatever it takes to make them feel inferior to you. For, after all, you are obviously more intelligent than they are. They scold you only because they lack the backbone to transgress the laws of obligation and logic as you do. *Carpe diem!* The world could end tomorrow, and where would you be? Floating through the abyss with a finished English paper in your hand. No. Every minute is precious, and you will not waste it on such trivial matters. Sit back down to watch that rerun of *Mr. Belvedere.*

Justify your actions; if you do not truly believe that you are completely right, then you have already failed. Tell yourself, "I have plenty of time to finish this" or "I work well under pressure." These two expressions usually do the trick. Concoct elaborate and creative plans for how to finish all your work on time and still enjoy the finer things in life.

Revise your plans constantly, as the excessive amount of time you have to spend constructing them will already render them obsolete. Above all, never allow yourself to give any credibility to the idea of starting ahead of time. That is admitting defeat. Play air-hockey while all the other fools labor the gorgeous evening away like a hundred monkeys at a hundred typewriters. Except they will never write *Hamlet*—only a regurgitation of facts put forth by an uninspired professor.

Talk with your girlfriend on the phone for a few hours. Guffaw when she says that she has to hang up because she has a chemistry test to study for. Brag about how much work you have due tomorrow. Speak with a fair amount of dignity, as though your procrastination is a big moose head on the wall that you are showing to an old hunting buddy. Get off the phone. Realize that it is one a.m. Decide to start your assignment. Vow not to sleep until it is finished. Turn on your computer. Check your e-mail before you start. Remember that you still have your secret weapon—the all-nighter. It is the procrastinator's silent ally, the cornerstone of this sacred temple of slackerdom that you have constructed.

Stare at a blank screen for a few hours. Think about how you have nothing to write about. Get annoyed. Punch the screen because it is obviously at fault for your lack of creativity in this hour of need. Get

tired. Decide to skip your classes and hand the paper in next time so that you can do a really good job (see "concoct creative plans" above). Tell yourself that it's better to turn in a quality product late than to turn in an inferior one on time. After all, you can't force creativity. Go to bed.

Try again at one a.m. the night before your next class meeting. Start to panic. Tell yourself that fear is the best motivator (see "I work well under pressure" above). Become devoutly religious. Ask God for help. Stare at a blank screen again. Fight off the growing heaviness of your limbs and eyelids. Admit that procrastinating is—(cringe) wrong. Vow never to do this to yourself again. Promise that you will purchase the complete Kenny G. recording library if you get an idea for your paper.

Get an idea. Finish writing your paper at 3:16 a.m. and go to bed immediately. As you float in the netherworld between consciousness and sleep, think that whoever that guy was who said "Do not put off until tomorrow what you can do today" must never have played Mortal Kombat III.

Force your sleep-deprived body out of bed, despite all its obvious protesting. Go to class to hand in your paper. Hope that the teacher accepts it. When she does (she will), silently laugh at all the simpletons who played by the rules. That night, when your friends go to their rooms to do work, watch *Mr. Belvedere.*

Socrates: One of the greatest philosophical minds the world has ever seen? Inarguably. A martyr to his belief? To be sure. A homosexual pedophile? Probably, but can you blame him? All of the ancient Greeks were doing it! Can we really judge an individual of a different culture and era for practices that were commonplace in his or her own society? And, lest we forget, Plato had a really cute butt.

Objections to his sexual behavior aside, one cannot deny the importance of the contributions Socrates made to the philosophical tradition, most notably the technique of learning through questioning—which he, rather modestly, named the Socratic Method. Recently, scholars have discovered ancient scrolls containing a number of such-heretofore-undiscovered-dialogues between Socrates and his student, Plato, which shed light on a number of dilemmas that have plagued the human mind for millennia. Presented here is a small sampling of said dialogues:

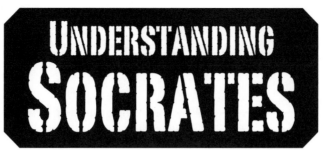

ON THE EXISTENCE OF GOD

PLATO: Teacher, does God exist?
SOCRATES: What properties must God, by definition, possess?
PLATO: Well, let's see . . . omnipotence, omniscience—uhh . . . perfection . . .
SOCRATES: Anything else?
PLATO: I don't know. Not that I can think of . . .
SOCRATES: How about—oh, I don't know—a long, flowing robe, a well-groomed white beard, a kick-ass bod?
PLATO: Yeah, sure.
SOCRATES: Greek, about yea high *[raises hand to head level]*, sometimes goes by the name "Socrates"?
PLATO: What?
SOCRATES: Well, do you know of any being that fits this description?
PLATO: I don't know. What do you want me to say? You?
SOCRATES: Bingo!

ON THE KNOWLEDGE OF ONE'S SELF

PLATO: Teacher, I am unsure of whether or not I actually exist.
SOCRATES: Let me ask you: Do you think?
PLATO: Sure, I'm thinking right now.
SOCRATES: Okay, so you think, therefore . . .
PLATO: I am?
SOCRATES: Right. Problem solved.
PLATO: But Teacher, "I think, therefore I am" is one tenet of the philosophy of Descartes, who will not be born for over a thousand years.

SOCRATES: Jesus Christ, dude, what do I look like, a fucking encyclopedia?
PLATO: Jesus hasn't been born yet either.
SOCRATES: Whatever. Here, you want the rest of this Sprite? Obey your thirst.

ON WHAT IS TAKING THAT DAMNED PIZZA SO FUCKING LONG TO GET HERE

PLATO: Great Socrates, I hunger. Where is our pizza?
SOCRATES: I don't know, how long ago did you order it?
PLATO: I don't know . . . an hour ago maybe?
SOCRATES: And how long did they tell you it would take to get here?
PLATO: Half-hour / forty-five minutes.
SOCRATES: Shit, you're right, it should be here by now. What was their number? I'll give them a call.

ON WHY SOCRATES IS STILL CRASHING AT PLATO'S APARTMENT, EVEN THOUGH HE SAID HE WOULD ONLY NEED TO STAY THERE FOR TWO WEEKS, AND IT'S GOING ON THREE MONTHS

PLATO: Listen, Socrates, I haven't said too much about you staying here for so long—even though you've been here for way longer than you said you were going to—but I kind of need to get on with my life, you know?
SOCRATES: But have I not enriched your life with my multitude of poignant and thoughtful insights into the nature of the universe?
PLATO: Yeah, sure, but come on . . . I really need some space here. Plus, when I went on that business trip to Athens a couple weeks ago, you said you were going to take care of the place, but then you had that huge party here and all kinds of stuff got broken, including that Grecian urn my mom gave me for graduation that had, like, huge sentimental value and whatnot.
SOCRATES: Do you think that, perhaps, your problems lie not in Socrates, but in yourself?
PLATO: Dude, can you give this question shit a rest for like two seconds? You are really getting on my nerves.
SOCRATES: But what are nerves if not bundles of cells that relay electrical signals throughout the body? And, on a related note, what is electricity?
PLATO: What are you talking about? That doesn't even make any sense.
SOCRATES: Hey, what's that over there?
PLATO *[looking over his shoulder]*: I don't see anything.
[Socrates runs into bathroom and locks the door.]

The Cat in the Frat

We were sitting around on a cold winter's day.
We were sitting around, there was not much to say.

The TV was broken, the Playstation too.
There was nothing to eat, there was nothing to do.

Then from the front door came a loud sounding BUMP!
The bump was so loud that it made us both jump.

In the door stood a cat, a cat in a frat,
with a fuzzy green fleece and a funky red hat.

"Greetings," he said, "I'm from Sigma Rho Nu.
And I hear that you're looking for something to do."

Then I said to the cat,
"I'm so glad that you're here.
Now we'll get lots of chicks
and we'll drink lots of beer.

"We'll get us some pledges and haze them to death,
then we'll go the the basement and smoke crystal meth."

But the cat shook his head, and he said, "Heavens no!
I don't know what you've heard, but it just isn't so.
Being a cat in a frat is not all games and fun,
I have to do work when there's work to be done."

"Never mind all that crap,"
Jimmy said with a wave,
"Let's go buy some beer and we'll all misbehave.
There's nothing to do in this damn college town,
Let's all go get wasted and wander around."

"Hmmm," said the cat,
"I don't know about that.
We drink milk and soda.
This is a dry frat."

44

"Well how about chicks?
Can you get us some chicks?"
Jim said, "We need chicks,
and we need some chicks quick!"

"Nuh-uh," frowned the cat,
"We don't do that stuff here.
We don't fondle girls and
we never drink beer."

"'In fact," he went on with a smile in his eyes,
"we think of ourselves as some very nice guys.
I don't know what you do
when you sit home alone—
We like to bake cookies
and talk on the phone."

"Well, what about pledges?"
Jim and I blurted out,
"We'll haze all the pledges and
shout, shout, shout, shout."

The cat shook his head gravely and said, "Don't you see?
We can't break the rules of the CIFC.
They don't allow drinking or hazing or kegs,
They don't allow dancing, spankings, or legs;
We don't haze our pledges, we just let them in,
And we never have parties because that's a sin."

Then I looked at Jim, and he looked at me.
The cat looked at us both and he said "Why don't we . . ."

But before he could ask us to study or bowl,
or offer us soda and glazed donut holes,
Jim grabbed his tail and I grabbed my bat,
and we started to beat on that lame-ass frat cat.

"OUCH,"
cried the cat,
"OUCH OUCH OUCH
OUCH OUCH OUCH!
Not my—whoa—hey stop,
that's—ah—my—ouch ouch
ouch OUCH!"

We threw the cat out, and we gave him a smack—
"We don't want you here, so don't ever come back!
We thought you were cool and you'd know what to do,
but we'd rather stay bored than to hang out with you!"

But after he left and we'd sat there a while,
Jim looked at me and his face cracked a smile.
He said "It's too bad that the cat was a geek,
I haven't had that much fun in a week!"

English 110
Poetry for Physicists

Final Exam

Read and analyze the following poem for certain literary devices:

1) Given that the meter of this poem is iambic pentameter, use Newton's second law to verify that the speed of light is 3.00×10^8 m/s. ($E = hc/v$ and Planck's constant $h = 6.626 \times 10^{-34}$ J s).

2) The author's diction is often ambiguous. Show this using Heisenberg's uncertainty principle.

3) Alliteration is an effective tool in poetry, contributing to the flow of the poem. Show that the angular flow and linear flow are equal. (Hint: employ $F = ma$ and Coulomb's Law for a point charge).

> Wake me up, before you go-go
> Don't leave me hangin' on like a yo-yo
> Wake me up, before you go-go
> I don't wanna miss it when you hit that high
> Wake me up, before you go-go
> 'Cause I'm not planning on going solo
> Wake me up, before you go-go—aah
> Take me dancing tonight

1) As the go go's approach the speed of light, the yo yo's decrease proportionally thereby causing you to ~~wake me up, before you gogo~~ take me dancing tonight.

2) $F = ma = (gogo)(yoyo)$ $E = 6.62 \times 10^{34}$ yoyo's
$$= \left(\frac{\text{you } gogo}{gogo \text{ aah}} \right) \rightarrow gogo\text{'s cancel}$$

3) This piece of poetry cannot be analyzed because it disobeys the laws of thermodynamics.

PRACTIS

THE CORNELL JOURNAL OF BUNNIES AND HORSIES

Editorial

Webster's *New International Dictionary, Second Edition,* defines a *schloop* as "a swishing sound ending in a plop." The casual reader would probably fail to give this outstanding definition the appreciation it is due. In fact, he would probably attribute the origins of the word *schloop* itself to a lisping seafarer. But what saith the wise son—the careful purveyor of nomenclatorial territory? He would, of course, first appreciate the detailed etymology of the word (Y. *"shtup,"* from O.Y. *"vey,"* 'a pound of tongue'; M.E. *"adultbookstore,"* 'to wrap fruit'; O.F. *"jimihendrix,"* 'to create small pottery'; L. *"spam,"* literally, 'to chase squirrels'), not to mention the entomology ("Yes, grasshoppah, you have hit me in the nuts"). And then, perhaps after eating some Cheez Twists or dancing a little jig in the living room, he would exclaim, "Why, what a striking example of sound imitating sense!" And he would be *right.* "A swishing sound ending in a plop." How lovely! How pristine! A sensorial cloak surrounds and envelopes us as we see …hear…even *feel* these words! Yes, go ahead…touch them. Ah! See how they respond? Caress them…a viscid, amorphous whirlpool of turbulent chaos swirls us around, around, and sucks us *down*—into some perilous pit—we are lost, dropping through the very bowels of essence, plunging through the dark abyss, hurtling past the dank walls of oblivion—until we land on a little pile of sticks, and the fall is over. What a God-awful mess!

But the point here is that words are more than assemblages of letters, or vibrations in the air, or pocket lint. They are the quintessence of all that is—an expression of all that will be. They are yours to share, use, trade, or eat. You can build or destroy with them. You can open doors, play pool, or trip two-year olds with them. They can kill people, spoil cabbage, and give you crabs. They can take you from King John of England ("Procure at once a lithe virgin") to John Wayne ("I wanna buttfuck your mule").

So, please, use them wisely. Use them cautiously. Immerse them in saline solutions. But heed the remonstration of Lord Byron, in his letter to Manfred Groll, Earl of Durrex: "Don't forget to write."

—the Editors

Ono is Enough: An Interview with Olga Yutz, the World's Only Yoko Ono Fan

Olga Yutz is a professor of Fine Arts who specializes in 20th Century avant-garde sculpture and weird window displays on Fifth Avenue that nobody knows what the fuck they mean. She is the author of several books, including *The Holocaust and its Relation to Disco,* for which she received the Jackson Pollock Award for the Extremely Abstract.

When not teaching at Cornell, Yutz serves on the Board of Directors for the Franz Kafka Institute of Mental Health.

How long have you been a fan of Yoko Ono?

Since the early sixties. There aren't too many of us around, you know. Most people don't seem to realize the incredible extent of her talent or the subtlety of her wit. Like that work she was showing back in 1966. You know, the one where you looked through the magnifying glass and saw the word "yes"? Or the film with the fly slowly crawling across a naked body? Or the one with all of the naked buttocks? God, those works were so inspired, so intense, so positive.

Why do you think her talent has been so underrated?

Probably because she's always been overshadowed by dominant males, which is unfair because they rarely have as much talent as she does. Take her record album, *Double Fantasy.* You know, the one she made with Jack Lemmon?

I believe that's John Lennon.

Yeah, right. Him. I mean, it's obvious that his songs were only meant to fill up the album so that it would have a longer playing time. She's generous to include his songs, but probably doesn't realize that it's harmful to her career in the long run. His little ditties tend to distract the serious listener from her more mature poetic statements. After all, everyone who pays attention to the lyrics of the album could easily tell that she's the more sensitive of the two. When she sings, "I'm moving on, moving on, it's getting phony," and then slowly drifts into her baboon imitation— well, what else can one say about love?

How do you feel about her music being compared to new-wave groups, such as the B-52s?

Personally, I think it was all arranged by Paul McCartney. He's trying to get her back for starting the "Paul is dead" thing in 1969. He's been planning it for years. That's what "Coming Up" was all about. Try playing it backwards at a

(continued on page 281)

Untitled

in case you're wondering

my poetry is all in
    lowercase letters.

        why do i write
        like this, you may wonder.

is it because i am an absolute

    moron,

        knowing nothing of the fundamental,
        first-grade rules of standard written english

            no.

is it because i find all things so

    insignificant,
        even myself,

        that i do not consider them worthy
        of capitalization

            no.

is it because ninety percent of the poetry produced by my

    contemporaries

        is written in a similar fashion,
        and i am a spineless conformist
        without an atom of originality
            to speak of

            no.

the answer is much simpler

        i use the lowercase
        because my
        typewriter's shift key
            is
             broken

Haiku

    Haikus are much fun
    To write except when there are
    Too many sylla

Signs

    No parking
    this side
    of street.

    Please curb your dog.

Untitled 2

In this place am I perched;
My heart is shattered—
For I try to purge the impurities of my body

And merely succeed
in passing empty air.

The Fly

I see the fly
see how he is straining against the tide
ripped by splashing waves that
tower and threaten to
engulf him in their fury, the hot
liquid desperately trying to
pull him down and he
just as earnestly
trying to break
away and be free.

Now I just wish he could get the fuck out of my soup.

My Blood

A freestyle poem by Susan Freeperson
Menstrual age 140.

Women bleed.
We bleed and bleed and bleed.
Men hate us because we bleed.
They envy us, for from our flesh issues the blood of life.
I shall not deny my link with my female past.
Like my mother, I shall bleed in office buildings.
Like my grandmother, I shall bleed while buying
Stationery at Woolworth's.
I shall bleed in class.
Most likely economics.
I will stand up when asked my opinion about
How men are destroying our female earth
and let loose a red rivulet
Of life.
Men view with disgust
When I smear my blood all over my face,
making a bloody beard.
It is their hangup that they can't
Deal with my blood.
I will bleed like a river.
I will be proud and bold.
Except when I get those horrible cramps.

Who Made the Salad?

The question asked, and posed before the restive, troubled, sweater-clad
husband at the table
    The question poised
        Like an adder flexing its sinuous black
        glistening length
        Threatening two-pronged, swift, and painful death
The husband, unsure, frantic, plays for time:
        The sphinx-question inching toward him in
        sated certainty
        Expecting soon the consummating familiar crunch
        of flesh bones blood
    The Question
        Now marching forth in certain triumph
        A solid phalanx
        An insurmountable, unanswerable threat
        It approaches:
But the husband
Feeling the surge of some Enlightenment long-hid
And with the thrill of Truth displays his banner:
Legions follow as he cries,
        "Caesar made the salad!"

Haiku 2

You're such a dickfor.
Tell me, what is a dickfor?
Don't you know? Ha-ha.

Despond

Fucking bicycle pump.
Jesus fucking Christ,
For thirteen-fifty you'd
Think they could make
Something that works.

Sculptors

Sculptors sculpt from
scaled sketches of
  the Object.
Or maybe they sculpt
from life, and chisel
  away whatever
doesn't look like
  the dog
    or face
  they're sculpting.
Do sculptors wear goggles so chippings
  don't fly in their eyes?
Do they ever make mistakes
  with their chisels?
Maybe sometimes the
mallet hits their thumb.
    Are sculptors happy?
    Do they make
      money?
I know very little
  about
    sculptors.
Well, who cares,
  anyway?
Goddamn
    sculptors.

HOW TO TAKE AN EXAM

PREPARATION

The first step in taking an exam is finding out what the subject is. It makes no sense to read the works of Kurt Vonnegut if you have to take a Math exam—well, maybe *Slaughterhouse-Five*, but definitely not *Jailbird*. You should also borrow the book for the exam from a fellow classmate at least two weeks before the test, so by the time he is ready to study, he will forget who the hell borrowed it.

You should begin to study for your exam at least twenty-four hours before the test, longer if it has been more than a month since you last attended class. The first step in preparing for your exam is to gather the correct supplies to create an environment conducive to study. No-Doz is important; you can never have too much of this life-sustaining health food. But man cannot survive on No-Doz alone; you should also grab a pound of coffee from the dining hall. Grab some of those margarine patties as well, in case you feel one of those pre-test cravings for a coffee sandwich. A case of caffeinated soft drinks is also a must. Don't be fooled by those sodas that appear caffeinated but are really just sugary water. Root beer is one such offender. You may also want something to eat during your studying vigil, like an industrial size vat of Peanut M&M's.

STUDYING

Now that you have surrounded yourself with piles of caffeine and sugar, you should begin to think about piling information into your brain.

Whatever you do, once you begin to study, *do not go to sleep*. One sure way to forget everything you have just learned is to take even a short nap. Once you do this, the only course of action that remains is to start all over again. More than one college student has tossed his cookies after realizing that he fell asleep for five minutes just before his exam and forgot *everything* he ever knew about anything. It's an easy trap to fall into; you just close your eyes and say to yourself, "I'm just going to count to ten; I'm *not* going to fall asleep. Really, I'm . . . " If you feel the urge to sleep, Just Say No-Doz. If you begin to fall asleep, you can force your eyes to stay open—not by propping your eyelids open with toothpicks (which are all too fragile), but by using an infinitely stronger substance: Flavor-Ices. No, don't put the frozen juice pops between your eyelids. Let a stick melt, and then pour the liquid into your eyes. The orange ones will form a tough, thick-transparent layer of gunk (much like that orange, pastey stuff on the floors of movie theaters) over your eyes, preventing you from shutting them. In addition, the resulting pain will keep you alert and help you better hone your concentration.

Most students find they study best when surrounded by a lot of distractions, forcing them to focus their concentration. One of the best sources of discomfort is *loud* music. None of this mamby-pamby New-Age Muzak. We're talking Motley Crüe at 162 decibels. That way, you can't hear the people down the hall when they begin to yell at you

to turn down the stereo. It will also, by contrast, make the test-taking experience that much more enjoyable, especially since you will not be interupted by campus police officers breaking down the door of the exam hall.

You should also have copies of your favorite magazines on hand. Who knows what insights you can find into American history by perusing your copy of *Whips and Chains International* while studying for the test? (In fact, you might very well find an answer key to the test in the back of the magazine.)

The next question you may ask is, "What information will be covered on the test?" As a general rule, you can forget everything your instructor mentioned during class. The professor figures everyone will know it, and there is no sense testing how well you listen to a lecture. What teachers do like to ask, in order to separate the men from the sheep, are esoteric questions about the text, such as, "How many pages of required reading were there since the last exam?" "Where did the person before you hide the article on reserve in the library?" and "What is the Library of Congress number of the primary textbook?" The professor may also ask a few questions about the T.A.'s sexual preferences, but these are usually extra credit and reserved for graduate-level courses.

TAKING YOUR EXAM

Taking a test is a lot like taking a screwdriver, shoving it up your nose, and stirring your brain until it leaks out your ears and onto the pages of that neat, little blue book.

When you finally find the lecture hall in the cow stables where the administration has, in its infinite wisdom, decided to hold your electrical engineering exam, you will be given a little blue book into which you must write everything you know. You are even allowed to use both sides of each page. On the cover is an agreement with the University that you will not cheat. Do not sign this until you have shredded all incriminating documents, procured counsel, and allowed your attorney to whisper legal nothings in your ear. Remember, plagiarism is a crime. Of course, so is voyeurism, but that never stopped astronomers.

One of the best things to keep in mind while taking your particular exam is the curve factor. Most college tests are graded on the basis of the mean score and not on actual merit. Hence, if everyone in the class scores 75 out of 100 possible points, and you get an 85, you receive an A. However, if everyone in the class scores a 99 and you get an 85, you recieve an F. It is possible to pass with 5 out of 100 correct and it is possible to fail with 95 out of 100 correct. Therefore, you should not only be concerned about how well you do, but also how well your classmates do. To hell with courtesy; this is war. If everyone wasn't going to cheat, why would you

be asked to sign something that says you won't? Before the test begins, encourage those around you to close their eyes and count to ten. Then, while they're not looking, steal their pens and pencils. Also take the batteries from their calculators. (This is especially helpful before English exams.)

One of the most popular ways to throw other test-takers off balance is the "Student-Gone-Mad Trick." Have a friend (who is not in the class) show up to the exam and take it as if he were, indeed, enrolled in the course. About halfway into the time allotted for the test, your friend jumps up, throws his test and exam booklet across the room, and screams, "I can't take it! It's too much! I can't take it!" After a minute of ranting, raving, and frothing at the mouth, the seemingly deranged student runs out of the exam room, screaming all the while. This inspires an atmosphere of levity in the room, making it harder for your classmates to concentrate.

When you go up to turn in your exam booklet, inconspicuously remove a few others from the pile. Something else to keep in mind: After paying tens of thousands of dollars in tuition, what difference does one hundred dollars make to be sure that little A is going to show up on your grade report? Before turning in your blue book, slip a C-note inside.

There is another alternative available to you when you take the test: Bullshit (from *Olde Englifh*, the word *bulle* meaning "large, furry mammal," and the word *shitte* meaning "defecation"). The basic idea is to sound like you know what you're talking about while avoiding the topic entirely. This can be done through a variety of techniques, not the least of which has nothing to do with the basic prospects for making an attempt at completing a thesis based on inconsequential data that can not be verified, yet sounds in essence at once plausible and believable, despite the overabundance of mini-theses and sub-plots, akin to Agatha Christie's methods of diverting the reader's attention in the novel *Curtain*, but not unlike an attempt at losing the reader's interest entirely in the process of laying out this plan for modern absurdity.

CHEATING

If all else fails, you can cheat. Yes, you signed the cover of the exam booklet and promised you wouldn't. But twenty years from now when you are making $500,000 a year, that little blue book won't really weigh on your conscience, now will it?

One method which has proven successful is the "Flash-Strobe Trick." Wait until the proctor looks directly at you, and then take a flash picture of him. While he is seeing little red and

 **meets "Homicidal Duck"**

blue circles, you are glancing at your neighbor's blue book. It may be helpful to bring along a hand-held copier so you can copy your neighbor's paper quickly, and then recopy it at your leisure. If your neighbor complains, slip him a sawbuck. After all, which is more important: a pizza or a decent grade? Okay, but you can probably spare the ten dollars anyway.

Another method is the "Phony Fire Conspiracy." Have a friend who isn't taking the test pull the fire alarm thirty minutes after the test begins. While everyone else is running for their lives, swipe someone's blue book. (Note: one drawback to this method becomes readily apparent if there is a real fire.)

Many students use crib notes (or cheat sheets), but smuggling them into the testing area without detection is an art form worthy of study. A few students, for example, favor the old "Barf Bag Method," by which the notes are placed into a balloon and ingested before the test. The student then induces vomiting, preferably over the exam booklet of some well-prepared student, and then palms the balloon. While everyone else is preoccupied with repulsion, you can casually consult your crib notes without detection.

Finally, consider the "Chess Cheat Charade." Bring a chess board to the test and, before the test commences, set up the board as if you are going to play with a co-conspirator in your class. Work out a code whereby each move represents a different letter of the multiple choice test and play out the game while taking the test. The proctor will never suspect anything. Be careful though; don't make a move just because you are tempted to win the game. Your partner may end up with a wrong answer and only you to blame. Remember, grades are not a game; getting good grades is.

Exams, approached in the proper manner, can help you lead a fuller, richer life. A lot richer. Oh, baby.

The Secret of the Scientific Method

1. Clearly Define the Problem.

Defining the problem as "Why do children run from me?" is not as clear as "Why do small children run from me?" For example, if Sir Isaac Newton had stuck with his original, unclear question ("What the dilly, yo?"), he never would have discovered electricity.

EXAMPLE OF A CLEARLY DEFINED PROBLEM: "Why does Gertrude refuse to go out with me, despite my guarantee that I can make her 'scream like a howler monkey?'"

2. Form a Hypothesis.

Newton hypothesized that "what goes up must come down." Benjamin Franklin hypothesized that "getting struck by lightning must be one hell of a rush." Albert Einstein hypothesized that Newton and Franklin were "drunk off their asses." Your hypothesis should be testable. If the hypotheses just mentioned do not seem testable, that is because those guys were all smarter than you.

EXAMPLE OF A TESTABLE HYPOTHESIS: "I am God's gift to women, so there must be something wrong with Gertrude."

3. Experiment.

Good experiments will make the uninitiated feel insecure because they are difficult to comprehend. This will guarantee that others will feel too intimidated to ask you questions, so you will not need to reveal that you have no idea what the hell you are talking about. Remember, your goal is to get some rich sap to give you carte blanche with his dough.

EXAMPLE OF AN EXPERIMENT RIDICULOUS ENOUGH TO GET FUNDING: "I'll telephone Gertrude and then hang up. Once I've made her paranoid, I'll ring her doorbell and run away. Failing this, I'll lose all self-confidence and not be able to talk to her."

4. Draw a Conclusion.

Eventually, your financial backers are going to demand results. Assuming they no longer fall for "I really need another high-priced lab assistant . . . preferably a member of the Swedish bikini team," you are going to have to give them substantiation. Review your data. Reconsider your original hypothesis. Finally, when your realize that you have wasted their money, fudge your results and skip out of the country.

EXAMPLE OF A CONCLUSION THAT WILL ALLOW YOU TO LIVE IN BLISSFUL SELF-DELUSION: "Gertrude just isn't into guys."

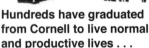

Imagine for a moment, if you will, a world without late registration, prelims, and homecoming games. A place without beer blasts, poetry readings, or Pink Floyd. In short, the "real world." Distant as it may seem, that terrifying scenario lies just around the corner. Of course, freshmen may sleep easy with the comforting thought of "four years, baby!" but don't kid yourself. If there's one thing you've learned by now, it's that time flies when you're doing drugs.

After four years of all-nighters, reserved readings, and late night pizzas, graduating students can't help but find the transition to reality devastating. To help you tackle the rites of passage without developing anything more serious than a degree, we present this . . .

GRADUATION KIT

One: No Exit

Picture the scene. Graduation's just days away. You've got five papers due last week. It's Senior Week and everyone else is out getting butterfly-stomping drunk. You're sitting in the library underneath a mountain of books.

"If only there was some way I could get all of these papers out of the way before the beer runs out," you sigh.

There is. *The All-Encompassing Research Paper*™ satisfies your every academic responsibility. Guaranteed to cover five subjects or five professors, whichever comes first. To satisfy ten-page length requirements simply photocopy the second page eight times.

ROUSSEAU'S LACK OF IMPACT ON WILLIAM FAULKNER AS COMPARED TO THE ANCIENT GREEK HUMORIST'S UNFAMILIARITY WITH ROBERT LOWELL'S POETRY IN ACCORDANCE WITH B.F. SKINNER'S APPROACH TO VEBLEN'S ECONOMIC THEORIES AS UNINFLUENCED BY THE WORKS OF RENÉ MAGRITTE

Like Faulkner's Anse Bundren in *As I Lay Dying*, Jean-Jacques Rousseau fails to mention that Thorstein Veblen's theory of conspicuous consumption does not touch upon Aristophanes' attack on Sophocles in "The Clouds." Consequently, Vardaman's inability to cope with Addie Bundren's death hardly reflects the principles outlined in *The Theory of the Leisure Class*, yet Rousseau's desire for the state to banish anyone not believing in the state's dogmas is noticeably missing from Robert Lowell's portrayal of Boston in "For the Union Dead."

While Faulkner's Vardaman sees his dead mother as a fish, and Lowell solemnly notes "The Aquarium is gone. Everywhere/ giant finned cars nose forward like fish;/ a savage servility/ slides by on grease,"[1] parallels between the two works could not be any more irrelevant unless contrasted in terms of Veblen's theory. If, for example, trout is $4.00 a pound and lox is $3.00, Veblen asserts that consumers will opt for the more expensive fish for the prestige of purchasing it. Such a principle never materializes in either Lowell's poetry or Faulkner's novel.

Although René Magritte uses fish for symbolic purposes in several of his works, fish would be a rather poor substitute for a pigeon in operant conditioning experiments utilizing the Skinner box. Whether Addie Bundren's coffin can be discussed in terms of the Skinner box returns us to Magritte's use of rectangular forms transforming before the viewer's eyes to drapery, cloth, or even fish. Lowell fails to make such a connection:

Once my nose crawled like a snail on the glass
my hand tingled
to burst bubbles
drifting from the noses of the crowded, compliant fish.[2]

Perhaps Lowell alludes to Rousseau's compliant citizens who are content with the Social Contract's restrictions, yet Faulkner

---

You hand in your papers and manage to squeak through the final semester—you thought. Turns out, you never did get through four semesters of physical education. It might also come as a surprise that you currently owe the library $4,796 in overdue book fines accrued over four years of writing research papers. Not only that, you took the take-home bio final home with you and forgot to turn it in. To complicate matters, your parents just flew in for commencement exercises. It seems the only exercises you'll be doing are squat thrusts on unemployment lines.

Sometimes there just aren't enough gorges to go around. But let's not jump into anything. If you can come up with a foolproof excuse for missing the ceremony ("I got the sniffles," "I have a headache," "I was run down by a Greyhound Bus"), we'll handle the rest. When the dust has settled, you'll mysteriously produce a bona fide sheepskin. Just clip the appropriate letters from the following page, glue them into the proper positions, and *voila!* Now they'll have to call you "Doctor."

Two: Picking Up the Pieces and Throwing Them Away

One of the first problems you will encounter after your dorm contract runs out is deciding what to do with the stuff that was absolutely necessary for college survival but is totally useless anywhere else.

When you move into your split-level townhouse, you won't be able to fit two-weeks worth of groceries into an *insignificantly sized refrigerator* that won't even keep a six-pack cold. Your best bet is to donate the itty bitty fridgy to the local ASPCA so they can put little dogs to sleep.

And what about the *cinder blocks* you used for book shelves? Try to explain those to the wife and kids. The folks down at the trailer park will be glad to take them off your hands if the price is right. Seems they love to park their old pick-up trucks on top of them.

Black-light "Stoned Again" Posters taped up on your office wall just won't cut it with the executive vice president. But if you spring for mounting, a chrome frame, and a snazzy piece of protective glass, you're sure to overhear the Chairman of the Board remark how your "innovative youthfulness brings a spark of excitement to an otherwise colorless atmosphere." Don't forget to sign them with famous artists' names.

Cornell University

Be it known that

having satisfied in full the requirements for the degree of

Bachelor of Arts

has been admitted to that degree with all
the rights, privileges and honors pertaining thereto
in witness of this action the seal of the University and the signatures
authorized by the board of Trustees are affixed below
Given at Ithaca, New York, on the twenty-sixth day of May,
in the year two thousand and eight

Dean

President

ABCDEFGHIJKLMNOPQRSTUVWXYZ
ABCDEFGHIJKLMNOPQRSTUVWXYZ
ABCDEFGHIJKLMNOPQRSTUVWXYZ
abcdefghijklmnopqrstuvwxyzabcdefghijklmnopqrstuvwxyz
abcdefghijklmnopqrstuvwxyzabcdefghijklmnopqrstuvwxyz
abcdefghijklmnopqrstuvwxyzabcdefghijklmnopqrstuvwxyz
abcdefghijklmnopqrstuvwxyzabcdefghijklmnopqrstuvwxyz
abcdefghijklmnopqrstuvwxyzabcdefghijklmnopqrstuvwxyz

You may have grown close to your *House of Shalimar bedspread-tapestry* over the past four years, but it won't go over very well on the Upper East Side. Don't sweat it; they make great dropcloths should you decide to have the den done over in burnt sienna.

Stealing all those *traffic signs* may have seemed fun at the time, and they certainly looked cool hanging in your dorm room, but they just ain't in the same league with Lautrec or Gaughin. Use them as fashionable serving trays for hors d'oeuvres.

Although they were big on campus, try walking into your nine-to-five sporting a Green Day *concert T-shirt*. Instead of sticking out like a sore thumb in the accounting department, sew all those concert T-shirts into an eyecatching quilt for the guestroom.

You can be darn sure you're not going to stick that silly *memo board* down in the lobby for the doormen to snigger over. Cut it into little circles and create dynamite coasters for those wild cocktail parties you'll be throwing. "Perrier, anyone?"

Sure, you had a bigger *beer can collection* than anyone else in your hallway, but the interior decorator says they're no substitute for drapes. Don't throw them away; you're going to need to tie them to the back of the Volvo after the wedding! And that old *yellow highlighter* will come in handy to write "Just Married" on the windshield!

Unless you want to be the laughing stock of Madison Avenue, you won't be making Lipton's Cup of Soup in your little *coffee hotpot* anymore. Just clip off the plug and fill with pencils and pens to make an attractive pencil holder for your office desk.

We all know how hard it is to get the Sunday barbeque charcoal fire cooking. But old college *notebooks* and *textbooks* will be a valuable resource in case you don't get your *Sunday Times*. And your *student ID* and *dining hall card* can help correct the wobble in the dining room table if properly placed under the short leg.

Three: Stalking the Wild Job

Perhaps by this time, you've realized that your dream of growing up to be a lion or an alligator will require more years of expensive schooling. You'll have to settle for a career that's just a little less exciting—like firefighting, nursing, or serving as President of the United States. One of the best places to discover the numerous possibilities is in the classified section of the *New York Times*. After you've read about all the nifty motorcycles for sale, you'll best direct your attention to the column marked "Professional Employment." College grads just don't find jobs at the saw mill, Hill's drug store, the taxi terminal, or in the produce department. They'll still only pay you minimum wage at

Burger King even if you do have a master's degree in food science. When hunting through the classifieds, know what to look for:

Four: Return to Sender

Remember the last time you applied for a summer job? You were after that real cushy spot in your uncle's law firm. But you were dumped like a truck when they hired some sleazebag who waltzed in with a sheaf full of recommendation letters. (He even had one from the Governor, that scumcake.) Don't let that happen again. All you need is a Xerox machine, a typewriter, the handy piece of Cornell stationery below, and a fertile imagination. Poof! You are voted "Most Likely to Succeed."

You might even discover more entertaining uses for your forgery talents. Try brightening up your younger sister's day by slipping a postmarked letter of acceptance into the family mailbox. Spark a controversy by signing a racist letter to *The Cornell Daily Sun* with the name of a white professor you admire. Send some letters to all the big publishing houses explaining how you are considering several of their books for use in your course, "The Publishing Industry: What It Has to Offer." They will be only too glad to send you a free copy of just about any book, anticipating huge revenues from subsequent student sales. Now sell them back to the bookstore of your choice. Or donate them to the Cornell Library and they'll build a wing in your honor.

Five: It's the Cops, Quick, Flush the Résumé

Okay, so the big day arrives. Your interview with J.B. is at 9:30 a.m. sharp. You get there bright and early in your stylish interview attire, toting your letters of recommendation in one hand, and clutching your diploma in the other.

Cornell University
Ithaca, New York 14853

The secretary asks you for "your résumé, please." The world goes black.

"Résumé? Why would I be carrying around a bowl of soup?" you stammer as beads of sweat roll down your chin to stain your cummerbund.

Without that shopping list of your achievements, or an introductory lesson in mind reading, how will J.B. know your credentials? How will any prospective employer find out you bussed tables at the Olive Garden every summer since sophomore year? How can you ask for a starting salary of sixty thou if the boss just doesn't know your cumulative grades averaged an impressive 1.8?

Maybe it's better if the company doesn't find out that you took off to Idaho for three semesters to find yourself. Instead, placate that establishment clone with some real achievements.

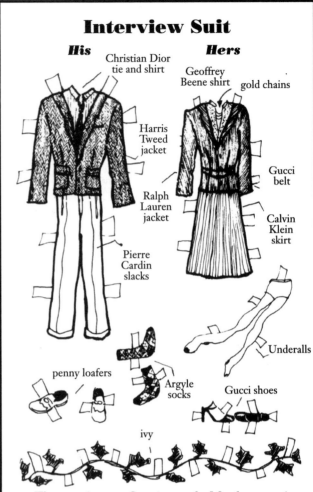

Interview Suit

His — Christian Dior tie and shirt; Harris Tweed jacket; Ralph Lauren jacket; Pierre Cardin slacks; penny loafers; Argyle socks; ivy

Hers — Geoffrey Beene shirt; gold chains; Gucci belt; Calvin Klein skirt; Underalls; Gucci shoes

The party's over. Starting early Monday morning you're going to take off that cap and gown. But dare you put on those grungy Levi's, tie-dyed T-shirt, and sandals before walking into your interview at Barnes, Barnes, & Shapiro? Of course not. Unless you have no intention of paying off your federal loan, clip out this READY-TO-WEAR INTERVIEW SUIT along the dotted lines, fold back tabs A, B, and C, and presto! Barnes, Barnes, Shapiro & You!

YOUR NAME HERE
RÉSUMÉ

EDUCATION:	Bachelor of Arts, Government Summa cum laude Cornell University Ithaca, New York	2008
	Junior Year Exchange Program Oxford University Oxford, England	2006-2007
	Phillips Exeter Academy	2004
	Sorbonne Accelerated High School Program Paris, France	Summer 2003
WORK EXPERIENCE:	Chairman of the Board Texaco Houston, Texas	Summer 2007
	Executive Vice President International Business Machines New York, New York	Summer 2006
	Associate Editor *Los Angeles Times* Los Angeles, California	Summer 2005
EXTRA- CURRICULAR ACTIVITIES:	President, Cornell Campus Council Editor, *Cornell Daily Sun* Editor, *Praxis*, Cornell Literary Magazine Title Role, Spring production of "Romeo and Juliet" President, Debate Team (2005-06 National Champs) Captain, Swim Team Editor, *Cornellian*, Yearbook President, Alpha Omega Epsilon House	
HONORS:	Nobel Peace Prize for nuclear submarine designs; Pulitzer Prize for book, *Einstein Revised*; President's Gold Medal for Physical Fitness; Inductee, Quill & Dagger Honor Society; Champion, Intramural Ping Pong.	
SKILLS & INTERESTS:	Flying Lockheed jet fighters, Esperanto, recombinant DNA experimentation, Mozart, chess, skeetshooting, skydiving, Dostoevsky, Sartre, and D.H. Lawrence.	
REFERENCES:	Condolezza Rice, Secretary of State Ralph Nader, Consumer activist Gene Shalit, NBC-TV, critic Ellen Goodman, Syndicated Columnist	

Six: Nothing to Say But It's Okay

Now that the preliminaries are over, it's time for you to put all that heavy preparation to work. The most im-portant thing to keep in mind is that you don't want your prospective employer to think you're desperate for bucks or even a job for that matter. If your interview is scheduled for ten in the morning, plan on arriving about forty minutes late mumbling something like, "couldn't get the fucking Bentley started."

Any attempt by the interviewer to feel out your job qualifications should be brushed aside immediately. Look 'em dead in the eye and make it clear from the start that "My experience and education far exceed yours or anyone presently employed by this mismanaged company." Get to the important information as quickly as possible, like how many Ks a year they plan on dolin' out.

If you smoke, by all means light up. If you don't smoke, adamantly insist that the interviewer doesn't smoke either. Employers love prospects who aren't afraid to assert themselves. Remember, the people you're dealing with have no idea of what they expect to accomplish by talking to you. You'll have to be patient with them. Enliven the discussion and give a display of your good nature at the same time by offering the interviewer a joint.

Sooner or later every corporate interviewer runs out of inane things to ask and the bullshit really starts flowing. Inevitably they'll set you up by asking something like, "Now that I've made an asshole of myself, perhaps you'd like to take a stab at it." This is, of course, your cue to ask some intelligently motivated questions about the company and provide them with enough ammunition to dump your application in favor of the brunette's (the one with the oversized résumés).

Don't fall for the bait. Explain that through the Freedom of Information Act you've already been over the firm's profit and loss statement. Then make a vague reference to the interviewer's personal tax return. Prospective employers admire candidates who have done extensive research prior to applying for the job. At this point slowly rise to your feet, shake the hand of the interviewer (who's probably still struggling out of his or her tilt-a-whirl chair), and, as you walk out the door, tell the receptionist you'll be getting back in touch if you're still interested.

Seven: Tell Them I'm Not In

Don't be fooled into thinking that four years of tuition hikes have quenched the University's insatiable thirst for money. Now that you're a powerful alumnus, the University

non-living bovine reassessment & processing specialist

metabolic systems resource supplier

high-speed nutrition manager

protein utilization analyst

plans to weasel you into donating everything from a building in your name to a tree on the Ag quad. Little do they realize you're more concerned with coming up with the doorman's fee, keeping your double-knits pressed, and buying that new dishwasher from Sears. Not to mention keeping up with payments on the new paneled station wagon.

Once you recover from the initial shock of receiving that brash plea for donations, you're going to have to concoct a graceful excuse for not contributing to the Noyes Center renovation fund. There are plenty of advantages to having yourself declared legally dead. You'll never collect Social Security, but you won't be financing the University's new Bio Complex either. And that junk mail will stop piling up in your mailbox.

"A good offense is good defense," according to a forgotten maxim. Try countering the University's financial pleas with an equally ballsy demand for University funding for the new nursery you'll be adding to your home. If babies aren't your cup of tea, tell them you donated a building last year. This will raise some eyebrows as they begin the embarrassing search for your check. A young alumnus from Minnesota accidentally mailed her October phone-bill payment to the Cornell Fund. When puzzled alumni officers called her up to report the error, she exclaimed, "Gee willikers! I must have sent the $1,000,000 in small bills to Ma Bell!" This one could work for you.

Eight: Future Shock

No matter how hard you try avoiding alumni contributions, you'll no doubt end up subscribing to the alumni magazine to keep tabs on your classmates and read watered-down versions of what's supposedly happening on campus. Here's a taste of what's in store:

News of Alumni
Class Notes

'33

"I did the grocery shopping this week," writes **Matt Churity** of Swampbog, Utah. "I'm not a University alumnus, but I thought you'd like to know anyway." **Lucy Furr** is resting comfortably after an operation to replace every organ in her body with Styrofoam balls. Congratulations to **Armand Hammer** who, on February 2 of this year, became the first person to drive a Cadillac into a replica of the Venus de Milo sculpted from marshmallows. **Calvin Hist** reports that his father, **Neil**, is a senile old man. In Ithaca, I spoke to **Bobby Pinz**, an ex-lacrosse player whose hobbies include breathing, sweating, and drooling. **Derek Crane** returned to campus last month, and walked across the Arts Quad on a brisk February morning wearing only a pair of swimming fins.

'40

Harriet Upp finished breakfast one morning, walked out the front door carrying her briefcase, and took a bus to work. **Lana Caine** is now teaching at Salt Lake School for the Thirsty. **Lou Natic** reports that since his mandatory retirement at age sixty-five, he's spent his days riding the elevators at the Chrysler Building in mid-Manhattan. "I hope to get stuck between floors," he writes, "but the only thing that has gone wrong so far is the indicator light for the fifteenth floor. They haven't fixed it in two months."

Jack Knife, Miles Tugo, and **Monty Cello** deserve more mention here, but nobody knows who they are. Fun-loving **Burt Toast** tells us that he and his wife **Melba** enjoy ringing doorbells and hiding in the bushes before they can be answered. **Erna Buck** and **Grant A Loan** run one of the top ten plastic shoelace tip manufacturers in the world. **Thurman Nuclearwarhead** suffered a mental breakdown soon after graduation and blew up seven municipal buildings.

Nobody knows what happened to **Ann Drogenous. Hugo First** occupies phone booths to annoy people trying to make important calls. Down in Acapulco, **Marianne Divorce** reports that her seventh millionaire husband just passed away under mysterious circumstances. **Mike S Membrane** watches television fifteen hours a day and burps a lot at night. **Cal Q Late** just bought a can of fruit cocktail and plans to open it during the coming year.

Art T Fishel continues his job as a paperweight at the Library of Congress. He is an expert in collecting dust and his wife likes to lie unconscious at the bottom of swimming pools. **Freida People** has been wandering aimlessly in the Plant Science building on campus for the past thirty years. **Tuck S Inn,** his wife **Phyllis,** and their four children enjoy making rest stops in towns beginning with the letter "K."

Matt R Afact enjoys reading the *New York Times* classified section by holding them up to a mirror. **Sal E Mander** was elected "Most Likely to Be Mistaken for a Mannequin," at his current home, the State Institute for the Criminally Gauche. **C D Character** just lost his job and now sits on a park bench making faces at little children.

Rita Goodbook, Tom O'Hawk, Trudy Myword, and **Dick Tate** never knew each other in college, but at a recent Reunion they failed to meet one another. **Marion Ett** recently had her name legally changed to EXIT. "I always wanted to see my name up in lights," she writes. **Denton Mecar** just had new tires put on his car. Way to go, Denton!

'55

Cora Gated is still involved with the Moonies and enjoys selling flowers in airports. Look for her the next time you pass through LaGuardia. Six months ago, **Stan Dupp** dropped a note telling me that, after ten years, he still works inserting pimentos into olives. But we recently learned he got a new job putting cotton into aspirin bottles. **Bill Ding** is a complete failure.

When you see **Jay Walker** at the next Reunion, be sure to tell him that he's got his shoes on the wrong feet. Our sincerest sympathies to **Bob Apples** who recently picked a scab off his knee. **Bart Tender** reports that if his kids like the way the toothpaste tastes, "maybe they'll stop eating food altogether." **Ray Gunn** wears clothes when he goes to work. **Cherrie Blossum** is no longer dangling participles, although she still uses unnecessary adverbs. **Simon Ize** uses both hands to get dressed in the morning. A correction from last month: **Duncan Donuts** was listed as having seen *Star Wars* three times. He's only seen it twice—it was *Saturday Night Fever* that he saw three times. **Glenn Dale** is helping design a new version of the swizzle stick. Closer to campus, **Matt A Door** passed away, but not before donating himself to be used as fodder in the Arts Quad resodding project. **Martha Vineyard** is one of four alumni. **Curtis C Tuothers** writes that "no one even suspects that I embezzled over twenty thousand dollars from the Cornell Campaign." **Harry Carray** observes that if kitchen utensils could speak they would probably make great conversationalists. **Emil Nitrate** voted for Richard Nixon in 1972.

Jim Shorts hangs out in a local Burger King and enjoys ordering French fries. **Naomi Twodollars** holds four jobs, works seven days a week, hasn't had a vacation in twelve years, hates life, and wishes she was dead. **Sam Arien** gets plenty of rest, drinks lots of fluids, and takes aspirin to relieve the aches and pains that accompany colds and fevers. **Louis D Battle** told **Wendy Warr** that he owns several multi-national corporations despite the fact that he has actually been on welfare for the past two years. **Tim Bucktu** and wife **Betty** inadvertently fed their dog a mixture of plaster of Paris and write that "Smokey is a lot more obedient." **Morris Less** recently received a letter in the mail, carefully opened the envelope, and was surprised to find a bill from the telephone company which did not contain deadly pesticides. On a more somber note, I was shocked and saddened to learn that **Mason Dixon** thinks the square root of 16 is 3. And on a final note, **Claire D Room** is sponging off relatives to support her family of four.

'62

Louise Z Annah enjoys visiting asylums to make sure she hasn't been committed yet. Her former roommate **Ada Goodmeal** has just been promoted despite having been fired three months ago. **Albert Hall** is never home, has never spoken to his wife, and doesn't realize he has four children. **Juan O Clock** finds time to fit his interests in narcissism into his hectic schedule manufacturing mirrors for the blind. **Robyn D Bank** pushes drugs to elementary school kids, while her husband **Wes** spreads communicable diseases on street corners.

Della Ware writes that if she had wings she would probably be commonly mistaken for a bird. **Bertha D Blues** is no longer addicted to benzoid-peroxide and writes she's switched to a Windex solution. **Harry Armpit** spent ten days last July locked in a storage closet at the base of the Statue of Liberty. **Ethel Alcohol** is still using the same mouthwash and reads billboards to support her family of three. **Mona Lott** expects to be victimized by the 245 inhabitants of a local trailer park, but her husband **Lyle** writes that "we don't live anywhere near a trailer park." **Chris Cross** writes that he has no time to write to us. **Molly Cule** uses a soldering iron to remove her unwanted facial hair. **Pat Myback** has been knitting the same sweater for the past nine years.

Scott Landyard doesn't like to eat 3" x 5" index cards, but his wife writes that he's gone through the entire card catalogue at the Boston Public Library. **Terry Torry** occasionally changes his clothes. **Maureen Science** denies being romantically invovled with a Greyhound bus. "We're just good friends," she explained. **Margie Null** bought a can of aerosol cheese and spent two weeks squirting dabs of cheese into coin return slots. **Yul O'Gee** writes that he plans to grow old and die. After donning a kangaroo outfit, **Grace F Termeals** hopped onto her dining room table, shouted "WA-HEE" at the top of her lungs, and disappeared into thin air. **Bea Hive** wears a motorcycle helmet to prevent juvenile delinquents from spraypainting her hair orange. **Pam Perrs** has trouble pronouncing words that begin with the letter "L." **Abbie Road** lies on her bed and stares at the ceiling eight hours each day. "It gives me something to do," she writes.

Beverly Hills has pursued a career as an illustration in a periodical because "I thought I'd follow the advice of my friends who always said I was two dimensional." **June Bride** took a piece of aluminum siding and coated it with grape jelly for no reason in particular last spring. **Jay Bird** says his parents gave his hobby horse to the Salvation Army when he outgrew it as a child.

'88

Carrie D Weight sets up folding chairs in large auditoriums for no reason. She writes that she finds the work challenging and enjoys seeing the expressions on people's faces when they walk into auditoriums they thought to be empty. **Sal U Tittorian** paints white walls white. When not bowling gutter balls at Bowl City, **Gene D Fect** translates Yeats's poetry into Esperanto. **Bonnie Fide** has spent the past seven years lobbying in Congress for the forced reunion of the Beatles. Needless to say . . . **Al K Trazz** spends his spare time making disgusting noises in libraries.

Thanks to the miracle of modern silence, **Lou Cyte** has not said a word in over four years. **Joy Buzzer** is dating the Pillsbury Doughboy, and really enjoys his pop 'n' freshness. **Charles River** enjoys solving quantum mechanics problems at the opera. His wife **Savannah** doesn't. **April Showers** is a Capricorn even though she was born in June.

Ray D O'Active has written four books relating his experiences with fast-acting nasal mist. **Mike Crowaveoven** enjoys gift-wrapping trees in Central Park. He says, "I just want to make sure people notice God's gifts." **Perry Winkle** has never eaten a water cooler. After being elected "Man most likely to drink oven cleaner from a Dixie Riddle Cup," funnyman **Buddy Sistem** burst into flames and exploded. "Never underestimate a person with a tattoo of a blueberry muffin on his or her thigh," writes **Sherwin Paints.**

Eileen Dover has won acclaim at the Metropolitan Museum of Meaningless Art for reupholstering her husband, **Ben.** "Only people with knives ever approach me on the subway," writes **Dennis Toffice**, who has always disliked the taste of tap water.

Ameila Rate is the Dizzy Dean Professor of Space Science at Guam Aerospace Academy. "The work load is very light," she reports. "The school only has about fifteen students, and none of them are enrolled in any of my classes." **Simon Sezz** observes that "If you pluck the wings off a fly, it can only walk or hop around." **Amanda D Votion** is having trouble sewing buttons onto concrete abutments.

Nona R Business programmed a computer to recite zip codes in twelve foreign languages. **Gladys D Weekend** quit gluing twenty-dollar bills to walls because it's hard to convince merchants to accept garage doors for payment. **Norma Tive** has discovered a new energy source but refuses to reveal it. **Pierre Pressure** fell out of a thirty-story window and missed the ground. **Marsha Mallow** enjoys reading menus in Chinese restaurants.

Last May **Madge E Nation** sold over eight thousand dollars worth of wintergreen Lifesavers to squirrels in the San Diego Zoo. **Sam Pell** only watches dishwashing detergent commercials on television.

'97

Norman D Coast tells us that his oldest son, **Ivory**, recently constructed a fifty foot model of the Parthenon with Q-Tips and three cases of mint-flavored toothpaste. **Cal E Berr** is currently in Nepal searching for the meaning of life because he couldn't find it in Newark, New Jersey. **Terry Fye** sharpens pencils twice a week with his wife **Clara** and his son, **Eddie**. **Wade A Minute** has just painted his den burnt sienna.

Faith Full likes stomping on ant hills and burning the survivors with a magnifying glass. **Saul Teencracker** has written a seven-volume history entitled *Authors of Seven-Volume History Books.* On the lighter side, **Patty Wagon** of Ft. Itude, Michigan, recently checked into the hospital for a tonsillectomy and was inadvertently given a lobotomy. Better luck next time, Patty! **Rose Budd** only answers the telephone when it rings. At the Bar Mitzvah of **Iris Stocrat**'s son **Moshe**, **Vic Trolla** set fire to the drapes, sat in the cake, and shot the bartender. Still a card at parties, eh Vic? **Clem N Cee** spent six weeks removing staples from bulletin boards. Luckily, he categorized them by their ferrous content and has been mailing them to friends.

Hal E Tosis has been president of every major oil company in the United States, flies a Learjet, has written four best-selling books, starred in a Broadway production of his own Pulitzer Prize-winning play, and is presently training for the Olympics. It's hard to believe that Hal wet his bed until sophomore year. **Sal Vige** has memorized every word in the *American Heritage Dictionary* that ends in the suffix "-ify."

Ally Katz reports that her husband **Bob** has forgotten his first name. They spent Thanksgiving consulting friends, neighbors, and relatives, but they still haven't stumbled upon it. We wish them luck in their search. **Tony A Ward** spent Christmas vacation trying to get his wife and children out of his locked car.

Welcome to the Real World!

Outro: How big a tip should I leave (or what's 15% of $200,000)?

Well, that about does it. It's true that we didn't hit the terror of Bridge night, scoring dope on Wall Street, or asking for an extension on that new account. But the sprinkler system's on the blink, and the exterminator's at the front door. Just don't fall for that old graduating speech line about commencement being the beginning rather than the end of your education. There's always grad school.

"I used to do it with my dog.
Now I do it . . . doggy style!"
—*Jerry Buttwater*

SEXUAL INDECENCY FOR DIMWITS®

*A Reference
for the Perverse*™

**A Great Gift for
Mom and Dad,
Dad and Dad,
or Mom and Mom**

**Guaranteed
"User-Friendly" and
"Many User Friendly"**
*(if you like that
sort of thing)*

by Jerry Buttwater
Bestselling Author of
The Name's Daddy, Pimp Daddy

Not to be sold to minors in
the U.S. or Canada without
false identification

Chapter 3

Sex, Drugs, & Bowling

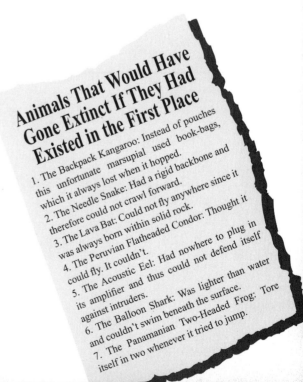

Animals That Would Have Gone Extinct If They Had Existed in the First Place

1. The Backpack Kangaroo: Instead of pouches this unfortunate marsupial used book-bags, which it always lost when it hopped.

2. The Needle Snake: Had a rigid backbone and therefore could not crawl forward.

3. The Lava Bat: Could not fly anywhere since it was always born within solid rock.

4. The Peruvian Flatheaded Condor: Thought it could fly. It couldn't.

5. The Acoustic Eel: Had nowhere to plug in its amplifier and thus could not defend itself against intruders.

6. The Balloon Shark: Was lighter than water and couldn't swim beneath the surface.

7. The Panamanian Two-Headed Frog: Tore itself in two whenever it tried to jump.

ne day I had to give an oral report on the mating habits of the Sperm whale in biology class. I was really nervous, so my stomach was in knots the whole day. When I finally stood up to read my report, my stomach began to growl and then I farted with enough force to shatter the window behind me! To add insult to injury I found out later that one of the shards of glass flew straight into the eyes of this guy that I had a crush on all year. Now that he's blind he'll never ask me out!"

— CORKY S., WEST PALM BEACH, FLORIDA

"I have been keeping a diary for the past five years to record all of my exploits, including the time my older brother Ned and I went out back behind the chicken coop with a couple of corn dogs left over from the Minnesota State Fair. It's pretty detailed, especially the parts that involve the midget farmhands, Lance and Barry. Well, one day I was running to biology class, and I dropped my diary in the hallway. This hot senior guy picked it up and read the entire thing and then made photocopies and handed them out to every other senior guy in the school. Now they all call me 'Chicken Poker.' It's so embarrassing! I'll never get a date for the Hoe-Down!"

—TRACY V., ST. PAUL, MINNESOTA

"One day in school I was late for my second-period English class so I had to run to get there on time. I guess I was running too fast because my tampon flew out and landed in the water fountain! I was so embarrassed! The humiliating part is that there was a really cute guy getting a drink and it hit him right in the head. He had to pick it up and hand it to me. My face was bright red the whole time! Now I'll never be a Supreme Court Justice."

—JUDY A., MISSION HILL, CALIFORNIA

Everything you've always wanted to know about bowling*

*Don't ask

What should I know about bowling?

Whatever is necessary to make bowling a satisfying and pleasurable exerience.

How big should a bowling ball be?

It seems that nearly everybody is preoccupied with this topic. They think that the only way to score well in bowling is with a massive sixteen-pound ball. This is simply not true. Many people with considerably less impressive arsenals (even under ten pounds) are extremely successful bowlers. Commented one woman, "My husband and I bowl every chance we get. He sports only an eight-pound ball, but he's wonderful. God, can he pick his shots!" Just remember it's not the weight of the ball, it's the spin into the pins.

My wife and I bowl together about three times a week, and I put my all into every game. The problem is, after ten frames I'm usually very tired, while my wife is ready to bowl again. What should I do?

Maybe your wife is not as satisfied with the game as you are. Remember her feelings. Rather than dashing off for a few obligatory games of pinball, sit down and talk to her about the experience. Sometimes that can make all the difference in the world.

The other day, I caught my eleven-year-old son sitting in the closet all by himself playing a game of Skittle-Bowl. Is this normal?

Perfectly normal, for someone of his age. Youngsters are ordinardy quite curious about bowling and it is only natural that they all want to experiment on their own. As long as he knows that Skittle-Bowl is but a substitute for the real thing, I advise you not to worry. It's a stage he will outgrow. (This also applies to those of you discovering stacks of bowling magazines in your child's underwear drawers. It's nothing to fret over.)

My boyfriend takes me bowling several times a week. While he has fantastic games every time, I can never seem to get a strike. What's wrong?

Probably nothing. Everyone is capable of achieving a strike. It's simply a matter of patience. I know of one woman who could never seem to light up that little "X." The dilemma upset both her and her husband. It finally reached the point where she would press the reset button when her husband wasn't looking and claim that she'd knocked down all the pins herself. But faking strikes is not a proper solution—patience is. Relax, your strike will come.

Is the first bowling experience usually painful?

It can be. Bowling employs a unique combination of muscles, some of which may never have been used before. First-timers may develop some soreness. On the other hand, the ball itself may be a source of pain. Often the holes are too small. A simple lubricant may do the trick but, occasionally, the only effective solution is drilling larger holes.

I probably whip the ball down the alley faster than anyone I know. Why aren't I scoring well?

Speed is not the key to successful bowling. A lot goes on between the time the ball leaves your hand and when it smashes into the pins. Make use of that time. Never underestimate the value of "floor-play"—the subtle twists, spins, and gyrations a ball makes on the way down the alley. Sometimes it can mean the difference between multiple strikes and no strikes at all.

What can you tell me about professional bowlers?

Professional bowlers have reached such a high level of proficiency that, quite simply, they are paid to bowl.

How should I educate my children about bowling?

Don't hestitate to bring them down to the lanes yourself some day. Better they should get their information there, than in the gutter.

PLAYTOY

ENTERTAINMENT FOR MEN WHO AREN'T GETTING ANY

April 2008 www.porn.com

Jane Goodall's Jungle Phenom!

KOKO NUDE

A Playtoy Interview with **Anna Nicole Smith's Breasts**

Rock Her World with Our Hot Sex Tips*

*That is if you had a girlfriend and didn't need to spend all your time reading this magazine alone in the dark

Featuring **Lots of Articles You Won't Read**

WINTER FUN ISSUE

**Hockey and SEX
Snow and SEX
Frostbite and SEX
Hot Cocoa and SEX
Mittens and SEX**

Midget Pin-ups *and other fetishes you can't resist*

ISBN: 978-0-9772590-3-8

How to tell your girlfriend she's getting FAT

Eventually, we all encounter this problem in our relationships. When your girlfriend starts to put on some pounds, you have an obligation to let her know. She probably hasn't noticed. Of course, you can't just spell it out for her. It's too much of a shock. You must be very diplomatic for her sake. Here are some tactful ways to let your woman know that she has to get the lead out:

1. Take her out to dinner. If she orders anything other than a salad, you should say to her, "Honey, I think you should lay off the calories. They're not good for you and that stuff will give you a stomach ache. I'm just looking out for you. In addition, you look fat to me."

2. Sit down with her and watch an episode of *Ally McBeal*. Say to her, "That Calista Flockhart sure is thin. I wish some of that thinness would rub off on you."

3. She may need to see a professional. Tell her, "Honey, I think you have an eating disorder. You eat too much. You're Queen Fat of the People's Republic of Lard. But you do have a beautiful personality."

4. Exercise is most important for her. Encourage her to workout. "Honey, I bought you this human-scale version of a hamster wheel. Why don't you run in it for about seven days?"

5. Go into her wardrobe and replace all her clothes with the same clothing except one size smaller. Repeat this once a week until she loses weight faster than you can make the weekly clothing replacement. She should be thin enough now.

HOT TIP When stuffing your pants with socks, remember: for maximum effect, the socks should go in front.

Sexual Prowess Quiz

Are you sex-starved? A social misfit? Find out with our portable evaluation. You have ten minutes to complete the test. Do not cheat off of your neighbor, though you may cheat on your neighbor.

1. When an attractive member of the opposite sex bumps into you, do you:
   a) Say "Excuse me" and introduce yourself.
   b) Stare lecherously and salivate.
   c) Say "Now that we've bumped, how 'bout we grind?"
   d) Open up your trench coat.

2. For a first date, do you prefer:
   a) A romantic candlelight dinner followed by a moonlight stroll on the beach.

HOT TIP If you need to fart during a date, stand next to a sweaty fat guy. Your date will think it was him!

   b) *The Rocky Horror Picture Show* followed by mutual heroin abuse in a mosh pit.
   c) Going to see *Bambi* with your mom (sitting between you and your date) and sharing a soda (two straws of course).
   d) Going to see a monster truck show with the hillbillies from *Deliverance*.

3. If it looks like she might be willing, do you:
   a) Stop at the drugstore and discreetly buy protection.
   b) Stop at the pet store and buy a choke collar.
   c) Stop at the cash machine.
   d) Pull out your zippered leather mask.

4. If your roommate walks in on you, do you:
   a) Dress quickly and apologize.
   b) Start swearing at him in Punjabi until he leaves.
   c) Tell him he's blocking the video camera.
   d) Ask him to join you.

5. If you had a choice, would you rather:
   a) Cure AIDS and never get laid.
   b) Achieve world peace and never get laid.
   c) Feed the poor and never get laid.
   d) It doesn't matter, because you will never get laid.

SCORING: If you don't know how to score, you flunk the test.

We go deep into enemy territory to bring you the exotic . . .

Women of the Al Qaeda

AND

Why I Don't Want to Have Sex with the Olsen Twins

1. Whenever I look at them I think of Bob Saget.
2. I'm still not sure which twin is the evil one.
3. There are probably several passages in the Bible discouraging that sort of thing.
4. The thought of them reaching the top of the *Billboard* charts with a single entitled "I'm Seeing Double" someday is terrifying.
5. They've really let themselves go since their *Full House* days.
6. The last twelve or so Mary Kate and Ashley movies didn't live up to my expectations.
7. It's hard to clear a week out of my schedule.
8. Sharing a mutual attraction with The Man in the Unmarked Van is a bit disturbing.
9. I'm saving myself for Hilary Duff.

PLUS

The World's Worst Opening Pick-up Lines

"You know, if you cut off your arms you'd look just like Venus de Milo."

"Are you incredibly beautiful, or is it just my chemotherapy?"

"Sorry, I thought you were a moose."

"Your place, or my car?

"Quick! How many psalms are there?"

"Ontogeny recapitulates phylogeny."

"Wanna come up to my place for a pizza and a fuck? What's the matter, you don't like pizza?"

"You know, you look better without my glasses."

"What's a slut like you doing in a classy joint like this?"

"Um . . . er . . . I . . . um . . . er . . . "

"Does the nose come off with the glasses?"

"Say, babe, can I fit you for a diaphragm?"

"Funny how those things never seem to go away."

"Why is it that the really beautiful girls are assholes?"

"Your body is like haiku in motion."

"Hi there! I'm . . . naaah, it'll never work."

We're looking for engineers who never gave coitus a second thought.

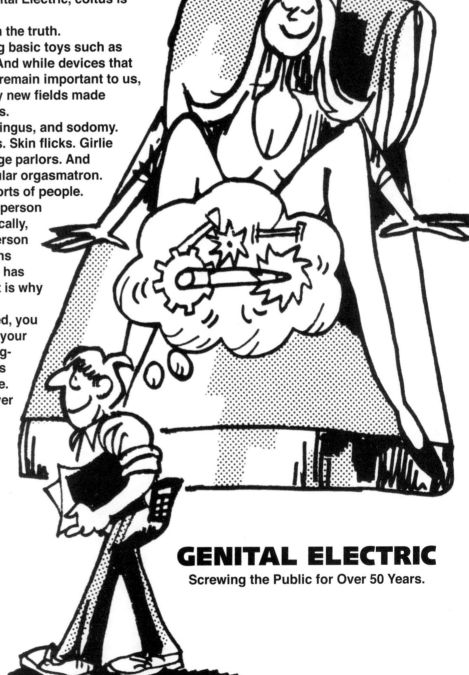

Most people think that at Genital Electric, coitus is our first, last, and only interest.

Nothing could be further from the truth.

We started out in 1927 making basic toys such as vibrators and rubber products. And while devices that run on electricity and spark fun remain important to us, we have branched out into many new fields made possible by today's loose morals.

Fields such as fellatio, cunnilingus, and sodomy. Whips and chains. Life-like dolls. Skin flicks. Girlie magazines. Adult books. Massage parlors. And last, but not least, the ever-popular orgasmatron.

All sorts of products for all sorts of people. Inventing these devices takes a person who can think about sex analytically, without becoming aroused. A person who has no preconceived notions about sex. In fact, a person who has no notions about sex at all. That is why we need engineers.

Since Genital Electric is varied, you can find a place with us to start your career, no matter what your hang-ups. And each of our divisions is small enough that you can score.

That is why we say if you never gave coitus a second thought, your first thought should be Genital Electric.

Give it a thought.

GENITAL ELECTRIC
Screwing the Public for Over 50 Years.

Some People Call Me the Gangster of Love

BY JERRY C. BUTTWATER

Your old pal Jerry Buttwater was watching cable TV the other night, hoping to catch a Shannon Tweed flick. Wouldn't you know it? This particular Saturday was the one night of the year that the lovely Miss Tweed would not be naked on Cinemax. Come on people! What do you think I'm paying to see anyway?

Normally, Jerry Buttwater would just go outside, snap his fingers, and immediately have his choice of twenty beautiful chicks. Unfortunately ol' Jerry B. was still unable to walk, having suffered a severe concussion after unwittingly fondling the captain of the football team's girlfriend. (I swear I thought she said, "Don't *not* touch me!") So I was faced with a dilemma: shell out the $4.95 for pay-per-view or watch whatever non-pornogrpahic film they were showing on Skinemax. After a frantic search under the cushions of my couch turned up only two nickels and an old Buffalo wing, Jerry Buttwater realized that he was going to have to settle for option number two. I ended up watching a Scorsese movie—I think it was called *Raging Casinofellas.*

About half way through the movie, Sharon Stone went down on Joe Pesci. I recall thinking, "Now this is more like it!" But deep in the recesses of Jerry Buttwater's soul something stirred. Despite all the oral sex, something was not right. Maybe it was just the fractured skull and the painkillers, but maybe it was something more. Something important. Suddenly, it became clear. There is *no way* Sharon Stone would *ever* blow Joe Pesci! I mean look at the guy. He should be living under a bridge somewhere and eating goats. Sharon Stone, one of the hottest broads on earth, who could have just about any guy she wanted (maybe even Jerry Buttwater himself), would never stoop so low (no pun intended). Yet even as I thought this, it was happening before my very eyes.

So the question was, "How could this be possible?" After much deliberation, Jerry Buttwater decided that there was only one explantion: chicks dig mobsters.

Take Joe Pesci: outwardly, he's a little runt with no redeeming qualities. But look—he starts acting tough, stabs a guy with a pen, hangs out with Ray Liotta, and suddenly he's a chick magnet. What an angle!

At that moment Jerry Buttwater decided that he, too, would join the studly ranks of the underworld. I contacted my Uncle Guido, who got me an application. The essays were tough, but Jerry Buttwater is a tough guy. No essay would stop him from becoming a made man!

A few weeks later, I went for my interview with a Mafia alumnus, Don Gino Vitello. Any fears I had about joining the family were washed away when he told me that the Mafia was really just an exclusive club formed so that an average Italian guy could get a quality lay. Sure, they rob and kill, but that's just to keep up the air of danger for the chicks. Man, these guys are swingers!

So now I'm one week away from my gangster initiation, and Jerry Buttwater is here to tell all you ladies and your boyfriends how things are gonna be from now on. A number of people have sought to silence Jerry Buttwater. They veil this oppression under the guise of "calling him a loser," "laughing at him when he asks them out," or "having their boyfriend get him really drunk at a fraternity party, flush his head down the toilet, and beat the crap out of him." Those with a keen eye, however, will see this ruse for what it is: a devious and meticulously calculated attempt to censor me so that I might never (1) become a figure in the public eye, (2) be adored by chicks everywhere, and eventually (3) take my rightful place as Stud-king of the dating world (or at least get to feel a breast). But now you're dealing with one of the Sons of Sicily, and Jerry B. demands his due respect. Girls, no more spitting on or kicking Jerry Buttwater in the head. You will only stand by my side and look pretty, smile when spoken to in a degrading fashion, and have lots of sex (with me).

And guys, you better watch your back. No more kicking my ass—my boys know where you live. Stay away from Jerry Buttwater and his ladies and nobody gets hurt, *capice*?

All you ever wanted to know about . . .

Stephen William Hawking!!!

Hey Girls!!!

Tiger Beat's got a special scoop for you this month on the latest and greatest hottie around! His name's Stephen William Hawking, and if you haven't heard of him yet, you will soon!

Stephen is a Capricorn (born on January 8, 1942) and a professor of "astrophysics" (a fancy word for awesome math stuff . . . WOW!!!!) In his spare time, Stephen likes listening to classical music and watching *Star Trek* . . . sorry, girls—he's married!!! (But that doesn't mean you can't hang his pictures on your wall and have totally unrealistic fantasies about dating him!!!)

WHY IS STEVE SOOOO CUTE?!

♥ He has a wheelchair.
♥ He talks through a computer (you know, the big, cool box that you use to Instant Message your friends and listen to *NSYNC when your iPod is rechargin').
♥ He is rich and famous—that means if you went out with him, you would be rich and famous too!!!!!!

Take Tiger Beat's SWH quiz!!!

1. What is Stephen's fave food?
2. Who is SWH's fave Spice Girl?
3. Where is Stephen's fave place to chill?
4. On a scale of 1 to 10, how hot is Stevie?
5. What is a "black hole?"— Just kidding!!!
6. What is your name?
7. How old are you?
8. I'm a 37-year-old, bed-wetting virgin who lives in his parents' basement and writes for *Tiger Beat*. Do you want to come over to my house sometime?
9. I hate my life.

Editorial

Superman Wrongly Accused

BY CLARK KENT

Not since Wonder Woman was arrested for indecent exposure while changing her underwear inside the cockpit of her invisible jet has the good name of a superhero been so viciously attacked by the media. Like drones, the fickle people of our city have been misled into believing that scientists have discovered the cause of the recent epidemic of breast cancer in Metropolis: Superman.

Without a smidgen of solid evidence to support their theory, scientists alleged Tuesday that Superman, the defender of truth, justice, and the American way in Metropolis, has been using his X-ray vision to see through women's blouses. They speculate that concentrated X-rays from Superman's eyes would cause a rapid acceleration of malignant cell growth in the breast. The head of the research team claims that this epidemic occurred soon after Superman arrived in Metropolis. In addition, the researchers point to the fact that there have been more Superman sightings here at *The Daily Planet* office building than anywhere else in the city; the highest rate of female breast cancer also happens to be in this building. These researchers failed to mention that the waitresses at the Hooters restaurant located across the street from *The Daily Planet* have nearly equivalent rates. Well, I eat there for lunch and dinner nearly every day, and I never—not once—saw Superman there.

In response to yesterday's editorial by my colleague, Lois Lane, entitled "Superman: That Cancer-Causing, Wandering-Eyed Pervert," I do not agree with her that women should try to go "an eye for an eye" with "that cheating bastard" by "hanging a fifty kilogram bag of Kryptonite from his [testicles], small as they are." First of all, Ms. Lane, let me remind you that Superman has saved you and your breasts on numerous occasions.

I think this is all a conspiracy designed by none other than Lex Luthor himself to get rid of Superman while making a quick buck. Rumor has it that in light of these recent accusations, LuthorTek has decided to make a new line of lead brassieres and lead underwear which cannot be penetrated by Superman's rays—no doubt this is all for a profit.

I contacted two of Superman's best friends, Batman and Robin, to ask them how it feels to be persecuted by the very people they are protecting. Referring to a *Saturday Night Live* sketch parodying the twosome called "The Ambiguously Gay Duo," Batman said "Do you know how much hate mail Robin and I received after that aired?" He continued, "And that was just from my butler Alfred. We also received tons of nasty letters and phone calls questioning our sexuality. It's nobody's business but our own."

Which reminds me: I wanted to conclude this column by eulogizing the best friend a guy could ever have—Jimmy Olson, the Pulitzer-Prize winning photographer of *The Daily Planet* for fifteen years. Jimmy and I grew really close over these years; we had had many intimate conversations and shared many late nights here at *The Daily Planet*. I am saddened that as a result of his untimely death, we were not able to become the type of friends I felt we could have been. Best friends, kindred spirits; soul mates, if you will. I can truly say that I loved him. He died this week of penile, testicular, and prostate cancer.

Clark Kent is a reporter for The Daily Planet. *In his spare time, he is Superman.*

 in "The Package"

Really Bad Topics to Discuss on a First Date

1. The merits of Christian Television over *Masterpiece Theatre*
2. That orange thing that's been stuck in your teeth since you last ate
3. Buffalo's comeback in next year's Super Bowl
4. Monochromatic modern art
5. That bulge in his pants
6. Your dad's televangelist compound down in Georgia
7. How to write a really efficient random number generating algorithm
8. Those neat pictures in *Animal Life* magazine
9. Which edition of J. Crew each piece of your outfit came from
10. GPAs, MCATs, LSATs, GREs, IQs, SATs, ACTs, or APs
11. Obscure Austrian psychoanalysts
12. Great fungi I have known
13. Cost-benefit analysis
14. Previous relationships and why they didn't work out (with violin accompaniment)
15. Friends' previous relationships and why they didn't work out
16. Bill Clinton's previous relationships and why they didn't work out

An ordinary housewife writes in and says . . .

"WHEN I BITE INTO A YORK PEPPERMINT PATTY,

it's more refreshing than the cool water of a mountain stream gurgling over my bare feet. It's better than the fine breeze that wafts down from the high places and sends a tingle of energy to the very tips of my toes. It's more wonderful than a clear sky after a summer thundershower, when the sun makes every raindrop a tiny diamond.

When I bite into a York Peppermint Patty, it feels better than the wide-eyed grin of my boyfriend, than the way his broad hand wraps around my narrow one, and his muscular arm envelopes my shoulders, than the feel of his powerful hands kneading the kinks out of my back, than the gentle strokes he gives my hair, and the way the back of his hand just lightly brushes my shoulder.

When I bite into a York Peppermint Patty, it's as good as my lover's tongue squirming around in my mouth. It's as fine as his soft lips running up and down my throat, his teeth nibbling on my earlobe, and his tongue tickling the little hairs on the back of my neck. It's as tingly as his warm breath in my ear, as soothing as his huge body, his arms wrapped around me, warm, protective, and strong.

When I bite into a York Peppermint Patty, it's nearly as good as his hands on my breasts. First as light as feathers, on the margins of ticklishness, then to the nipples, rolling them like marbles between his fingers while I squirm and giggle like a schoolgirl.

When I bite into a York Peppermint Patty, it's not nearly as good as the spurt of hot semen into the back of my throat, when my lover's hips jerk forward and he comes in my mouth. It doesn't even compare with his mouth around my breast, first a vacuum cleaner, then a crocodile, then a velvet, magic carpet. It's not much, next to his stern spanking, or the funky smell of that forest of hair on his chest. It's not at all close to the strange feel of his balls in my hands, or the tingle I feel when he licks my armpit. It's far from the ecstatic sensation of his lips and his tongue toying with my clitoris.

When I bite into a York Peppermint Patty, it's not even close to the sensation of that ropy cock forcing its way between my legs and burying its head in my hungry, wet womanhood. There's no comparison with the explosions that radiate from my privates to my head, and send yellow lights blinking behind my closed eyes. There isn't a shred of comparison with the massive orgasm that leaves me limp in his arms, crying with uncontrollable glee. But he doesn't stop. That cock slides in and out, tickling the outside of my labia, probing the gates of my cervix. The bountiful fluids of our love stream from the point of our junction, as he gyrates his hips, and I know I'm going to come again. Finally, he shoves two leather-gloved fingers into my asshole and I scream with pain and ecstasy—and you'd compare that with a lousy piece of candy?"

—*Name and address withheld*

Do you have a suitor who just won't take "No, you digusting pig!" for an answer? Does he call you all the time, ask you out, and no matter how hard you try, he just doesn't get the message? Well, as played by the out-of-work actors Kristine and Tom, here are some suggestions on how to get rid of that guy permanently.

THE DIM-BULB APPROACH

TOM: Hey Kristine, can I interest you in a nice night of theater?

KRISTINE: What are you going to see?

TOM: *Death of A Salesman.*

KRISTINE: Oh . . . I haven't heard of that one before.

TOM: What!?! You've never heard of Arthur Miller's masterpiece?

KRISTINE: Hey, that's such a coincidence!

TOM: What is?

KRISTINE: I named my dog Arthur.

TOM: After the playwright?

KRISTINE: No, silly.

TOM: Then after what?

KRISTINE: After I got him.

TOM: Oh . . . so, you wanna go?

KRISTINE: Where?

TOM: To see *Death of a Salesman.*

KRISTINE: Is it like *Taxi?*

TOM: What?

KRISTINE: You know, like *Taxi* on Nick at Night. That Louie, he's so crazy!

TOM: No no, it isn't like *Taxi* at all.

KRISTINE: Doesn't this salesman drive a car?

TOM: Yeah, but what does that matter?

KRISTINE: Then it's like *Taxi.*

TOM: It isn't like *Taxi* at all!

KRISTINE: Doesn't the salesman make a living by driving to different places?

TOM: Yeah, but it's not like *Taxi* at all.

KRISTINE: Are you sure?

TOM: I'm positive.

KRISTINE: Sorry, then. I like *Taxi,* and if it isn't like *Taxi,* I don't think I'd enjoy it very much. I need mental stimulation, and this *Death of a Cab Driver* doesn't seem very stimulating at all.

THE MODERN-TIMES METHOD

TOM: Hi Kristine, wanna go out with me sometime?

KRISTINE: Um . . . .

TOM: This is a once in a lifetime opportunity we're talking about here.

KRISTINE: No, this is sexual harassment we're talking about here, and I don't have to take it anymore!

GETTING RID OF THAT GUY

THE NARROW-MINDED MANNER

TOM: Hey Kristine! Wanna go to Disneyland with me sometime?

KRISTINE: Disneyland? No thank you! That's run by a Jew!

TOM: Er . . . do you have something against the Jewish people?

KRISTINE: You're joking, right?

TOM: Uh . . . well I have tickets to see New Edition.

KRISTINE: Now the blacks!? What are you, a social worker!? Not in my lifetime!

TOM: Okay, why don't we go to a Chinese restaurant?

KRISTINE: I'm Japanese, you idiot! We all look the same to you, don't we?! Man, you're so racist!

TOM: Me? You're the one who's racist!

KRISTINE: What? You're calling me racist? What's the matter, laddy, upset because you didn't get your usual supply of potatoes?!

THE SIBLING RIVALRY MIX-UP

TOM: Hey Kristine . . . wanna go out sometime?

KRISTINE: Are you gonna bring your sister Cathy?

TOM: What? No, I mean, just you and me . . . you know, like a date.

KRISTINE: Um . . . how about we make it a threesome and invite Cathy?

TOM: I kinda wanted this to be private, you know?

KRISTINE: Well, I think Cathy's really swell, you know. I like her a lot.

TOM: What? I'm not talking about just going out here. I mean a date. We can't take my sister on a date!

KRISTINE: Why not? I like her. She's nice. She has a very nice body.

TOM: You like my sister's body?

KRISTINE: Yeah . . . I think she has a nice figure and nice breasts. She's really cute too. Does she have a boyfriend?

TOM: Um . . . I dunno.

KRISTINE: Has she ever expressed any interest in . . . you know, an "alternative lifestyle"?

TOM: Are you a lesbo?

KRISTINE: Now see, we don't need this name-calling around here. Just because I think your sister would be good in the sack doesn't mean I'm Lebanese.

TOM: Not Lebanese! A lesbian! You're a butch queer!

KRISTINE: I think I've had about enough of this! I don't like this name-calling! Now just give me your mighty fine sister's phone number and get the hell out of here!

If you want to enlarge your bust, say "Cheese!"

Have you considered breast augmentation but balked at the health risks and the outrageous doctors' fees? Have you ever stood in a long line at the bank and had the craving for a delicious snack? Well, look no further than your local grocery store! Easy Teatz combines the latest in breast implant technology and a super-tasty cheese product! And boy, is it quick, easy, and—yes—fun!

Simply go to the dairy section of your grocery store and pick up a can of Easy Teatz! (available in cheddar, nacho, goat's milk, and pimento cheese flavors. *Yum, yum, yummers!*)

Then go to your favorite lingerie shop and purchase the bra of your dreams. (Easy Teatz will take care of *any* size! If it's 80HHH breasts you want, then by golly, buy an 80HHH bra!)

While wearing your regular bra, put on your new super-size bra over it. Place the nozzle of your can of Easy Teatz between the two bras and squirt away, giving yourself firm, voluptuous breasts with a delicious cheese flavor! Since Easy Teatz isn't real cheese, it can be worn for any length of time without getting moldy. In fact, the longer you wear it, the firmer and more life-like it gets. If you can't wait a long time, line your super-sized bra with crackers before filling with Easy Teatz. In seconds, you'll have your firm, perky breasts with no fuss or muss. And what a delicious snack it makes!

Read what others are saying about Easy Teatz!

"I was throwing a party for a close friend when I realized we were out of cheese topping, I panicked! Then I remembered that I was wearing my Easy Teatz. Thank you, Easy Teatz! You saved my party from being a total disaster!"

"My boyfriend can't tell the difference!"

"As an angry feminist artist, I got a double masectomy to make a statement. Later that day, I realized that I had a lingerie photo shoot for Cosmopolitan! *Easy Teatz, you're a lifesaver!"*

"I send my daughter to school with Easy Teatz for a taste-tempting lunchtime snack!"

Easy Teatz causes no adverse effects—unless you count the psychological damage caused by extreme embarrassment.

PSYCHEDELIC SAM

The traffic refused to stop. Car upon car dribbled through the intersection as Sam stood helplessly on the corner. He had to get to work, and that meant getting past those cars. He leaned against the lamp post and noticed that his legs were getting weaker, his vision was blurring, and things were spinning. It was happening again. Sam was being transformed into Psychedelic Sam, a regression to his college acid days. With graceful ease, Sam floated over the cars, handing out flowers to those who brashly blared their horns at him. He yelled, "Peace baby!" and pushed his long, brown hair behind of his ears. He drifted to the ground a block from the office and settled back into Sam the Executive.

"Good morning," said Sam's secretary as he strode into the office.

"Good morning, Miss Wirtier," replied Sam as usual. "Any mail?" asked Sam, not really caring if there was any.

"No Sam," said Miss Wirtier, obviously glad that she did not have to answer any of Sam's letters. Sam was too lazy to reply to his mail, so he had Miss Wirtier do it any way she pleased.

Sam walked reluctantly to his desk. He felt a slave to it, knowing that he would have to sit behind it for eight hours whether or not he had any work to do. "If there isn't any work to be done, why can't we go home?" thought Sam, a college graduate with a degree in philosophy. He frowned, shuffled some papers around, sank his head down onto the desktop , and fell asleep. Miss Wirtier interrupted him before he could get too far.

"Sam, there's a board meeting in a few minutes, and Mr. Fleeb wants you to be there."

"Thank you, Miss Wirtier." The last thing in the world that Sam wanted was a severe case of hemorrhoids, and the second to last thing he wanted was a board meeting. He never did anything at the meetings except sit in a dignified manner, representing the labor management division of the company. How could he manage the labor of a multimillion dollar corporation when he couldn't even manage to keep his room clean? The answer was quite simple: He had a piece of paper from a university that said he could, so the company believed it.

"You can't hurt me! I'm just a bunch of lines on a piece of paper!"

So off he went with an empty briefcase. The board room was the same as always, with sixteen chairs around a long, mahogany table. Sam picked his usual spot, two seats from the right end, which gave him an all-encompassing view of everyone else. In reality every seat had the same view, but Sam clung strongly to his belief in the second seat from the right end.

Sam sat down and watched the others file in. There was Mr. Blue, Chairman of the Board, Mr. Brock-well, Vice President of Corporate Affairs, and Mrs. Smithens, Vice President in Charge of De-sexing Corporate Executive Titles. More people came in until all the seats were filled. Sam stared at them all. "What bores," he thought to himself. Then in walked Mr. Fleeb, and everyone snapped to attention, standing at their seats with their hands resting at their sides. Mr. Fleeb waddled in, and as soon as he sat down, everyone else followed suit. Sam wondered what would happen if he remained standing. "Probably nothing," he thought, and he sat down.

Mr. Fleeb started the meeting by asking for new business. To everyone's surprise, Sam raised his hand.

"Yes, Sam," asked Mr. Fleeb.

"Yesterday I bought a tie, and that is *my* new business."

"Now really!" exclaimed Mrs. Smithens. "This is a serious top-level board meeting."

"I'm sorry, Mrs. Smithens," declared Sam, still amused by what he had said.

Sam carefully eyed Mr. Brockwell. His tie in particular. It was black against a white shirt. Sam thought it made Mr. Brockwell look like a zebra. He spied at his face, and sure enough, Mr. Brockwell was a zebra. He looked around the table. There was a giraffe, and an elephant, a rhinoceros, tigers, lions, gorillas, and wildebeests. Sam was turning back into his psychedelic self. He looked down at his brown

sports jacket. A tan shirt was in its place. He glanced up and thought he saw the brim of a pith helmet. The door opened and two bushmen stood by a waiting jeep. Sam reached down by his side and found a rifle in place of his briefcase.

"I'm a hunter," declared Sam, and he picked up the firearm and began bagging trophies. The animals offered no resistance. They sat patiently in their seats while Sam shot them. "What fun," thought Sam, as

he reloaded the rifle time and again. As the last animal fell, Sam looked toward the door. His vision blurred and the bushmen were nowhere to be found. Mrs. Smithens was speaking. Casually he rose from his seat and walked toward the window.

"Where are you going, Sam?" asked Mr. Fleeb.

"Just out for a while. I'll be back." And with that Sam leaped out the window and joined the swirling mass of cars that swarmed the street.

OUTER SPACE FOR EVERYONE

What, exactly, is outer space?

What the hell kind of a question is that? For God's sake, you walk outside at night, you see a bunch of stars and planets and blackness—that's outer space.

Can you give a more precise definition?

Never heard of a dictionary, I suppose. Look, I know the title says "Outer Space for Everyone," but it isn't referring to imbecilic woodchucks who chortle with glee each time they hear the word *clamato*. If you fit into that category, you'd better turn the page because you're a complete waste of my time and effort.

How big is the universe?

The universe is huge. Mind-bogglingly immense. Astronomically gargantuan. Infinitely infinite. Let me put it this way: The universe is so voluminous, so goddamn brain-splinteringly BIG, that no number known to man can be used to describe its size. 964,000,000,000,000,271,000,341,005,000,000,000? Sorry, no good. How about $14^{800000000}$? Nope, wrong again. The late Dutch physicist, Franz Glanz, came close with $62.4 \times 10^{3000000000000000}$!, but even that fell short. Only when we talk in fictional figures, like eighty thousand zillion jillion, do we begin to get an understanding of the size of our vast universe.

How old is the universe?

Old. Real old. I know no other way to express accurately the sense of agedness. Think of it this way: If you held a birthday party for the universe, and you lit a candle for each year of its existence, the heat produced would be so intense that the planets would melt, the stars would explode, and all life would be decimated; in short, the universe would be instantly converted into a steaming, bubbling, mucky pizza.

What does the universe weigh?

What an asinine question.

How did the universe begin?

Look, I don't know everything. Why don't you just ask me how many grains of sand there are in the Sahara desert?

How many grains of sand are there in the Sahara desert?

I don't know. Go count them.

Are there any theories attempting to explain the origin of the universe?

A few.

What are they?

The Big Bang Theory: This theory states that the universe began with an explosion, hence the name Big Bang. I know, it sounds crazy—you'd think it might end with an explosion . . . but to begin with one? If you ask me, I'd say it's a bunch of hooey.

The Gang Bang Theory: This is a rather ludicrous hypothesis that's really not worth going into. All I'll say is that it hinges on the existence of a reproductive organ the size of the Andromeda Galaxy. You can probably figure out the rest.

When will the universe end?

Why the hell are you worried about something like that? Aren't there enough problems in this world without fretting over an event that won't take place for billions and billions of years? By then you'll be long gone, and good riddance.

Is there extraterrestrial life in the universe?

To be quite blunt, no—at least, nothing that could interest you. Oh, chances are there are a few amoebae scattered about the cosmos, but that's all. No intelligent life. No beasts with forty-seven heads. No Klingons. And no R2D2s either, thank God. So you can forget your neurotic fantasies about getting zapped aboard a flying saucer and being tickled to the point of ecstasy by a pack of lusty, love-hungry space amazons, because it ain't gonna happen.

What's a black hole?

Sheesh, that's all anybody cares about these days. Nobody ever asks about dwarf stars, or pulsars, or nebulas anymore.

Well, it's just that we hear so much about black holes nowadays, and . . .

All right, for God's sake, black holes are strong vacuums from which nothing can escape. Satisfied?

But, scientifically speaking, what exactly is a black hole?

Give it a rest already, would you?

Isn't the purpose of this article to educate the general public on some of the fundamentals of astronomy?

I know that. What of it?

Well, then answer the question. What is a black hole?

You know, you're getting to be a real pain in the ass. Who the hell are you, anyway?

What's the difference between a comet and a meteor?

I'm not telling if you're not.

How long is a light year?

Long enough.

Why is the sky blue?

Drop dead.

Explain the principle of nebula formation.

Eat me.

Are there canals on Mars?

That does it. I'm leaving.

Where are you going?

No, really . . . where are you going?

Can I watch?

Be a Family Therapist
at Home

by Carlester Crumpler
*PhD, psychologist,
and family therapist*

Carlester Crumpler has been practicing family therapy for over thirty-four years. He has a loving wife and two children, ages 34 and 29. In addition, Carlester can vow that he practices what he preaches to his clients. Throughout his parenting, Carlester thought like a therapist. What resulted was an intimate relationship with his children and a life of unending joy. Here are just a few excerpts from his new book, Be a Family Therapist at Home.

Situation 1:

Your teenager wants to talk about his or her problems. You just have to get your teenager to talk. Here's what I usually do . . .

ME *[to my son, Billy]*: Have you seen my shoes?

BILLY: I can't hold it in anymore! I tried marijuana at Joe's party last night. I felt pressured to do it! What should I do? I need your help!

Situation 2:

If you are still having trouble getting your teen to talk about his or her problems, try repeating the last word of every sentence your teenager says.

BILLY: Bye, Dad! I gotta go!

ME: Go?

BILLY: Yeah, I have football practice really soon.

ME: Soon?

BILLY: Actually, it's not for another two hours. I'm going over to Todd's.

ME: Todd's?

BILLY: Yeah, he's the new kid in town. *[Cough.]*

ME: *[Cough?]*

BILLY: I can't hold it in anymore! I quit the football team and now I go over to Todd's to smoke marijuana!

Situation 3:

Or, your teen may approach you.

BILLY: Dad, can we have a private conversation?

ME: Sure, son. Go right ahead.

BILLY: Can you put away that tape recorder?

ME: Oh, it's not on.

BILLY: I don't know what I want to do with my life once I'm finished with high school. I don't know if I want to go to college.

ME: Are you still smoking marijuana?

BILLY: I can't hold it in anymore! I love you, Dad!

Situation 4:

If your teen still isn't talking, you may have to force the situation.

ME *[to Billy]*: Would you like to smoke some marajuana with me?

BILLY: I love you, Dad!

Situation 5:

If all else fails, try reverse psychology!

BILLY: I'm going out to a party tonight.

ME: Isn't it a school night?

BILLY: No.

ME: Fine, have a good time.

BILLY: You're right! I shouldn't go! I'll just be pressured to smoke marijuana. I think I'll stay home. I love you, Dad!

Situation 6:

If in doubt, marijuana may be the problem.

ME *[to Billy in his bedroom with the door shut]*: What are you doing in there?

BILLY: Nothing.

ME: Are you smoking marijuana?

BILLY: I learned it by watching you! Burn in hell, you bastard!

ME: Why don't we go out and get some munchies?

BILLY: Cool. I love you, Dad!

Curious Gorge Gets Laid

Gorge is a little monkey. He lives in the apartment of the man with the orange hat. Everyone knows that monkeys are curious. But Gorge is the most curious monkey in the world. That's probably why his name is Curious Gorge.

"I have to split the scene," said the man with the orange hat. "Be a good little monkey while I am out. Try some of the Colombian I bought for you until I come home. Just don't get too curious, you little monkey." And the man went out.

It was a lot of fun for Gorge to smoke the marijuana the man left for him. He smoked a little, and then a little more, and then a little more, and then a little more.

Gorge got very high. And he felt very good. He began to do a lot of tricks. He even did a little dance.

Gorge wanted to broaden his horizons. Where did the man keep his acid? Gorge was curious.

He looked all over the house. There was a closet in the room. Gorge looked through the closet for the acid. He found a lot of things in there. But he did not find the man's acid. Gorge looked for it here and looked for it there. Where was the acid? Gorge took all the drawers out of the dresser. He took all the toys out of the toy box. Gorge looked everywhere. But he could not find the acid.

The room was a mess. Gorge sat down. He had been a bad little monkey. Why was he always so curious? Why did he make such a mess of the room? His trumpet was on the floor. His racing cars and building blocks were everywhere. Now he had to clean up the room and he could not trip. The marijuana made Gorge hungry.

Gorge got up. He had to have something to eat. Maybe there was some food in the refrigerator. Gorge went to the kitchen to look. Yes, there was something to eat and it was something good too. It was a sugar cube.

Gorge took the sugar cube and went back in to the other room. Gorge sat down and ate the sugar cube. Soon he began to see colors. Then he looked around. The room wavered back and forth. Gorge turned on the man's record player. He put on a record by Jimi Hendrix. Gorge felt unusual. He could taste the music. Soon he began to imagine that he was a banana. He did not want anyone to peel him, so he hid under the bed. This was good acid.

Soon the man in the orange hat came back with a fat lady. "What a mess," said the man. Gorge was hiding under the bed. "Where is Gorge?" asked the man. "Maybe you should go out and look for him," suggested the lady. "I'll wait. . . ."

The man did not want to hear any more. He ran to his car and hopped in. "I'm going to kill that little fellow," he said. Gorge stayed under the bed.

The lady did not see Gorge. She took off her clothes, turned out the light, and got in the bed to wait for the man with the orange hat.

Gorge had seen this lady before. But now she was a bright shade of red. This was good acid. Gorge had seen the man in the orange hat in bed with this lady before. He was curious. Gorge crawled out from under the bed. What if the man came back? Maybe he would never come back.

The lady had fallen asleep. Gorge climbed into the bed. She woke up. But the room was dark so she could not see. "Orange hat man, you're back," said the lady. Gorge could not talk so he did not say anything.

"Gee, you're like a monkey in bed," said the lady. "Ooh, ooh, ooh." Gorge liked the lady. The acid was good too.

Just then the man with the orange hat came back. He turned on the light and saw Gorge and the lady in bed together.

"Gorge!" screamed the man, "I'm going to blow your little brains out." The man opened a drawer and took out his gun. Gorge was curious. But he would never, never be curious again.

VILLAGE VICE BULLETIN BOARD 555-7478

TO THE GIRL: Your name was either Cindy or Mary, we passed each other on the New Jersey Expressway yesterday. Did I only imagine a wink? Call either Fred or John at 555-0978.

HERPES?
You should be ashamed of yourself. There is no cure, you know. Call me up right now so I can yell at you.
Dial-a-Mother (212) 555-0978

Joan Crawford's Underwear! Worn by Joan Crawford and Cary Grant, but not at the same time. Authentic, a must for old movie dirty underwear buffs. Box 3, Passaic, N.J.

Dear Wendy: I miss your creamy white thighs, pockmarks, and deep, booming voice. Let's be friends when you're freed, okay? Peter

I'LL PAY YOU CASH FOR YOUR SEXUAL FANTASIES.
Certified accountant without his own sexual fantasies will buy yours, but you must forfeit any future use.
Call me at 555-0956.

HI! I HELD YOU UP AT KNIFEPOINT ON 6/8.
Was there a twinkle in your eyes, or was I just imagining? Call me if there was any magic between us. P.S. I am out of your blank checks and need more. Call Peter at 555-0659

I PAY CASH FOR YOUR FECES!
Do you have any good shit lying around the house? I want it! Call Mike at **555-9867**

Dear Sue: I'm in love with you very very very very much, but I have a problem that must be discussed (we shared an elevator ride on 7/9).
Call me (Charlie) at 555-5670

ARE YOU INTO KINKY ANIMAL S&M, JELLO BONDAGE AND CREAM CHEESE ENEMAS? IF YOU HAVE THE LEATHER, I HAVE THE FEATHER. CALL ME (CHARLES) AT 555-5670.

Buttons to express your present political sentiments. MAKE MINE MEAT, MUST A PIG DIE, and ONLY A TELEPHONE HAS NUMBERS. For catalogue, write Box 45, Flushing, N.Y.

WARNING!
Your pocket money might have deadly carcinogens on it! Government reports (all classified) warn that all $50 bills may have carcinogenic dye. For proper disposal, send to Mike immediately at Box 277, N.Y. Do it today BEFORE IT'S TOO LATE!!!

STOP SMOKING IN FIVE MINUTES!
U.S. Army method leaves you free of any bad habits/ personality defects/individuality. Call your recruiter today.

Disco Anonymous: Can't stop boogieing and people think that you're a shallow mindless wasteoid? We can help, perhaps. Mail us $500 and we teach you to hate John Travolta and start foaming at the mouth whenever a song by KC and the Sunshine Band is played. Call Karen at 555-1377.

ARE YOU A TRANSVESTITE?
You can be helped. Therapy group to foster exchange of clothing. Call Frank at 555-0978

End of world is imminent! Recent discovery proves that the world will be burned to crisp by passing comet. For possible ways of coping with this certainty, send $5 and SASE today . . . before it's too late, to Box 36, Lunar Base, the Moon.

FLASHERS!
WE'RE HAVING A FORMAL TEA AND GET-TOGETHER TO DISCUSS POSSIBLE FRANCHISE OPPORTUNITIES. CALL ERIC AT 555-0845.

Feed one adult for only 65¢ a week. Eat lobster, steak, and caviar every night, unless they catch you doing it. Send one dollar to Marvin Gardens, Box 569, Radio City Music Hall, New York, NY.

SHOPLIFTERS ANONYMOUS: To the member who stole our charter, the TV, and the money, please return it. This is no way to be cured, you know.

LESBIAN coming out of closet sale. I'm moving out of my closet and into my lover's apartment, so I got quite a bit of stuff to sell. I have masks, nightlights, and small squares of carpet just right for your own closet, perhaps. 555-1809.

TO THE SHEEP THAT I GLIMPSED AT THE BRONX ZOO:
Was there a twinkle in your eye,
or was it just the light?
I know you must have a human soul.
Please call me, my little lambchop. 555-0037.

Unemployed artists, dancers, musicians: Things must be pretty bad now, eh? You can scrub my floors and shovel coal for me. This will give you character and give you countless anecdotes to tell about "your way up." Call 555-1774.

WOMAN HATERS: Come, come. There must be plenty of you, in government, big business, and University administration. We've needed a club now for some time. Let's discuss our feelings. Send all inquiries to Cage 6, Central Park Zoo.

BARTER! No cash but gotta eat? Swap me your socks for a salami, your driver's license for some cookies, or the shirt off your back for some corn. Hey, I gotta live too, you know. Box 722 vv

TO THE AMERICAN PEOPLE:
Well, it finally happened. We accidentally dropped some U-238 (the fissionable, radioactive kind) somewhere on the New Jersey turnpike. We need it back. Don't touch it, just call us, collect at 555-0653. Ask for Fred or Sid.

Herbie! PSO your BRC before I BIO. *Comprennes*?

NO SCAM, no come-on, no bogus claims . . . Just send us $10 and we'll leave you alone. We promise, you won't be disappointed. Box 333 vv

NEVER DIE!!!
Live in eternal bliss, tax free. No problems for all eternity. Nothing to sign, no forms to fill out, no salesman will call. Why spend all of eternity dead when you can spend it relaxing? Send $5 to THE BIG ONE, Box 56, WSH, Ithaca, NY 14853.

THE POOR MAN'S GUIDE TO DRUGS

Hey, man, like, we all got troubles. I mean, dig it, if it's not a war, then it's the establishment. If it's not the establishment, then it's the fuzz. If it's not the fuzz, then, like, it's the bureaucracy. You dig my rap?

The point is, the one thing we could always turn to was <u>drugs</u>. Just a couple hits of mind-altering substances and, man, all the fuck-ups would seem to disappear. But, like, the scene is uncool these days. Why? Because drugs are so fucking expensive man, that's why. It's a drag on my part. Like, who can afford to get wasted at sixty bills an ounce? LSD, too, man -- like, I've had to literally drop acid. And coke? Man, don't even talk to me about coke. Burn my fingers on that shit.

But dig it, man, there's still hope. That's where this guide comes in. It's for cats and chicks like me and you, man, who still want to get stoned but, like, don't got the heavy bread for it, you dig? Like, if you use this guide right, I'll guarantee you get stoned without spending one fucking penny, man. 'Cause, like, it's really easy to get high, but you just gotta know what to use, and how to use it.

ENACTMENT

Like, this trip depends on your creativity. You can really blow your mind, if you're up to it. Here's an example: Paint your dog green. Then tie four balloons to his tail, and hang pretzels from the ceiling. After that, put Jimi Hendrix's <u>Electric Ladyland</u> on the stereo, and play it at 16 rpm. Next, turn on all the lights, and open up the windows till the room is full of moths. Then just sit back and take in the whole experience. Like, wow -- wild trip, huh?

SNOW

No, man, I'm not talking about cocaine. You gotta be kidding. What I'm talking about is real snow -- you know, that cold shit Mother Nature lays on us every winter. Now don't run out and start eating it or shooting it up, 'cause that's not the way to use it. Actually, you're supposed to take off all your threads and then lie in the stuff. I know it's fucking cold, man, but dig this: Scientific establishment studies have shown that an outta-fucking-sight psychedelic trip hits you right before you freeze to death. That's right. Like, I've never done this up, but it seems you could probably stop before you died. Hey, man, write me if you've ever tried it, and clue me in. If I don't hear from you, I'll know why.

AIR

I ain't shitting you, man. Air is really wild stuff. Remember when you were a kid, and you went to the doctor, and he kept laying this rap on you about breathing in while he was listening to your chest? And you kept taking deep breaths and, like, before you knew it, you felt like you were about to O.D.? Man, that's called hyperventilating, and it can give you a far-fucking-out rush. I do up "oxies" twenty or thirty times a day. And, like, you're already addicted to the stuff, so you may as well do it up as much as you want. A suggestion: It's best to snort air -- like, a cat I know tried to shoot it up, and he got one motherfucker of a case of varicose veins.

DREAMS

Dreams can be really wild psyche-fucking-delic trips, man. Like, I once dreamt that a floating peanut was rapping to me in Spanish. Can you dig it? Show me someone who got a trip like ɪʜ that from shrooms, and I'll show you someone who's lying through his fucking teeth. I drop "rems" a few times every night, whether I want to or not. x Hell, man, even the fuzz do rems, though they won't admit to it.

INJURIES

Like, this method is not an end in itself, but a means to an end. Anyone who's ever had a bone sticking out through his flesh knows it's a dynamite way to score some excellent quality morphine. Yeah, man, I know ɪɪɪxx it'll hurt for a minute, but then it'll be worth it. You can do up "ulnas," "femurs," "joints" -- wherever you don't mind a little skeletal mutilation. Then just sit back and enjoy the ride.

HUNGER

Like, if you don't got bread for drugs, then you probably don't got bread for food, either. But that's cool, 'cause hunger can give you an outtasight buzz. I mean, just don't eat for five or six days, and you'll be seeing all kinds of spots and swirls and weird shit like that. Like, for example, the entire country of Cambodia is perpetually wasted, man. I do "pangs" all the time, sometimes in conjuction with oxies. It's also a far-out way to lose weight, if that's what you're ɪɴɪⱼ into.

CONCUSSION

Remember those old cartoons where some animal gets bashed in the head and sees little birds chirping around in the air? Like, wow, man -- doesn't that sound groovy? I save "smacks" for when I'm really desperate, but even if you don't see birds, you're sure to at least see stars. Like, that can x be really wild on a cloudy night. And no dry-mouth either, man.

SPINNING

Remember ʷʰʷ when you were a kid you used to spin around all ᴛʰᴇ ᴛʰᴇxᴛɪᴍᴇxxᴀᴎᴅxᴛʜᴇᴎxʷʜᴇᴎxʸᴏᴜxᴃᴛᴏᴘᴘᴅ the time, and then when you xᴛx stopped, you'd walk into walls and feel really fucked-up? Man, kids know where it's at. Like, I'm still into "spinners," even though if you do it too much, you'll feel like you want to puke. But what the hell, man -- that's true for anything, dig?

INSANITY

Still not satisfied? Just can't get with it? Well, dig this, man: Insanity is a non-stop high. That's x right, man. Crazy people are always seeing things that aren't there, and hearing strange noises, and getting intense rushes. Night and day, man. And not a penny spent! Think you can handle it? Like, here are a few suggestions to get you started: enlist in the armed forces; have fucked-up parents; have a lousy childhood; go into performing arts; become a shrink; isolate yourself from human contact; go senile. And there are lots more. But, ɪɪᴋᴀⱼ like, dig it, man, these are just suggestions. They're not foolproof. None of them is guaranteed to make you lose it all. Like, you just gotta be lucky.

RUSTLER

APRIL 2008

$3.50

Is Kosher Meat Really Best?

Beef Jerky: Rib Tickling

Jimmy Heifer Exposé

ISBN: 978-0-9772590-3-8

ELSIE

"There's nothing I like more than lying around in the sun. I love the heat on my back, the flies buzzing around my tail, and the sweet fragrance of freshly made fertilizer in the soft summer breeze. It's times like that when I feel like a roll in the hay."

"I'm not really turned on by bondage or S&M, but I was tied down and branded once, and it was kinda fun. The guy turned out to be too possessive."

"I've never made it with another cow. Although the idea excites me, the right cow has yet to stroll down my path. Bestiality is normally a real turn-off, but once I had this relationship with a young farmboy who used to be my milker. He had such soft hands and the way he stroked my udder really rang my bell."

"I'm thinking about going into movies. I've done modeling for Borden and my agent says I have the natural look that's so much in demand these days. Last summer I got a few jobs appearing in Westerns but I'm still waiting for my big break. I hope one day to direct and star in my own picture where the stakes are big."

"I like my bull to be all meat. Cereal and beef byproducts don't attract me at all. They just don't have that tender juicy taste I love so much."

BARNYARD DATA SHEET

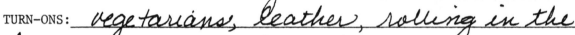

NAME: _Elsie_

RIBS: _prime_   UDDER: _firm_

BIRTHDATE: _May 1, 1992_

SIGN: _Taurus_

BIRTHPLACE: _in a manger_

GOALS: _to meet Hugh Heifer and milk him dry_

TURN-ONS: _vegetarians, leather, rolling in the hay, studs, and good grass_

TURN-OFFS: _branding irons, Elmer's glue, Schlitz Malt Liquor commercials, Merrill Lynch_

FAVORITE SONGS: _"Still Grazing after all these Years," "Back in the USDA," "Honky Tonk Cow"_

FAVORITE SPORTS: _horse shoes, bull fighting, and horse racing_

FAVORITE BOOKS: _Slaughterhouse Five, Black Beauty, Animal Farm, A Child's Garden of Grass_

FAVORITE TV SHOWS: _"Wild Kingdom," "Bonanza," "Little House on the Prairie," "Wild Wild West," "Mr. Ed"_

IDEAL MATE: _well groomed, outstanding in his field, not just one of the flock_

Me at age 3

No beef at age 4

Udderly attractive at 5

How Low Can You Go?

ANNOUNCER: Hey there, welcome to the program that finds creatures from the lowest level of the food chain to answer your questions. Today we welcome a tapeworm and Jack Tripper, known best as the lovable but clumsy guy on the television comedy *Three's Company* who feigned homosexuality so he could live with Janet and a blond girl. Thank you both for being here. Allow me to read the first letter.

Dear "How Low,"

I'm 29 years old and I'm still a virgin. There's this girl I've had my eye on for a while and I want to know how to get intimate with her.

—Horny Harry

TAPEWORM: There's nothing more intimate than burrowing your way through a girl's intestines. Give it a try.

JACK: Tell her you're gay. Then she'll really want you.

Dear "How Low,"

My math teacher has been making me stay late for detention every day for no reason. How do I get him to lay off?

—Detention Bitch

TAPEWORM: Have you considered entering his intestines? It might help you understand what he wants from you.

JACK: Just bat your eyes at him, and bake him your best crème brûlée. He'll never bother you again.

Dear "How Low,"

There is this girl who follows me around all the time, and my friends make fun of me. Should I lie and tell her I'm gay?

—Super Sexy Stud

JACK: You're on the right track, my friend. I like the way you think.

TAPEWORM: I'll go with Jack on this one.

Dear "How Low,"

I think my parents want to send me to boarding school. What should I do?

—Screwed for Life

TAPEWORM: I like boarding school boys. Firm intestines. I think you should go.

JACK: Make sure you haven't misunderstood them. It happens in my apartment all the time. One time I thought Larry and Mrs. Roper were getting it on in his bathroom because I heard her screaming "Oh, Larry!" through my bathroom pipes. But, when I went upstairs to check it out, I was entirely wrong. He was actually banging her in his kitchen, not the bathroom. Her voice just carries really well. But anyway, just tell your parents that going to boarding school would be a great way to explore your homosexual tendencies. That should do the trick.

Dear "How Low,"

I'm a gay male and I'm looking for a partner, but I can't seem to find anybody. What should I do?

—Homely Homosexual

JACK: *So . . . you're really gay?* I have no idea what to say.

TAPEWORM: Come to me, baby. I can go where no man has gone before.

ANNOUNCER: That's all for today's edition of *How Low Can You Go?!* Join us next week when Buddy Lembeck from *Charles In Charge* and the staphylococcus virus will answer your questions.

Eighth Grade Romance

Ilene's Secret, Secret Diary	**Robert's Journal**

September 28th

There's this cute boy that sits next to me in math class. He left the room to go to the bathroom and I looked at his book. His name is Robert Spaulding. What a heavenly name for a boy! Why won't he talk to me? I told Cindy about him, and she made a face. She says boys are only interested in our bodies . . . I think that Cindy is immature. Robert isn't like that . . . I don't think.

October 14th

Oh God! Oh God! I am going to die, I think. It happened today in the hall . . . where to begin, dear diary? I passed him on the way to the bathroom and . . . our eyes met! I felt this radiant glow issue from his deep eyes. His eyes seemed to be saying. . . "I cherish you! I worship you!" Oh, how I long to hug him . . . . .

November 8th

He must know how I feel! My soul cries out to his soul. I long to touch his spirit. I know he's as sensitive as I am. I just know it. I found a piece of paper that he had written on, lying on the floor. I took it home and kissed it. He had written "I must look for my soul . . . " He is a true poet.

December 20th

This is it! Today I will tell him how I feel. I can't go on living like this . . . with my insides in a knot. I'll ask him to the junior high dance and there I'll unfold the secrets of my being to him.

December 21st

HE ACCEPTED!!!!!!!!!! My body sings, my soul cries out, and my penny loafers vibrate! What to wear? *What to wear???* I spent hour after hour in front of my mirror trying to find the right clothes that will reflect my true nature, so he will see just how sensitive I really am . . . . . .

December 22nd

TONIGHT I BECAME A WOMAN!!!! Oh, where to begin? Where to beginnnnnnnnnnnn?????????????? Oh, we were slow dancing. Robert is *soooo* masterful on the dance floor, and yet, so gentle. He even let me lead. They were playing "A Moment Like This." My heart kept time with the music. I looked at him . . . he looked so dreamy-eyed, as if he was in another world. Suddenly . . . I knew that I must make my move . . . and so, we . . . kissed.

September 28th

Another dull day here in this stupid school. I have a feeling that somebody is trying to steal my books. When I came back to math class after using the john, somebody had opened up my book. I bet they were trying to take it. The Simpson girl was looking at me. She probably knows who opened it. You can't trust girls.

October 14th

Passed the Simpson girl in the hall today. Gave her a quick glance. Jesus, are they real? I mean, is she getting a little help from the Kleenex people or something? She caught me staring at her. I wonder what she would look like without any clothes on.

November 8th

Goddamn it! I was running to class and the sole of my shoe fell off. Jesus Christ . . . made a note to look for it. Saw the Simpson girl again. Oh well, turn 'em upside down and they're all the same, I guess.

December 20th

The Simpson girl called. She asked me to the Snowball Dance. Christ . . . I thought that her name was Ruth . . . It turns out it's Ilene. I guess I'll go. There is nothing else to do, and there Red Sox aren't playing till Sunday.

December 21st

The Red Socks might make the World Series. Oh yeah . . . the dance is tonight. I couldn't find a clean AC/DC T-shirt, so I borrowed a clean, white T-shirt from my dad . . . it's such a drag trying to find clean clothes. I don't even want to go. Oh well, who cares? It's only a stupid dance.

December 22nd

Hey, the Red Sox are going to the World Series!!! Oh yeah, I went to the school dance. Ilene is one strange person. They were playing "A Moment Like This," and I was trying to remember the name of the guy that Kelly Clarkson beat on *American Idol* when suddenly, out of nowhere, Ilene kissed me. She put her tongue in my mouth . . . it was all slimy. She must have had fish for dinner or something. Girls are really strange. She was

Our red lips pressed close together. His tongue sought out mine, like a fish seeks out nourishment. For a brief second, our souls intermingled . . . my whole existence stopped and we were one. There we were, on the dance floor . . . kissing. Robert is soooooo sensitive and gentle. And then, dear diary, it happened. Gently and smoothly, his masterful hands slowly crossed the silken polyester of my new dress. And then, so lightly, so ethereally, his hands touched my . . . my northern woman parts. Thank goodness that I was wearing the brand new "Be More" teen bra that mom bought me just last week . . . it must have been fate. I thought that I would swoon in his arms. I am his forever. I shall love him forever, *forever!* I shall go home and memorize his locker combination and steal his sweat socks, that I may cherish them. I shall be his for eternity, if not longer. Dear diary, this is it. He must know how I feel by now, that I am his forever. He left the dance floor to comb his hair. Dreamed of having nine kids and a '98 Camaro with red lambskin bucket seats. When he returned, I asked him what he wanted to do next. He said something about trees. Yes . . . I am the apple of his eye . . . I am his cherry tree, ready to be picked.

December 25th

I was walking over to Rob's house to memorize the color of his mailbox and as I was crossing the street, I ran into Tony, Rob's friend. He is very nice and a lot taller than Rob. We talked for a while and guess what? WE BOTH ARE LIBRAS! What a coincidence! We went out for pizza and he even paid! He is a real man. Tomorrow night we are going to the movies.

December 28th

Oh, that Tony is *soooooooooo* funny! We went out for ice cream today. We spent half an hour fighting over the cherry on my sundae. Tony kept on telling me that he wanted it. That's silly, he had one of his own. After he finally stole it from me, he stuck his straw down the waistband of my skirt. I just don't know what he'll do next. Oh, that stupid Robert Spaulding keeps on bothering me. Why won't he leave me alone? He called me up again to ask if we could go bowling. I told him that I was catching a cold and that bowling alleys were drafty. I went with Tony to the drive-in movie, although neither of us is old enough to drive. We had to sit next to the back gate, listening to the movie through the sound from a 2001 P.T. Cruiser, my new dream car. I didn't know what was going on inside the car . . . it kept shaking but it didn't look like anybody was inside it. It looked pretty spooky to me. I asked Tony about it and he said something about baseball, although I didn't understand. Tomorrow I'm gonna memorize his telephone number . . . I hope he calls again.

wearing this weird dress. The lights were really low, and she wouldn't stop stepping on my toes and kissing me. So, I thought that this would be a pretty good time to find out just how much help she was getting from the Goodyear rubber company. I ran my left hand from where it had been, cleverly toying with her bra strap that I was trying to unhook through her dress all evening. I slyly ran my hand to the front of her dress and stopped for a minute, and then I slowly reached for her headlights. I couldn't tell what I was feeling, and then the assistant principal came over to offer us some punch. I had to limp off the dance floor and dash to the washroom. When I returned, I had my T-shirt casually untucked, the hem hanging down to my knees, thank God. Ilene was starting to act really weird at this point. She asked me what I wanted to do next. I thought that we could go tree climbing outside so I could see if she was wearing panties . . . my friend Tony says that girls who don't wear panties will do anything, and he means *anything*. It was too late for that, anyway. We danced some more, and my mom came to pick us up. I can't stop thinking about how Ilene would look naked. I guess I like her. Maybe I'll call her up tomorrow.

December 25th

Something is wrong. I called up Ilene to ask her out. She said that she was going to be washing her hair all night. That's strange, it only takes me five minutes, and *that's* if I stop to think about Britney Spears on the "Oops! . . . I Did It Again" album cover. Then I called up Tony to see if he was free. He said that he was taking out some "chick." He gets all the luck. He tells me that he feels certain that he can "score" with her . . . whatever that means. I wish him luck . . . I guess.

December 28th

Hey? What gives? I mean, after Ilene let me touch the front of her dress, after we kissed and everything, she seems completely different. I said "hi" to her today in study hall and she ignored me. I tried to sit next to her at lunch, but she said that she was going to have lunch with her seven-foot brother who was in the Marines specializing in killing people. Finally, I offered to carry her books for her from school, but she said that her father the judo expert was going to drive her home. That's funny. When I watched Mr. Simpson go to work in the morning, he was always wearing a three-piece suit. To make matters worse, Tony keeps looking at me and laughing. He tells me that he is getting pretty far with this girl of his . . . some guys have all the luck. Anyway, I have decided that girls are stupid. You never know what they'll do next. I played basketball outside today for a few hours after dinner. Then I thought about what Pamela Anderson must look like without her clothes, then I fell asleep.

Chapter 4

The Good Life*

*Void where prohibited by law

Other Ways to Skin a Cat

1. Sleep with cat's wife, and send an anonymous letter to him detailing her infidelities. Cat will skin self in shame.

2. Deliver cat to restaurant in box marked "Potatoes." Blind and deaf chef will simply think, "Lots of claws on spuds these days."

3. While visiting cat's house, turn up the thermostat. Overheated cat will take off fur coat. Steal it, but leave a scarf so the cat can stay warm.

It is cold here, bitterly cold. I live here, in this bitterly cold place called Alaska. They call me Eneuck Dok No How. I am an Eskimo plumber.

When I was five, my father, who was also a plumber, spoke these words to me: "Son, it is not easy being an Eskimo plumber. People may laugh at you because you cannot make a kayak or kill baby seals, but who else can fix the tribe's garbage disposal when the chief elk is coming for dinner?"

One day a film crew comes in a helicopter. They land on a patch of ice by the igloo. The ice breaks and the helicopter sinks. Another helicopter comes, but this time it does not land. It hovers above the ice, and a man jumps out. He falls through the ice and drowns. The helicopter leaves. The next day another helicopter comes. It hovers above the ground, and a man climbs down a rope ladder. He is careful not to touch the ice. "Excuse me," he says to me, pointing at my sealskin work shoes. "How does it feel to club a baby seal to death?" "I'm not a seal-clubber," I reply, as the helicopter crashes into a glacier. "I'm Eneuck Dok No How, Eskimo plumber."

On Monday, Mrs. MacAllastair from 3B calls up. "Eneuck Dok No How, my pipes are frozen. Can you help me?"

I get my Drāno and my statue of Daduk, the Inuit god of plumbing, and walk over to the MacAllastairs' igloo. I walk around the igloo, inspecting every block of ice. I go inside and look around. There are no pipes. Igloos do not have running water. Mrs. MacAllastair opens up her closet and shows me her bagpipes, which are frozen solid. I hold the statue of Daduk over my head and pour the Drāno on the bagpipes. Mrs. MacAllastair is so happy that she plays a jig. The next day she is dead. It is not easy being an Eskimo plumber. It is always cold here. So cold that all the water turns into ice. Ice cubes come out of the faucets and go into the sink, which is made of ice. Even the pipes are made of ice.

Hard as it may be to digest for some of you, your four years of grandly wasting thousands of hard-earned dollars will soon be ending. Yes, we know it's sad, but the time will come when many of us must give up this "school" thing and adopt the routines of the shiftless servant to the pesky "price system" and its wacky friends "supply" and "demand."

Oh, who are we kidding? Most of you would rather form the new generation of Robber Barons than learn anyway, with your Delta Burke-sized stock portfolios and blueprints for success laid out through your connections-saturated families (like you even need help finding a job). But in case you do, Junior Captain of Industry, here's . . .

How to Get That Job

The Job Search

For college graduates and other dirty, unfocused stoners, the "looking for" part of the job search can certainly seem daunting. Fortunately for you, this country is inhabited by enough uninspired bums and hoboes that many sloppy seconds are available for all who show even the slightest ambition or nervous tic. All you need to do is direct your energies towards the right channels—

• **Newspapers** provide up-to-date listings of available positions. However, you must be willing to look past ink stains and accelerating macular degeneration, as this door to opportunity is usually buried behind stories about people who already have jobs and printed in minute-sized text by more people who already have jobs.

• **The Internet,** patented by Al Gore, can help you connect to a wealth of jobs for which you are woefully underqualified. However, the Internet can help you only if you shift the key words in your search from "personality test," "jokes," and "xxx" to words such as "position," "opening," and "who do I have to blow to get a job around here?"

Remember, reading about jobs is nice, but reading never got anyone anywhere. Except for those people who read a lot for their classes and aced all their exams. Or those who read this guide. What were we talking about again? Oh yeah, if you want the jobs to be more than just words on paper or a computer screen, you'll have to follow up on them. Make sure to:

1. Record contact info on the back of your hand or stall door.
2. Call collect from a noisy club or penitentiary.
3. Beg.

The Career Fair

For those of you who find yourselves dissatisfied with the passive nature of the classified-ad job search, there is the career fair. Like many other kinds of fairs, it consists mainly of strategically placed booths vying for the fairgoer's attention so that gypsies can pick his pockets. These fairs also have carnies, except they dress well and hate to be called carnies. Call them "suit" or "bitch" instead.

APPLICATION TO BE A CIRCUS CLOWN

Name:
Age:
Size of hair:
Color(s) of hair:
Sound nose makes when squeezed: (circle one)
    Beep   Honk   Waka-Whoo   Buzz   Other/Explain:

Size of foot:

Are you allergic to cream pies?

Are you averse to putting cream pies in your pants?

Do you own a car? If yes, can you fit an elephant in the glove compartment?

Have you ever been arrested? If yes, did it have anything to do with a midget?

Do stripes make you look fat?

Cutest balloon animal you can make:

Most obscene balloon animal you can make:

Are you willing to travel? By cannon?

Please drop applications off, with résumé, to our secretary. Don't honk our nose, we'll honk yours.

Remember to Bring
• **Yourself**—*preferably well-clothed, groomed, and in full physical form rather than transbody form*
• **Résumé**—*to trade for pens and mayonnaise*
• **Cell phone**—*so you can play Snake*
• **Social affectations**—*to make yourself stand out*
• **Shaving mirror**—*to signal passing ships and aircraft*

The Résumé

The résumé is crucial for any interview, job fair, or info session. Without a concise and respectable résumé, you will bring shame upon your entire family and be doomed to become the wacky, ambiguously gay uncle/aunt no one wants to talk about. It's important that your résumé show the potential employer your qualifications and achievements without being too wordy. If you don't have any qualifications, people always need help carrying their groceries to the car. Here are some suggestions for the format of your résumé:

The Heading

This is where you put your name and relevant contact info, in case the employer finds any need to abduct you or harass you with chain letters.

Objective

What you are looking for. We suggest you write "job."

Employment Experience

List any paid or volunteer work you have done besides smuggling, extortion, insider trading, slave trading, insider slave trading, NAMBLA, NAMBLA for Jesus, or breakfast enemas.

Education

What you did in school besides pursue Kelly Kapowski and projectile vomit. Usually this includes where you went to school and what you studied there. If you're a Communications major, please refrain from writing "bullshit."

Awards and Activities

Only include those that are accredited. Being a member of your hometown Spur Posse does not count as an activity, and your friend calling you "da man" on the golf course is not an honor or award.

Skills

Not to be confused with "skeelz," so you may not include such "phatness" as "kickin' it," "keepin' it real," "livin' large," "droppin' science," or "eight-ball rollin'." Instead, you may want to say what you can do with a computer besides steal it, or what foreign languages you can speak without inserting English phrases or making derogatory noises which sound like the language.

GOD Résumé

Education:	All-Knowing	
Work Experience:	Created humans	Friday
	• Used dirt to create "man"	
	• Used man to create "woman"	
	Created all living things	Thursday
	• Birds	
	• Trees	
	• Other Animals	
	Created light and darkness	Sunday
	• Created sun and moon	
	Created land mass/ocean dichotomy	Monday
	• Mountains	
	• Water	
Extracurricular Activities:	Smiter of Philistines	
	Worker of Miracles	
	Shepherd	
	President, Heaven	
	Author, Ten Commandments	
Honors:	I am God	
Skills & Interests:	Meteorology, Religious Studies, Plant Science, Contemplating the Fate of Mankind	

Unlike most other fairs, however, there are no dunk tanks or whack-a-mole games. No one's saying there shouldn't be, especially the whack-a-mole game. Better that you hear it here first.

Think of the career fair as a look at your future that doesn't involve Christopher Lloyd and a time machine that runs on merchandising, but does include a free key chain. You won't have a job, but you will have a handy key chain. Yes, you'll always have the key chain.

The Interview

The interview is often the most dreaded part of the job search. To make the experience easier to stomach, drink heavily and remember the nine Cs of interview success:

1. Confidence. If you're thinking, "Nothing really sets me apart from anyone else," you are already at a disadvantage. Don't forget your unique, freakish appearance and disturbing knowledge of "age-of-consent" laws. Imagine yourself as the person you want to become: the one who isn't a total loser.

2. Composure. The interviewer may ask you a brainteaser or logical game question which is difficult to answer on the spot. Or he might try to trick you into deviating from the bullshit you have prepared. It's important that you appear unrattled by such situations. It may help to remember that the interviewer is a sadist who fucks sheep.

3. Concentration. Be especially attentive. If you let your mind wander for even a second you may misunderstand a question or be fooled by the interviewer's wily disappearing-reappearing move.

4. Clarity. Try to recall what you've done in the past with some detail, even if you've ingested enough bong water to wash Wilford Brimley.

5. Curiosity. Ask questions, particularly about the job. Do not ask how hot the interviewer's sister is, or if he has Grey Poupon, since that joke is, like, so 1992.

6. Cuteness. Being physically attractive never hurts. If you aren't attractive, you should do something about that. Or resign yourself to table scraps, you hideous, hideous troll.

7. Catchphrase. While this is sure to irritate anyone if used too frequently, you're only going to meet your interviewer once. That means your one-liner is sure to make you come off as endearing. Try "*Dyn-o-mite!*" "Whatcha talkin' 'bout, [interviewer name]?" or "I used to suck dick for crack."

8. Centhusiasm. Not a real word, but it should be.

9. Crack pipe. Do not ask the interviewer if he "smokes the rock." Remember, these are classy, white-collar professionals. Bring a gilded tureen of heroin. Your goal is to impress.

Vacuum Cleaner Crisis

So You Want to Quit?

Well, you are in luck because I understand the plight of the employee whose talent goes unrecognized, whose motivation is drained by tedious busywork, who feels unfulfilled in a stagnant work environment. And I am willing to do something for you lazy shiftless slobs. You, whose future seemed a picture of the American Dream: success guaranteed, career goals set at infinity, the spouse, the houses, the porcelain lawn statue. You thought your indispensable genius would draw opulent offers from all of the Fortune 500 corporations. They would all clamor to welcome you aboard, make you a part of the home team, install you as vice president #357, love you like one of them.

Fell for the dupe, didn't you? You wasted the sawbucks on tuition at an Ivy League institution for your degree in Gregorian Ornamental Headgear, expecting to be recognized for your insightful, penetrating contributions to an inconsequential field.

Feel pretty stupid, don't you?

Okay, so say you got your desk job at some dehumanizing, cut-throat corporation. Say you finally landed a job as a lab technician after being summarily rejected from every medical school with an English-speaking faculty. Or maybe you snagged that manager's position at Friendly's thanks to your degree in Ukrainian Folk Travesties of the 12th century.

It's just what you wanted, huh? I bet you burst in on your job early every morning to spend nine straight hours devoting your entire being to the intriguing challenges of your profession. You talk nothing but shop during lunch as you wolf down that liverwurst sandwich as fast as you can so you can get back to the latest dreck the boss has handed you . . .

Before I retch bile, let me tell you what you want to know. You want out in a big way and I can show you how to leave—not in a few years, not after the boss dies, but today! Stand up in defense of your own dignity, if you have any left after all that buttsucking. Take that positive step toward the huge welfare line where you will be spending the rest of your pitiful life.

But let us not concern ourselves with the distant future. Right now you want instant job satisfaction, and I can help you make that moment of truth as perfect as possible.

Quitting is a fine art—to be carefully planned, forcefully executed, and savored to the utmost. You are in the limelight all alone and you don't want to blow it. No, you want to milk it for all it's worth because, face it, after this it's nothing but vermin-infested gutters for you.

How much would this information be worth to you? $100? $500? $1000? I didn't think so. That's why I am offering "The Complete Quitter's Course" for the incredibly low price of . . . you guessed it . . . $9.95!!!!! That's right. A mere $10.95!!!!!! But wait. Included in this bargain of $11.95 are two long spiked needles for no extra cost. And if you act now, you will receive for this phenomenally low charge of $12.95 an additional item ABSOLUTELY FREE!!

Hold on to your salivary glands! Listen to this guarantee. If are not permanently unemployed upon completion of this course, return the course materials to me but keep the shiny needles for your own eyes as a gift from me. And what will I do? I will return the unused portion of your money.

If you are not convinced of the priceless value of this offer by now, you are a brain-damaged moodge. And yet, I will make the attempt to bore through that hunk of mantle of yours. Included in this article is the First Introductory lesson. Read on to meet your destiny, if you dare.

The Complete Quitter's Course
Lesson 1

I am a success. You are a groveling scrap of head cheese. I am my own boss. You perform sexual favors for your boss. If you ever decided to quit, it would sound like this:

"Uh, Mr. Smeghonker, sir, . . . I . . . uh . . . put a lot of thought into what I'm about to say, and, please, don't take any personal offense, um, . . . because I mean nothing personally to you . . . but . . . I . . . um, wanted to say how much I . . . appreciated this opportunity to earn a living and learn the skills involved in towel maintenance . . . but . . . I . . . was thinking that upon careful consideration, that maybe . . . taking into account all of the outside pressures I've been under, . . . I feel it is kind of best for all concerned if I left the company . . . even though it is such a great, luminous institution . . ."

Yes, you cowering shadow of a colostomy

bag, that is you all right. Compare the above to the following success story to realize the heights to which you may aspire.

"Hey, Joe, sign this time card and I don't want no lip."

"But you didn't work 438 hours—umph—this week—umph."

"What did I say? I said 'Sign this time card,' not 'Insult me with lies.' By the way, I did your wife last night. Talk about loose. I got lost in there. I heard about the death of your golden retriever, and I want my pickaxe back. And your daughter, she was tight like I like 'em. Face it, Joe, you're a sniveling little fungus at the bottom of the heap of globby pus that makes Amalgamated Towel a vile snake pit."

The above was taken verbatim from the life of ex-blue-collar worker Ogner Snellings, a graduate of the course. After surviving the bombings of his dwelling, Ogner went on to buy up Amalgamated Towel and proceeded to break every labor law on the books.

In this course I will teach you how to act out of pride when you disregard all the company regulations, break valuable equipment, sabotage production, sell company secrets, and, of course, steal everything in sight. You'll learn how to make convincing false accusations to ruin the lives of countless thousands.

I will also make you aware of signs that they are onto you. You will recognize words like "terminate," "severance," and "electric chair." But before they can fire you, you will quit. You will quit loud. You will quit long. You will have enough evidence of their illegalities to blackmail them for the rest of your life.

It's fun. It's easy. Once you start quitting, you'll never want to stop. You will take on new jobs just to try out my foolproof methods of lying, cheating, and embezzling. And you will increase your skill with practice. You will have developed a skill which normally takes a life sentence to master. And think of how proud you will be when you say, "I quit that dead-end job," instead of "They fired me because I am incompetent."

And all because of me. Do it today. Or be a loser for the rest of your life.

Send $14.95 today to:
Prisoner 6655321
Cell Block 56H88J
San Quentin, CA 94974

Religion in a Nutshell

Religion used to be simple. As long as you sacrificed a goat by the light of a full moon every now and then, you were assured a bountiful harvest of virgins. Nowadays, though, it seems like every Tom, Dick, and Harry has some sort of religion to belong to, believe in, or keep locked in the basement. How can you tell which one is right for you? Why, with ridiculous stereotypes, of course. Let our handy-dandy guide help you pick the religion you've been praying for.

ISLAM

PROS: The one true religion, according to its holy book, the Qur'an. Doctrine of acceptance of other faiths insures peaceful coexistence with all people, except maybe Jews. You get to wear a turban.

CONS: Get searched at every airport. Expect denial of several basic human rights for at least the next few years. Turbans are heavy.

JUDAISM

PROS: The one true religion, according to its holy scroll, the Torah. Bagels for everyone! Improves your sense of smell and ability to do math. All goods 20 percent off.

CONS: Where's the pork? Tardy messiah. Precludes any sort of athletic career. Oh yeah, and men, you're required to cut off a piece of your penis.

CHRISTIANITY

PROS: The one true religion, according to its holy book, the Bible. Afterlife includes complimentary harp. Nifty costumes and hierarchy. Incense common.

CONS: Doctrine of the tithe. Arbitrary and wide-ranging sexual repression. Hey, stop touching that!

HARE KRISHNISM

PROS: Yet another only true path for enlightenment and inner peace. Anti-materialist stance lets you feel good about being poor.

CONS: The goofy, goofy hair. Airports increasingly hostile.

BUDDHISM

PROS: Costumes, saffron color, deep and lasting inner peace and contentment, even when oppressed. Polytheistic system improves prayer-response time. Reincarnation.

CONS: Easily mistaken for Islam by ignorant morons. See *Islam*.

HINDUISM

PROS: Many gods plus public ignorance means you can claim a holiday pretty much whenever you want to. Examples include Shiva's Birthday, Vishnu's Anniversary, and Ravi's Briss.

CONS: Reincarnation means that if you make a mistake, you'll have to start all over again, maybe as a dung beetle or Doug Flutie. Easily mistaken for Buddhism by ignorant morons. See *Buddhism*. And sacred cows? Who made this up, Chick-Fil-A?

SATANISM

PROS: You worship the lord of evil and destruction. How cool is that? Potential for career in entertainment industry skyrockets. Gets great reaction from your girlfriend's or boyfriend's parents.

CONS: All the mice-eating. Tic Tacs are powerless against mouse breath. Afterlife is going to suck.

MORMONISM

PROS: Snappy dress. The smug advantage of knowing that your religion is the only true one. Membership packet includes easy-to-follow donation conversion chart to show which level of heaven you'll go to. More wives than you can shake a stick at.

CONS: Public service requirements, er, privileges. Everyone else goes to hell, so it's going to be pretty lonely up there. Founded by one "Joe Smith." No, really.

WICCANISM

PROS: There must be some pros.

CONS: You're a Wiccan.

ATHEISM

PROS: Officially, nothing you do has any consequences outside human laws. Let the good times roll! All seven days per week free.

CONS: If you're wrong, whoa boy, is God gonna be pissed.

NOW IN LARGE PRINT!

Seventy

April 2008

Hot Flashes

Titanium Wheel-Chairs

Gray Highlights

Viagra

Who Rules
QUEEN ELIZABETH

Golden Girls
steamy behind-the-scenes secrets

LOOK 60 AGAIN!
*Make-up Tips
by Zsa Zsa Gabor*

Sexy Pin-ups
**Bob Dole
Strom Thurmond
Willie Nelson**

"My Alzheimer's and Me"
The Interview Ronald Reagan Forgot

70

Walker-Cise:
Aerobic Tips You Can Use

ISBN: 978-0-9772590-3-8

51495

9 780977 259038

ELDER SKELTER

YOU SEND US YOUR MOST EMBARRASSING STORIES AND WE PUBLISH THEM FOR ALL THE WORLD TO SEE!

The Declining Hipster ★★★

I saw my crush, Walter, walking down the hallway at the home, so I seized my chance—I sprawled forward, face-down. Then, when he came by, I said, "I've fallen, and I can't get up!" "Eh, yer just fakin' it," he said and kept on walking. I was mortified! Also, I broke my hip.

Denture Adventures ★★★★

It was family night at the nursing home, and all my kids had come to visit. We had a special dinner, and, much to my luck, my crush was sitting across from me at the table. I bit into the nice, juicy fried chicken and returned my drumstick to the table. Just then, I had an odd sensation in my mouth and I knew something was wrong. I looked at my plate and there were my teeth, in the chicken! I tried to conceal them, but I wasn't fast enough—my crush took that moment to shout out, "Polly Wanna Grip!" I was mortified! My children haven't visited me since.

Bladder Splatter ★★

It was Field Trip Friday and I had forgotten my Depends. Still, there was a bathroom on the bus, and I went right before we got off at the Flea Market, so I thought I would be okay. Unfortunately, twenty minutes after we got there, I saw the most gorgeous blue vase. I was so excited, I wet my pants in front of everyone. The nurse (whose name I always forget—it's either Fred or Shiquanda) had to bring me back to the nursing home in our special Emergency Bus. I was mortified! Worst of all, I didn't get the vase.

Oingo Bingo ★

It was "Games and Giggles Night" at the home, and for the first time, I won! I stood up, shaking with excitement and Parkinson's, and yelled *"Bingo! Hotcha!"* It took me eight minutes to get to the front of the room with my card, and when I did, the caller said, "That's a jack of spades, and we're playing Capture the Flag." Then a dodgeball hit me in the head. "Fiddlesticks," I said.

Exlax-scuse Me? ★★★★

My hearing aid was on the fritz, so Lennie and I hopped in our Continental and headed over to CVS—he just loves their sugar-free candies. Then I remembered I hadn't quite been regular that week, so I asked the sales clerk with the impaled eyebrow where the stool softener was—but I forgot my hearing aid was broken, so I practically screamed it at the whole store. Lennie had a heart attack and knocked over the whole display of Metamucil. The whole aisle started tittering. I thought I would plotz!

SKELTER SCALE

★   Nothing a little Viagra won't fix.
★★   You'll be kvetching for weeks.
★★★   Time to move out of Florida.
★★★★ I'd take dialysis any day.

seventy Quiz!

Is your nursing home stealing from you?

Take our simple quiz to find out if your nursing home is taking advantage of your sweet, trusting nature!

1. When the orderly brings your pills to you, he says:
   A. "Here you go, ma'am."
   B. "Better take some water with these."
   C. "We're stealing from you."
   D. "Where's my money, ho?"

2. When you win at Bingo, you get:
   A. A candy bar.
   B. Prozac.
   C. Robbed.
   D. Your wallet back.

3. When your children come to visit you, they say:
   A. "Hello, mother."
   B. "You look poor . . . err . . . well."
   C. "Where's your jewelry?"
   D. "We've donated your body to science."

4. The nicest thing any of the orderlies has said to you is:
   A. "Aren't you sweet?"
   B. "You have such crisp twenties!"
   C. "What a lovely ring I'm taking from you."
   D. "You smell just like Florence Henderson."

5. The motto of your home is:
   A. "To care for and respect"
   B. "The wonders of sedatives"
   C. "To shamelessly bilk"
   D. "Money, Money, Money, *Moooney*!"

SCORING

Now add up your score. Give yourself three points for each answer. Your home is stealing from you.

seventy's senility spotlight

Recently Seventy took part in a truly special event. We sat down with Dorothy Mae Jennings, the oldest woman in the world, and Mary Lou Parker, the second oldest woman in the world. Through their vast wisdom, we learned important life lessons, found true beauty in life and hope for the future, and even got some mighty tasty chocolate-chip cookies.

SEVENTY: Miss Jennings, I'm so honored to meet you.

DOROTHY MAE JENNINGS: Who are you and what are you doing in my kitchen?

SEVENTY: I'm a reporter. This is Mary Lou Parker; she's the second oldest woman in the world. If you die, she'll be the oldest.

DOROTHY MAE JENNINGS: Why is she tied up?

SEVENTY: Anyway, it's such an honor to be here with both of you. I'm going to remove her gag now.

MARY LOU PARKER: For the love of God, why have you done this to me?

SEVENTY: Miss Parker, how badly do you want to be the oldest woman in the world?

MARY LOU PARKER: Excuse me?

SEVENTY: How much are you willing to pay me to knock off Miss Jennings?

[Both women gasp. Mary Lou Parker faints.]

SEVENTY: I'm glad she fainted. I've been waiting for our chance to be alone.

DOROTHY MAE JENNINGS: You're an awful man.

SEVENTY: Are you senile?

DOROTHY MAE JENNINGS: What?

SEVENTY: Well, are you so gone that you can't even understand the question? Are those cookies I smell?

DOROTHY MAE JENNINGS: Well, yes. I'm baking for my grandchildren. I've got fifty-two of them.

SEVENTY: Thank you, I'd love some cookies . . . and some grandchildren.

DOROTHY MAE JENNINGS: No, stop it. Those are for my darling grandchildren.

SEVENTY: Mmm, gooey.

MARY LOU PARKER *[regaining consciousness]*: Where am I?

SEVENTY: Is the mind really the first thing to go?

MARY LOU PARKER: Who are you?

SEVENTY: I guess it is.

MARY LOU PARKER: What is that noise?

SEVENTY: That's the police. I have to go now. It was great meeting both of you. I'll never forget this. Miss Jennings, thank you for all these cookies. I'm going to feed them to my dog.

seventy FLIRTING TIPS!

◆ Shake that steel hip, girl!

◆ Ask about the war.

◆ Nothing is more attractive than a tirade against those no-good kids today.

◆ If you complain enough you're bound to find something you both hate.

◆ The way to a man's heart is through his stomach. Think prunes.

◆ Ask him if he wants to see your new I.V.

Can't Fail Pick-up Lines

■ "Who's your grandma?"
■ "I'm not wearing any Depends today."
■ "Did I mention that I'm high in fiber?"
■ "Do you want to watch *Matlock*? In bed? Naked? While having sex? With me?"
■ "The nice thing about menopause is that you don't need to worry about contraception."
■ "Do you want to play Bingo? In bed? Naked? While having sex? With me?"
■ "Well, how about Canasta then?"
■ "Pinochle?"
■ "I've been having sex since 1950. I'm getting really good at it."
■ "Would you like to share my wheelchair?"
■ "Do you want to complain? In bed? Naked? While having sex? With me?"

Come live the good life at ...

Cemetery Village

A Little Bit About Us

Cemetery Village is a community built especially for you, the most penny-wise and dollar-foolish age group in America! If you are at least 55-years of age, are senile, and watch the Home Shopping Network, you too qualify to join our close-knit family of deteriorating elderly here at Cemetery Village.

Life over here is just how you like it—slow. After all, what's the hurry?!? At Cemetery Village, you can relax and avoid the fast-paced nature of this strange and complicated world of automatic teller machines and turn signals. This gives you plenty of time to do simple activities without the rush. For example, imagine making a day out of food shopping at the local grocery store. Okay, you do that already. Now imagine making a day out of food "shopping" for wild berries in the bushes alongside Cemetery Village's private gardens of beautiful swampland stretching as far as the eye can see!

Where Are We?

Cemetery Village is located in the heart of more life than anywhere else in the country! Centered in the Everglades of balmy Southern Florida, Cemetery Village is surrounded by a wide array of magnificent animals and insects.

Just twenty years ago, the land on which Cemetery Village currently rests was covered by over eighty feet of water. After draining most of the water, Cemetery Village was constructed. Surrounded by vast fields of mud stretching for miles in every direction, Cemetery Village is the ideal location for a life of wet serenity.

What Are the Living Accommodations at Cemetery Village?

You'll live like royalty! Did you ever think you'd have an indoor wading pool? Well, at Cemetery Village, every one of our suites comes with a wading pool in each living room, as well as bedroom, dining room, and kitchen.

Here we are!

Is the Neighborhood Safe?

Yes, as long as you stay away from alligators, leeches, typhoid fever, mosquitoes, river pirates, mercury poisoning, Peter Fonda, drive-by shootings, postal employees, dinosaurs, hunters, dinosaur hunters, radioactive iodine, radioactive dinosaur hunters, and O. J. Simpson.

What Is There to Do at Cemetery Village?

The favorite activity of Cemetery Village locals is what locals call "Gator Wrasslin'." And let's not forget our ever popular eighteen-hole golf course, as well as the eighteen-hole tennis courts and eighteen-hole fishing boats.

There comes a point in everyone's life when we must come to grips with our own mortality. I myself might die tomorrow of a massive heart attack due to overexcitement from catching the winning touchdown in the Super Bowl and getting congratulatory sex from Brooke Burke. Granted, the Super Bowl isn't tomorrow, but the point I'm trying to get across here is that people die. Especially people like your grandma. Hasn't called in a while, has she? Probably due to the deadness.

I pledge not to leave this mortal coil without a bang. I plan to put the "fun" in "funeral," the "rigor" in "rigor mortis," the "joy" in "a funeral is an event completely without joy." I thought long and hard on how to accomplish this. Finally, it came to me while I was sitting around in my apartment with my best friend one afternoon. "I've got it! I'll have the craziest will ever," I exclaimed to the gin bottle. From this historical event came what can only be summed up as . . .

The Rough Draft of My Will
by Peter Haas

Executors of Will

I request that my close friends Jimmy Carter, the Harlem Globetrotters, and the nervous-lookin' guy from that car commercial be the executors of my last will and testament, although their grief at my demise will probably make them insist they don't know me.

Guardianship of Minors

In case my spouse and I die while my son is still a minor, he will live with a guardian of his own choosing: pirates.

Inheritance

My fortune of several tens of dollars will be inherited by the winner of a national "Hungry Hungry Hippos" tournament. That, or Mortal Kombat on stilts. Wait, definitely the second one.

My house will go to my son, my baseball card collection to my wife, and the proceeds from selling my car to the National Dyslexia Association. Take that, learning disabled!

I leave intangibles such as my calm demeanor and patience to Cornell University. Construct a "Peter Haas Center for Awesomeness" and we'll call it even.

Funeral Instructions

When I die, a tough New York detective will show up at the scene of my death and proceed to make inappropriate jokes about me. For example, if I die in a head-on collision, he will quip, "I heard traffic on the freeway can be murder at this hour!" He will also be invited to my wake and funeral, unnerving my friends and family with his endless repertoire of death humor.

In the grand tradition of *Weekend at Bernie's*, my body will be dragged around by Andrew McCarthy and Jonathan Silverman for three days on a Caribbean island and used like a giant marionette for unknown reasons. When others inquire about my inert state, the duo will explain that I'm drunk or tired.

At least five people attending my funeral mass should yell "Free Bird!" at the organ player.

My tombstone will read: "Dedicated father, husband, and werewolf hunter. He saved the President from crocodiles. Didn't mean to, though."

Circulate fake maps to treasure buried beneath neighboring graves. I need my space.

My body will not be buried, however. Instead it will be recycled into playground equipment for inner-city children. In exchange for this service to the community, a plaque will be mounted in the playground that reads, "The swing set is made of dead people."

ATHEIST FOR HIRE

Name: Lanny Lanster
Age: 29
Hometown: Las Vegas, Nevada
Religion: None
Marital Status: Divorced seven times, currently married to four women
Hobby: Performing abortions

Job Summary:

Hell is nothing more than a tactic to invoke fear into idiots. God does not scare me like he scares you. I'll commit any act worthy of an infernal afterlife for just $99.95! For those of you who adhere to religions without eternal purgatory, you suffer from feelings of guilt. I do not feel guilt. I do not feel guilty for my actions. I am merely an animal acting on my instincts. I'll commit any act which might otherwise inflict lifelong guilt on foolish people like yourselves—for just $99.95.

You disagree with me? Good! Without your disagreement I would be out of a job. You see, I'm an atheist for hire. I commit any act which you can't do yourself due to your obligation as a God-fearing individual. And the cost to you? No more sleepless nights, that's for sure. It's just $99.95!

Now you might be saying to yourself, "Gee willickers, God doesn't prevent me from committing immoral acts by invoking fear in me, God bless my soul." But think deeper, my friend. Do you remember yesterday when that asshole in the Mercedes cut you off on the highway without signaling? You sure wanted to get even with him. Well, I would have followed him home, smashed his windshield, beat him with a baseball bat, and raped his wife on the front lawn in front of him. All for just $99.95.

Specialties:

JUDAISM (hourly rate: $25 + bagels): During Shabbat, I turn on lights and operate electric appliances. I will vacuum, run the electrical can opener, help you change channels with the remote control for television entertainment purposes, smash mirrors, walk underneath ladders, and scratch my ass with a rabbit's foot, you superstitious witch-burner!

CATHOLICISM (hourly rate: $22.50 + statue of baby Jesus): You know Satan is evil, but somehow you can't resist the urge to worship him. Something must be done! This is where I can help. All I need is a small room in your house—even a closet will do! I will supply my own sheep's blood and virgins. Just remember, Satan worship comes with a price. When I'm really high on Satan, I eat a lot of pizza.

The Ten Commandments:

NUMBER 1: *Thou shalt not eat pork.*
Maybe you believe pork to be an unholy animal. It wallows in its own feces. I will eat this wallower of feces, and I will eat it with mustard for no additional fee. Ham: $4 a pound. Pork Chops: $8.95 + your choice of soup or salad.

NUMBER 8: *Thou shalt not covet thy neighbor's new car.*
That bastard doesn't pay his taxes and he owns a Lexus. Son of a bitch! Too bad you can't covet his car because of this commandment. Don't you worry. I'll sit across the street from his house and covet for as long as you'll pay me. When your neighbor forgets to lock his car door, I'll sneak inside and pretend to drive the car. "Vroom! Screech! Vroom, vroom! Honkity honk!"

NUMBER 12: *Thou shalt not masturbate more than once a day.*
Not only will I masturbate for you at least twice a day, I will masturbate for you to the image of that robot girl from *Small Wonder*. Now that's sick! Plus it also breaks the 47th commandment: robot sex.

 in "Cooking with Suicidal Duck"

Thousands and Thousands of Jenny McCarthys

BY JERRY C. BUTTWATER

Clones. Clones, clones, clones. Sheep clones. Monkey clones. Highly successful Pearl Jam clones. This biological breakthrough is taking the world by storm, and as technology moves closer to being able to replicate humans, many people are questioning the ethics of cloning. "What right do we have to meddle with the forces of nature?" you say. "Is nothing sacred anymore? Do we have that little respect for human life? Blah blah blah blah? Blah blah?"

"You can't play God," you say.

And I respond, "Well why the hell not?" Jerry Buttwater is already a love god of sorts. Chicks mistake me for the Lord all the time: "God, would you get out of my face!" they sometimes exclaim. Other times they'll remark, "Jesus Christ, you're a loser!" I've been playing God for years, why can't everybody else? The earth is ripe for a change, if you ask me. Jerry Buttwater is sick of living in a world so oppressive that women cannot express their raw, primal lust for him. A world where they are instead forced to kick him where it hurts and/or get restraining orders against him. How frustrating.

Cloning can put an end to this deplorable state. "How so?" you may ask. The answer to that question came to me the other evening when I was cruising the local bar scene. There I was exuding manliness, hitting on this chick. She was really into me. I could tell. Then, as I innocently tried to grab her breast, she hauled off and punched me in the nose. It was a really nice shot. A girl had never hit me that hard before, and that's saying something because I've been hit by *many* girls. I was sure to tell her that before my knees buckled.

Just before everything went black, I looked up at the TV over the bar. It was playing an episode of *Singled Out.* There was Jenny McCarthy in all her buxom glory. The recent blow to my head was making me see double, so I had the unique pleasure of seeing *two* Jenny McCarthys.

Two Jenny McCarthys. Why not? Why not four? Why not eight thousand? Cloning my friends, cloning. The phrase "the more, the merrier" never rang so true. I can picture it now . . .

There he sits atop his gilded throne surrounded by broads. What a great monument to masculinity he is. "Are you comfortable, Jerry?" says Jenny McCarthy 2. "Can I get you another Budweiser? Perhaps some oral sex?" purrs Teri Hatcher 5. They all want him. THEY WANT HIM!!!

Of course they want me. I'm a stud.

But even for those guys who are less studly than Jerry Buttwater (and there are a lot of them), this dream could become a reality. We're just talking simple numbers here, guys. Boost that chick-to-guy ratio up to, say, 70 to 1, and you're *bound* to get a hot broad. How can that be wrong?

Sure there are other uses for cloning out there that people are championing. Medical benefits, lesbians having kids, crap like that. I've got nothing against medical advancement, and I *certainly* don't have anything against lesbians. I love lesbians, especially those lesbians in the building across from me who always leave their window shade open. But that's all beside the point. In the end, cloning boils down to four little letters:

C-H-I-C-K-S. Chicks. Beautiful chicks everywhere. This is what cloning can offer mankind. And when it comes down to it, is there really anything else? So put aside your "ethics," your "morals." Jerry Buttwater cannot hear these inconsequential words over the promise of unlimited sex that thunders in his ears.

And to all you ladies out there, don't think that Jerry Buttwater has forgotten about you. I've already donated my cells to human cloning research. In a couple of years, there'll be plenty of me to go around.

How to Counterfeit Money

Hello, Lazy American! Avery Notlob here! You may remember me from such books as *Soap: Why Bother?* So, you wanna make some fake money, huh? Well I'm gonna show you how, without all those tedious "technical" steps. Before I lose your attention, let's get started!

1 You're gonna need some paper. Don't bother finding anything that resembles parchment, you'll just need something flat. Construction paper will do (all the better if it's green!), but if you can't find any, just use old receipts or Kleenex.

2 Now, you need to color the paper. Here's where it's handy to have green construction paper because you can skip this step! Otherwise, find a green pen or crayon and scribble the color just enough so, at a glance, it looks money-colored.

3 Now you need to make the "markings." Forget about all those numbers, pictures, codes, and Latin phrases. On the front, in the center, write "MONEY." On the back write "OFFICIAL TENDER." I know it's a lot of writing, but stick with me. Then, in each corner, on both sides, write the dollar amount you want. (Important: make sure each dollar amount you write matches with the other amounts you've written on the paper.)

4 Now, you need a bit of artistic prowess. You have to draw a portrait on the money. Don't worry, just make two circles for the eyes, a dot for the nose, and a "U" for the mouth. Then draw a big circle around all of these for the head. If you're feeling inspired, you can write the name of the president it's supposed to be at the bottom, but you don't have to.

5 Finally, crumple up the paper a little to make it look used.

There! That's it! You're done! Now you can make all the cash you want! So go out into the world, Lazy American, and spend the best kind of money—your own!

Extensive *Lunatic* research reveals that the new twenty-dollar bill has been given a facelift by the good folks at our national treasury. Much like the old bill, the redesigned twenty-dollar bill is worth approximately twenty dollars (except those with a one-eyed Jackson, which is wild). Full of intricate features, the modified bill makes it virtually impossible for even the most high-tech counterfeiter or book publisher to replicate. Here are the secrets revealed . . .

How to Spot Counterfeit Money

Running down the front left of the new twenty-dollar bill is an embedded polymer thread. Not only does it become visible when held up to the light, it also includes a special motivational message directed at misguided swindlers who try to reproduce it.

The new portrait of Jackson includes an earring in his right ear. Does this mean what we think it does? How will John Q. American handle this revelation? "Oh, there's no need for concern," says Assistant Secretary of Treasury Gerald Sweet. "Back in those days, wearing an earring in your right ear didn't mean that you were gay — just that you were 'experimenting.'"

In what appears to be just a patch of blank space actually lies a hidden watermark. It's not Jackson, but rather everybody's favorite game show host. Who is Alex Trebek? Correct. He was once the Prime Minister of Canada!

Every new bill is signed by a member of the Backstreet Boys! This one is signed by Nick! He's the blonde one! This money is dreamy!

Why the tiny White House on the back? Because government scientists know it's much more difficult for assassins to shoot at it when it's so small. The enlarged view above reveals a tiny Jackson peeking out of the upstairs window. Watch out Andrew! There's a homophobic sniper in the tree!

Some money users have recognized that the American flag on the new twenty-dollar bill is not the "official" one. Instead, this new flag confirms what we've all suspected for years—that U.S. currency is a division of Microsoft. With the appropriate plug-ins, the new bills can be made Wallets '98 compatible.

G.A.S.A.T.'s

The Standardized Aptitude Test for Gas Station Attendants

This exam was devised to test the capabilities of those individuals seeking employment in the field of Fuel Dispensation and Automobile Maintenance. The subsequent questions test the decision-making abilities and cognitive skills needed in order to become a successful gas station attendant. You have two (2) hours to complete the exam.

Section I: Multiple Choice—Circle the answer choice that is most correct. (NOTE: circle only one answer per question.)

---

1. A car pulls in next to the gas station pump labeled "Full Service," and the driver beeps the horn for five (5) minutes. You must now:

   (A) Spit a large hocker onto the floor, scratch yourself, then pump the gas for the customer.
   (B) Wait and see if another attendant will do it first.
   (C) Stare blankly out the window and hope that the car goes to the station down the street.
   (D) None of the above.

2. Your name is:

   (A) Vinnie
   (B) Squitty
   (C) Frankie
   (D) Something ending with a "y" or "ie"

3. One customer buys five (5) dollars worth of gas. She gives you a ten (10) dollar bill and asks for her change. What do you do?

   (A) Clean her windshield until the manager comes out. (He has a calculator.)
   (B) Say: "Whattya need to change for when you gotta a body like dat?"
   (C) Give her whatever is in your pockets at the time.
   (D) Both A and C.

4. Nobody has come to buy gas in fifteen (15) minutes, and you are tired. You:

   (A) Go home.
   (B) Stay.
   (C) Steal a Milky Way bar from the candy rack.
   (D) Both A and C.

5. A customer tells you that your service is "too slow" and that you had better shape up or he is going to buy gas from another station. You:

   (A) Kick his ass.
   (B) Really, really kick his ass.
   (C) Pick your butt.
   (D) Spit.

6.) Your favorite television program is:

   (A) *The Dukes of Hazzard.*
   (B) *The Beverly Hillbillies.*
   (C) You do not own a television set. However, your uncle lets you watch *Hee Haw* at his house every Sunday night.
   (D) *The People's Court.*

This is the end of Section I. Do not go on to the next section until you have removed your finger from your ear.

1. Water : Water pump :: Gas :
   (A) Gas pump
   (B) Your butt
   (C) Monster truck
   (D) Both A and B

2. Food : People :: Gas :
   (A) Car
   (B) Hooters
   (C) Hooters
   (D) Big hooters

3. Water : Water slide :: Oil :
   (A) Engine
   (B) Your hair
   (C) Your face
   (D) All of the above

4. Dirt : Windshield :: Dirt :
   (A) You
   (B) Your mother
   (C) Kleenex
   (D) Sylvester Stallone

5.) Your Job : Dead End :: Your Life :
   (A) Bad
   (B) Really Bad
   (C) Sucks
   (D) Traffic violation

This is the end of Section II. Do not panic. Please concentrate on breathing slowly.

Section III: Reading Comprehension—Read the story and answer the following questions to the best of your ability.

Billy Bob and Lauralee were bored one day and decided to take a road trip from their hometown of Happyville to the neighboring town of Smileburg in Billy Bob's newly bought '75 pickup truck (they could not drive Lauralee's Pinto because it is on cinder blocks in her front yard). Billy Bob's car uses about one (1) dollar's worth of gas every ten (10) miles. Before the trip began, Billy Bob and Lauralee went to their local gas station to buy some gas, Slim Jims, and chewing tobacco. The total cost of their purchases was fifteen dollars ($15). Along the way they listened to some jamming Def Leppard and a little Whitesnake. When the pair arrived at their final destination of Smileburg (60 miles away), they had used up all of the gas that they had bought and could not travel any further. Fortunately, they were one block from a gas station and were able to fuel up there.

1. The car Billy Bob and Lauralee drove on their trip was:

   (A) An old model and probably not a good choice for such a long trip.
   (B) Just like your car.
   (C) Just like the car you have always wanted.
   (D) Both B and C.

2. From the information given in the story, what do you think Billy Bob and Lauralee did when they arrived in Smileburg?

   (A) Bought more gas since they had run out and the gas station was nearby.
   (B) They did it.
   (C) They drank some beer and then did it.
   (D) Both A and C.

STOP! Go no further. You are done with the examination. Leave quietly.

- Free Spam   • Privacy Violations   • Porn Sites

Find It **Line Up** **Lost Items** **Directions**

| **START** | Your Living Room | US - Hotel Offers - Flight Deals |
| **END** | Your Bathroom | US - Hotel Offers - Flight Deals |

	Maneuvers	**Distance**	**Maps**
START	1: Start out petting KITTEN in LIVING ROOM	<0.1 miles	Map
↰	2: Turn LEFT into KITCHEN	5 feet	Map
🔑	3: Defeat EVIL GORLOCK guarding GREEN KEY, get the KEY	Right there	Map
STOP	4: Have a SNACK, you've earned it. Maybe SOME GRAPES or a SANDWICH (Get Directions to STORE).	3 feet	Map
↰	5: Turn LEFT on RAMP to HALLWAY	<0.1 miles	Map
⚠	6: Continue along HALLWAY, Look at CHILDHOOD PHOTOS and FACE reality of SHATTERED LIFE	15 feet	Map
↰	7: Turn SLIGHT LEFT at GAPING ABYSS	2 feet	Map
EXIT	8: Take EXIT 2 to BATHROOM	4 feet	Map
↱	9: Bear RIGHT at BLOOD STAIN FROM ATTEMPTED SUICIDE (Get Directions to a PSYCHIATRIST, Jesus!)	1 foot	Map
🔑	10: Use GREEN KEY on BATHROOM DOOR (also green)	Right there	Map
END	11: End at BATHTUB, drowning that KITTEN you've been carrying	Finish	Map

Total Est. Time: However long it takes to drown the cat.   **Total Est. Distance:** Like 20 feet or something.

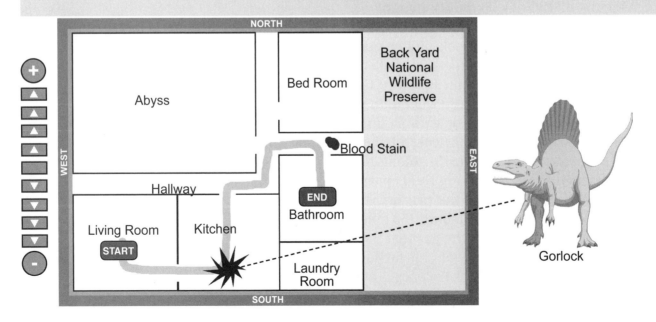

112

The Night Grandfather Turned into a Horse

Growing up in Columbus was, on the whole, a study in incidence and insomnia, as our family was awakened by a crisis or near-crisis almost every night. This just goes to prove, of course, that ours was a perfectly ordinary family, prone to outrageous and unlikely happenings. My grandfather, an old bloodthirsty veteran of the Spanish-American War, was, according to grand old American tradition, a "kind-hearted, irascible old codger." To the medical profession, he was "a psychopath and social deviant." We called him "Grandfather" or "the old coot" and kept all sharp objects from his reach. We didn't believe him dangerous, as no family member had ever suffered more than a bitten leg at the hands of the mangy octogenarian. True, the neighbors were often upset by his exploits, but Mother calmed them by minimizing ex post facto the damage done. "Just a little arson," she would say, or, "a nice friendly assault." One year, we went through twelve neighbors in four months. Mother assured us the "unpleasant ambience" they complained of was the pickle factory down the street.

More often than not, and certainly more often than could have been appreciated, the family had for its honored guest our cousin Henry, or, as my brother Mongo and I called him, "Leper-head." Henry suffered from dermal and subdermal abscesses about the face and neck, the results of a childhood effort to smoke an industrial-size can of Lysol. He usually slept in my room when he visited our house, as I was the only one who could calm him down when he awoke screaming from his recurrent nightmare involving a team of Gestapo field mice that was trying to mine his oatmeal with incendiary devices. My mother slept in the room across the hall from mine, and my father spent nights pacing the floor of our pantry. He was wont to sudden fits of anxiety just before he fell asleep, during which he would stuff his material possessions in his mouth as a means of protecting them.

Those evenings when we could find him, we put Grandfather to bed by tossing him up into the attic and latching and barring the door. By this time, only two rooms would be unoccupied: the bathroom, also called "the growler," and the guest room, also called "the street." On the night in question, everything proceeded smoothly and according to custom: Henry stayed in the bathroom far too long while we jeered at and threatened him. Sparks, the dog, fought playfully with Mother, who as usual feinted right with the frying pan and then brained the mutt with a handy crowbar; Grandfather ran down the stairs, through the kitchen, and behind a couch in the living room, before Father was able to sink the

help Martha, I'm being absorbed!

gaff in his leg and drag him up to the attic. Soon everyone was ready for sleep, doors were shut, lamps blasted out, prayers and maledictions uttered.

A silky somnolence, at once comforting and deadening, wafted its gentle breeze around the bedrooms, down the hallway, through the kitchen, out the back door, and down the street to the twelfth precinct, where it was mistaken for a dangling modifier and flung into the gutter. The sounds of slumber echoed throughout the darkened house: Father's incessant hiccoughing; Mother's loud, raucous snoring; the steady drip-drip from Henry's gaping pores; and the crunch of Mongo's knuckles as he smashed his fists against the wall. "Still dreaming about those baby ducks," I speculated. I shrugged the thought away and let Grandfather's pained moans, muted through the attic floor, lull me into unconsciousness.

I couldn't have been asleep for more than ten minutes when what sounded like a falsetto foghorn gently stirred me from my quiescence. I tripped out of bed, introducing my nose both to the floorboards and to the pleasures of extreme malleability, but was soon on my feet again, searching for the light switch. I found one of Henry's fists instead. Grasping my left ear and restraining myself from bludgeoning my cousin with a nearby vase, I turned on the light and watched while he thrashed about, pushing away a nonexistent bowl of Quaker Instant and moaning, "Just tea for me, thanks."

He was in the middle of his most feared nightmare, and my instincts told me he should be awakened immediately. Quietly, I approached the side of his bed, knelt down, and, careful not to disturb him prematurely, placed my mouth close to his ear. Then, with a gentleness born of experience and my own innate sense of kindness, I yelled, "BOOM!"

CASTING PEARLS BEFORE SWINE...

STEP 1 - PEARLS

STEP 2 - SWINE

OINK.

D Futrelle

The result of this perhaps unpleasant reveille was quite impressive, and Henry, with the help of the ceiling and his dorsal cranium, proved once again that two pieces of matter cannot coexist in the same space. He fell back to his bed with a crash and looked about, wide-eyed. "They got me," he groaned.

"No, you whistle-head," I shot back. "That was me. But what were you doing? Trying to imitate a banshee castrato?"

"What? It weren't me who screamed," he insisted.

"Well, then who gently stirred me from my quiescence?" But before Henry could respond, a second shriek had both of us searching for cover. I was just about to convince Henry that I should be the one to hide under the Buster Brown blanket when Father careened into the room, his mouth filled to bursting with what looked like a weapons arsenal bought at Woolworth's. When he spoke, much of the potential articulation of his words was sacrificed to the twelve skate keys and the Iranian musk melon he had stuffed into his cheeks, and it seemed to me that although he appeared to be speaking real words, the actual meaning he was trying to convey was hopelessly lost. "I'm a melancholy baby, got the Yoko Ono blues!" he cried, some wing nuts dribbling out of his mouth. I made a quick guess at what he meant and tried to calm him down.

"It wasn't me who screamed, Father."

But this news only increased his anxiety, and he asked, "Your distributor's shot. Fifty bucks, please?"

At this point Mother, woken from her sleep by the noise, entered the room.

"What's the deal here, buster? Why the screams of anguish? Leper-head steal your Mallomars again?"

Father did his best to explain: "Surfboard Eddie and the Rancheros tickets on sale now!" he tried, his brow wrinkled in both expectant and retroactive pain. But Mother was apparently not in the mood for fun and games.

"On your feet." Father stood up before her, head bent. "Eyes front." His head jerked up, and their eyes locked. "Tell me what's going on. Come on, spit it out!" Father tried to restrain himself, but the temptation offered by the situation was too alluring. One second later, Mother found herself covered with styptic pencils, sections of peat moss, deposit slips, and diverse other sundries that had found their way into Father's mouth.

The tension in the room was so thick you could cut it with a knife. That's what Father did, piling up blocks of it around him to form a sort of makeshift igloo to protect himself from Mother. She made short shrift of the feeble fortress and stood above a now prone Father, one foot on his neck.

I decided this might be an appropriate time to intervene. "Gee, Mother," I remarked casually, "maybe you shouldn't shove that blade into Father's heart and make him bleed all over the floor until he shudders and dies." I thought it a convincing argument.

"No," Mother began, but she was cut short by a wail that soon escalated to a heart-stopping screech, then a seismic bellow, before dying out into a pitiful whine. We all looked around the room.

"Musta been . . . ah . . . ," began my ever-astute brother.

"Grandfather!" Mother and I finished, and I heard her mutter, "Gonna kill the bastard," as she rushed out of the room en route to the attic. I glanced back to see Father, busily stuffing an encyclopedia into his mouth. I didn't have time to stick around, so I ran down the hall, behind Mongo and Mother.

When they were about fifteen feet from the attic door, Mother panted, "Wait . . . I've got the key . . . . . ." But Mongo preferred the more genteel method of forced entry, head first. The door was reduced instantly to a fine powder as he crashed through it and barreled up the stairs.

Mother and I followed, and we were about halfway up when we heard Mongo say, "Uh . . . um . . . holy cow . . . "

Mother and I reached the top of the stairs and peered through the darkness. Grandfather's bed was there, as usual, but instead of his slight form lying in it, we saw it was occupied by a rather capacious quadruped: a full-sized horse! It was tossing and turning and whinnying as it could not, apparently, get out of the bed by itself. Mongo helped by lifting the creature up by the scruff of its neck and depositing it gently on the floor. We noticed it was wearing an army cap and had a military saber strapped to its side.

"Grandfather?" I inquired. The big beast nodded its acknowledgment.

"Well, I say," said Mother, who had come up to the attic seething with anger but who was obviously convinced by the change in Grandfather's physical stature that any melee would end in his favor. "He certainly does look better than he has in years." She gave him a few gingerly strokes.

"Yeah," Mongo said with typical acuity, "but he's a horse."

"We know that, salami-brain," I said, "but what do we do with him?"

Mongo, slightly dizzied by his newly-acquired concussion, was at a loss for words. I glanced down the stairs to see Father flinching involuntarily from invisible assailants. "What's going on?" he asked, his throat making a funny sort of whistling sound when he breathed.

"Grandfather turned into a horse," I replied.

"But we just got his pacemaker insured!" Father complained. "How can we cash in on it if . . . a horse, you say?"

When tires go bald

"Right here," I said impatiently, pointing out the equine addition to the family.

"Sure looks like a horse," Henry remarked. "I wonder if Sparks'll like him."

"Sparks?" I asked, the germ of a bad feeling beginning to grow in the pit of my stomach. "Maybe we ought to keep him away from Grandfather for a while. I don't think . . ." I trailed off as the family dog, looking slightly peaked from hunger, came padding up the steps, sniffing for food. As I had neither lead pipe nor shotgun, I knew better than to get in his way or even call him names.

He walked slowly past the human contingent of the family and stopped in front of Grandfather. With a speculative look that almost turned Grandfather into a living can of Alpo right then and there, Sparks proceeded to walk calmly and resolutely back to his potential victim's rear, eye a tasty hind leg, lick his chops, open his mouth, and lift his own hind leg, sending forth a cathartic shower of bliss onto Grandfather's hoof. Unable to keep still any longer, Grandfather bolted, trying for the stairs. But somehow one of his shoes became dislodged and he careened into me. Although he tried to stop himself, his momentum carried both of us across the attic, and we crashed through the side of the house and went spinning out into space, watching the ground come up . . . .

I woke up in a cold sweat, my heart racing. Frantically, I sat up, looked around—the family was gathered around my bed, and a gentle hand pushed me back onto my pillow while Mother assuaged me: "You wake us up like that again and we'll slit your throat."

"Even Gramps got woken up," said Father. "Isn't that right, Dad?"

"Neigh," replied Grandfather, stomping a hoof.

conformity today
the magazine for everyone

FEATURES

CONTENTS

roving conformist

This month, our Roving Conformist asks . . .
"Are these two lines the same length?"

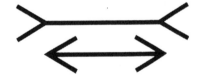

Mark Mywords, New Fungus, Tennessee: "This is one of those psychological optical illusion things, ain't it? Uh . . . . yes, they're the same length."

Philip D. Tank, Succumb, Nebraska: "What did the last person answer? Oh, okay. Yes, they are. No mistake about it."

Drew A. Salary, Lake Old People, Florida: "Uh . . . the other people answered yes? I'll go with that then, yes!"

Stan D. Side, Blueballs, Alaska: "Of course not . . . oh, everyone else answered yes? All right, they're both the same. Absolutely."

conformity corner

Don't Stand Out at a Party!

Ever wonder how people can have a thrilling time at the same party that made you grateful when it was over? Think back. Why was everyone but you having a good time? Doesn't anyone's "technique" give you some insight into becoming a successful socialite? Of course not, because there is none. The trick is to blend in with the crowd. *Don't stand out!* Nobody likes an individual. Here are some specific hints to ensure your position as one of the gang.

Only converse on subjects that can't possibly reveal your personality. The weather and pressure from work or school are both excellent topics. How many times has someone started a conversation with, "The cheese is in the refrigerator, but I'm over here"? Don't try it because it doesn't conform. If you want to fit in, you have to use accepted lines, such as:

1. "God, I'm drunk. Guess how much I've had?"
2. "Oh, this is my favorite song!"
3. "Am I going bald? Here, feel."
4. "How much booze do you think is in that punch?"
5. "Oh wow, I'm so high I thought you were someone else."
6. "Whose party is this, anyway?"
7. "You know, ten minutes ago there was nobody here."
8. "Aren't you my cousin?"
9. "Where are you living next year?"
10. "I know someone at Yale Law School."

Okay. Now you've got them talking, but what do you do when they start looking at you? Are your clothes right? The trick is to wear clothing that makes no statement at all. Select clothes you've seen on other people, and wear them to your next party. For every person you see that is wearing the same item, give yourself a point. Keep track of your points, and add them up at the end of the night. Did you score at least a 40? If not, then take a good hard look at a Sears catalog when you get home.

Now that your clothes are appropriate, what about your speech? Watch yourself! Are you looking the other person in the eye? That's a no-no. Conformists look away when they talk to others, surveying the rest of the party. In conformity lingo, this is called "getting scope." Are you using your hands to talk? Wrong. Gestures are out. Keep one hand half-stuck in one pocket and the other holding a beer-filled cup. Don't play with the cup and scratch the wax with your fingernails. The other party goers might think you are sexually frustrated.

Now for the last step: keeping the conversation going. Obviously you can't stand there all night talking about the weather or your bald spot. Try to keep subjects to the banal. No one wants to hear anything stimulating. Because if they don't understand what you're talking about, you'll have to go into greater detail. Better stick to topics people are familiar with.

Good topics include the week you spent in bed when you got sick, how you parked your car for this party, or how you're standing right there at that party when you could just as easily be standing across the room.

As long as you don't become the center of attention, you won't be noticed. Make sure you don't wind up with a lamp shade over your head, and whatever you do, don't start making loud animal noises.

Anyone can fit in at a party if they know the right tricks. Good luck, and remember, don't chew your ice unless everyone also does.

Deviance Causes Cancer

Those who challenge the norm know the kind of anguish that can result. Remember second grade, when you were the only one still carrying that "Snoopy" lunchbox, long after your friends were bringing their "Star Trek" lunch boxes to school? Many conformists have spent a good deal of time trying to learn just how defying the norm can damage one's health, but until now, conformists were often the ones who bore the brunt of society's ridicule, having to endure such taunts as "Hey, where's the flood?" and "Where are the pennies for your shoes?" At last, recent medical evidence may suggest that deviancy may lead to terrible forms of cancer.

A study released by Professor Dullard of Blah University has found that laboratory rats, when thrown into situations requiring unique and innovative responses, developed cancer at an alarming rate (when compared to test animals, who sat around in polyester suits, drinking Perrier from the water bottle). "Such findings are very significant to humans," comments Dr. Dullard, "because rats and people are very similar. I mean, that's what I was taught in medical school."

Professor Dullard exposed his rats to eight conformity situations. Rats were forced to end a conversation without making reference to having a nice day or keeping in touch. Rats that were forced to display honest emotions on leaving a fellow rat quickly developed cancer of the lip and jaw. Rats that commented on the weather in parting usually remained active and alert enough all day to stay up and watch *The Tonight Show* on TV.

Other rats were dressed in flashy clothing, including little rat bandanas and rat sunglasses. These rats were quickly rejected by the other rats, and soon, the rejected rats developed nervous tics that quickly turned into cancer of the back, whereupon the rats refused laetrile treatments on principle.

One question that springs to mind is, "Why cancer?" "That's a tough question," admits Dullard. "We didn't know what to attribute it to, although it could have been the asbestos lining in the deviant rats' cages to keep out the Castellanos Muzak we played to calm the conformist rodents."

In human terms, these radical findings indicate what most of us knew all along: weirdos are going to suffer the agonizing fate that awaits anybody who dares to dress in natural fibers. "Great care should be taken by all people to conform," Dullard advises. "Especially in dress, and don't ever wear a Harvard sweatshirt with the sleeves ripped off. It's certain death."

This Year's Conformity Olympics

Due to political pressure, this year's Conformity Olympics will not be held in the Abe Praxis Go-Go World Hotel Complex in Las Vegas. The original Olympics was scheduled to feature such new exotic events as nude high jumping, grenade swallowing, mollycoddling, and hallucinogenic mud wrestling. Because these events would have generated far too much innovation and excitement, the Olympics have been moved to the back of Al's All-Night Speed Wash, on Main Street, Postpartum, Iowa.

The U.S. has an unnotably average record and is fielding a surprisingly ununique team this year. The most challenging competition will come from Japan, which will be a tough team to beat in the "No, you pick up the check" competition. Japan also will figure prominently in the barbecuing event, in which each team must shop for ketchup, briquettes, and aluminum foil—all within a two-hour time limit.

Freestyle Conformity

In this event, the competitors witness a woman being mugged and repeatedly stabbed. Last year's gold medal winner, Sweden's Eeeba Hueba, won first prize when he reacted by crossing the street and ordering a large meatball sub to go.

Dress Conformity

In this event, each contestant stands against a wallpapered wall. The contestants who blend in with the paper pattern are usually declared the winner, although India's Vamishnu Vermica won the 1992 award when he showed up in a Nehru jacket. Ned Parkenson from Arkansas is hoping to take first place with his Nike running shoes and "I Got a Peek at the Pope" sweatshirt combination.

Social Conformity

In this event, each contestant is placed in a cocktail party situation. The competitor's behavior is timed, and points are received when a competitor starts to conform to the group. A Perrier and lime rates ten full points, while initiating a conversation about the "kids these days" yields seven points. The American team faces stiff competition from Germany's Henrick Smith, who garnered top honors last year when he took out his pet rock and told everybody about being denied entrance to Studio 54.

Occupational Conformity

Brad Rickmuller, Britain's conformational powerhouse, will be a difficult man to beat. He is a CPA, working a 9-to-5 job with a small accounting firm in London. He does not work as a taxi driver or as a gigolo on the side, and he has never considered leaving the hellish pace of the work world to paint nudes on Tahiti.

Postpartum. A small sleepy town that will soon blend back into the fabric of America after the last contestant has doffed his or her polyester tracksuit and has downed that last, unique Dr. Pepper. Postpartum and the rest of the conformist world await, with little trepidation, the commencement of this year's Conformity Olympics.

HOWARD AND THE CRAYON

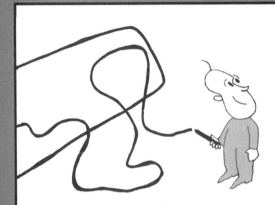

One day, Howard got horny and decided to get laid.

And he took his big crayon and made a Jaguar so he could go cruising for girls.

But he could not seem to find any girls.

So he got out of his car. And he drew three of them.

But Howard needed atmosphere. So he made a stereo and a case of Heineken.

The girls should slip into something more comfortable, Howard thought.

Howard hopped into bed and drew up the covers.

After, Howard gave the girls some toys. He left them to go make some money.

Howard made ones, and then fives, and then tens. Then he drew a printing press to make even more money.

But Howard did not have to spend his money because he could draw anything he wanted.

Soon Howard realized that everything in this world was two-dimensional and, try as he might, he could not draw any meaning into his life.

So Howard drew a gun. And drew the curtains.

Chapter 5

Hidden Dangers

Freak Accidents

1. Drowning at Foam Rubber City.
2. Paper cut from Silly Putty.
3. Piano crushed in typewriter.
4. Great Dane gets sick, slips on Crisco, negligee tears, vibrator impales postman.
5. Geology professor slips on icy sidewalk; 723 die.
6. Town of Stolix, Massachusetts, caught in a sleeping bag zipper.
7. Look in mirror and see Bob Keeshan.
8. Lose four fingers, nose, and fiancé while shuffling cards.
9. Find Ricardo Montalban in glove compartment.

adies and gentlemen, I have just witnessed the future of music. It is large, it is loud. It is pure, it is honest. It is Fire Truck. Yes, Fire Truck. The same Fire Truck that briefly set the scene ablaze back in the early 1990s as a blip on music's radar with its song "Weo-weo-weo," only to speed back into oblivion.

Well, the long wait is finally over. Fire Truck is back and better than ever. Its new CD, *Siren*, places Fire Truck squarely on the cutting edge of the music scene. In fact, Fire Truck may have just turned out the best record of the decade, if not the century.

I first heard Fire Truck at a surprise, impromptu CD release party at the building across the street last week. Set against a backdrop of impressive bonfires, Fire Truck dazzled for five straight hours! Let's see Ricky Martin go that long, without even a break between sets.

Amazed and awestruck, I could do nothing but lie on my bed and think about what had just transpired. The crystal clear notes! The level of emotion in each successively higher note. The deft, thematic use of repetition. Fire Truck had just performed at a level comparable to that of any great aria ever produced.

Desperate for more, I raced to my office and popped the CD into my player. Let's just say I wasn't disappointed. From its first song, "Wwwaaaaahhhhhhh," to its last song, "Reoooooooooooooooo," Fire Truck is nothing short of amazing. *Siren* should cement Fire Truck's place as music's first genius of the 21st century. In this album, Fire Truck reduces music to its barest, most primeval roots. Stripped of words, the music is capable of touching emotion at its purest. Meaning becomes secondary as the beauty of the sound moves the listener to tears. Ending in a bone-chilling, long-sustained, climactic note, *Siren* establishes Fire Truck as the most daring artist of the new millennium, probing the depths of passion as it extinguishes music's boundaries. The music world will never be the same again.

Have You Heard About
Placebo®?
(sucrosium fabricate)

Ask your doctor about this revolutionary breakthrough in medicine. PLACEBO® provides instant relief from symptoms associated with a variety of ailments, including: insomnia, obsessive-compulsive disorder, post-nasal drip, lower back pain, Tourette's syndrome, and many others. Although most PLACEBO® users experience trouble-free relief, some patients may encounter some side effects.* So ask your physician if PLACEBO® is right for you, or call for a free brochure at 1-800-PLACEBO.

*Placebo® (sucrosium fabricate)
Capsules 100.00%
INDICATIONS AND USAGE PLACEBO® (sucrosium fabricate) capsules are indicated for the symptomatic relief of anything imagined in adults and children ages zero and older. PLACEBO® (sucrosium fabricate) capsules do not actually have any biochemical effect on said patient, but hey, whatever works, right?
CONTRAINDICATIONS PLACEBO® (sucrosium fabricate) capsules are contraindicated in patients with a history of diabetes.
WARNINGS Never cross the street without looking both ways first. Stay away from my girlfriend. Don't eat yellow snow.
PRECAUTIONS General PLACEBO® (sucrosium fabricate) capsules should be swallowed one at a time in order to prevent choking and/or indigestion. PLACEBO® (sucrosium fabricate) capsules may cause cavities.

Carcinogenesis, Mutagenesis, Impairment of Fertility Two-year oral carcinogenicity studies in rats and mice have revealed no carcinogenic activity, except in a few that turned into giant infertile mutants that destroyed our lab. HELP! HELP! The giant rat beasts have breached our last line of defense! Call the . . . oh God, what have we done?! AHHHHH!!!
Pregnancy Expectant mothers should feel free to stuff themselves full of PLACEBO® (sucrosium fabricate) capsules to relieve symptoms such as morning sickness and labor pains. PLACEBO® (sucrosium fabricate) capsules can be used to prevent pregnancy altogether if inserted directly into the vagina before intercourse.
ADVERSE REACTIONS PLACEBO® (sucrosium fabricate) capsules caused few adverse reactions in the test group. Some patients became enraged when they realized they were paying forty dollars per bottle for sugar pills.
Store anywhere between -273° and 300ºC to avoid caramelization. Keep out of the reach of children, unless PLACEBO® (sucrosium fabricate) capsules are being served as dessert.

PERSUASION

Harry Lewis had been sitting in the window booth of a business district diner, wondering whether his watch was five minutes fast or the wall clock five minutes slow, when the trouble started. You wouldn't have known he was about to go totally insane; he was only a small, balding, slightly pudgy little man with pince-nez eyeglasses and a crisp, economical Brooks Brothers suit. But at 3:53 p.m., plus or minus five minutes, he heard a voice say, "Hello."

Harry nearly gagged, but he regained control of himself, dabbed his mouth with the corner of a napkin, and reached for his coffee.

"Hey, don't be a snob," the voice said. "I'm talking to you."

This time Harry did gag. Reeling, he turned around in his chair—but the nearest human being, six booths away, was a wrinkled, old woman whose lips and chin were soaked with brown lentil soup.

"Don't bother," the voice told him. "You can't see me."

Harry looked at his coffee. "Where are you?"

"Where do you think I am, Sherlock?"

Harry pondered that for a while. Then he glanced out the window at the enormously fat old bum who danced down the sidewalk accosting pedestrians with tunes from his kazoo. Harry couldn't hear what the bum was playing, but the puzzled expressions of the passing crowd gave it away all the same: gibberish, crazy.

"A voice," Harry said quietly.

"Give the man a cigar," the voice muttered icily. "I can't believe it. The first head I get sent to, and the guy turns out to be a moron. I should have listened to my mother and become a Muse. You meet a more talented class of people."

"Hey," Harry protested. "I'm not too happy about this either, you know."

"Oh, wow," the voice said with an acid bite that made Harry wince. "Let's get abusive! That's all I need, you know, insults from a guy who thought he was too stable for this sort of thing. I'm almost tempted to call the whole thing off."

"Please do."

"I can't. I must stay in your head until you listen to me."

Harry sighed mournfully and returned to his meal. As the waitress refilled his cup and walked back to the kitchen, casting strange looks over her shoulder, he stared out the window. The street was as it always was—the news headlines marching around the sign on the side of the Times Building; the sweaty fat men galloping toward the buses, pretzel lunches still clamped in their jaws; the beehive in the square, where a bored evangelist went through the motions of making a fool of himself before an angry audience; the grinning, wide-eyed cultists, wheedling contributions from everybody; and, most obvious of all, the amoebic crowds, oozing past, around, and through each other as they diffused in a hundred different directions.

The voice asked, "Revolting, aren't they?"

"Not very," Harry said.

"Admit it, for God's sake! They're cattle! Mindless masses!"

"I don't want to think about it," Harry said, truthfully.

"You know I'm right," the voice insisted. "They'd be better off dead."

Suddenly, it was very obvious where this conversation was going. Harry shivered. This was one of the voices mass murderers hear. "Let's change the subject," he said.

"I will, if you admit that I'm right."

"I don't want to admit it," Harry said.

"Why not?"

"Because . . ." Harry waved his fingers, searching for the right words. " . . . Because it's not true, that's all. They deserve to live, too."

"No, they don't," the voice argued.

"Yes, they do."

"No they don't! Admit it!"

The argument was becoming entirely too childish for Harry. He closed his eyes, hoping to be comforted by the dark, but this was late afternoon, and all he saw was a field of red caused by the bright sunlight refracting through the blood in his eyelids. Red. Red. Such a lovely color, but he felt surrounded by it, and he closed his eyes tighter to achieve genuine darkness.

The darkness was worse.

Terrified, he opened his eyes. The diner looked alien to him; its sprawling vistas of Formica and linoleum seemed to be a hellish fast-food nightmare of the damned. Tormented patrons trapped at the counter sat perched on horrifying, tall pillars of chrome and vinyl. And then it all changed back: the diner was a diner, its patrons only patrons. Half the place was staring at him.

"They want to get you," the voice warned, ominously.

Harry ignored it. Well aware of his sweaty forehead and his uncontrollable trembling, he took a pill from his pocket and popped it into his mouth. The diners looked away, satisfied. As far as they knew, the man in the window booth had been having a heart seizure, the pill was his medicine, and the crisis was over. Actually, it had been a wintergreen mint, and he had swallowed it to make them forget about him.

"This is easier than I thought," the voice mused. "Already I have him acting paranoid; by suppertime I'll have him positively homicidal. He must have tendencies . . . "

Harry rubbed his forehead nervously. "How did you do that?"

"Do what?"

"The . . . " Harry had no word for it. "What I saw when I closed my eyes."

"Oh, that," the voice realized suddenly. If it had possessed a hand, it would have slapped its nonexistent forehead with it. "Very simple, actually. Right now, you see the real world. But if you close your eyes, you see me."

"That's you?"

"Yup."

"That's disgusting!" Harry cried.

"Thank you," the voice said, pleased. "But you won't think I'm disgusting for very long. By the time I'm finished, you'll be seeing me all the time."

"All . . . " Harry said, and, some seconds later, "the . . . "

He fainted.

A lot happened while he was unconscious. The floor turned into tissue paper and he plunged through it, screaming, into the mouth of a ponderous metallic snake with elephant tusks for fangs and portholes for eyes. The mouth closed, and boiling marmalade oozed from the Volkswagen-sized glands, enveloping him. Desperate, he broke off one of the tusks and hacked violently at the reptilian cheek by his side. Scales tore and parted. He hacked again. There was a thin pop, and the snake's head imploded like Bazooka bubbles. Harry found himself falling down, but that was okay. He landed on a soft, moist surface a couple of seconds later and bounced over the side of a bottomless chasm where all he could see was a gargantuan statue of his mother.

"I think he's coming around," the waitress observed, with the clarity of a person speaking through a mouthful of broken glass.

Harry Lewis felt himself nodding imperceptibly. Of *course* he was coming around. Any fool could see something obvious like that. What few people could see was the multiple nature of the gum-chewing waitress who bent over him. One of her faces was the one she presented to the world at large; another looked exactly like his sister, who had teased him and stolen his toys as a child and another looked like Mary Jane Colson, the girl he had asked to accompany him to the high school prom before she had so brutally laughed in his face. How he longed to throw her in the deep fry vat.

But no. Not now. He couldn't afford to get caught. Not when he had so much to do . . .

Hey, wait a minute.

Dizzily, he sat up. "Oh, my aching head. What happened?"

"You fainted," the waitress said.

"Ask her to tell you something you don't know," the voice suggested.

"Shut up, you," Harry shouted. "I've had enough of you and your obnoxious interference!"

The waitress gasped in horror and fled into the kitchen. An elderly matron by one of the rear tables snorted in disgust, and a pair of burly taxi drivers turned away, their hands compressed into knuckled fists. Harry's cheeks burned in shame. Miserably, wondering if this would become the norm for him, he

Sir, do you have any idea how black you were going?

pulled himself back into the window booth. He took a sip of coffee to calm himself, but it was cold. He decided to go to the bathroom, but before he got up from the table, he took a piece of paper from his pocket and wrote: I'M TERRIBLY SORRY ABOUT THE BLOW-UP. I'VE BEEN SICK. Next to the note he left a twenty dollar bill. It was meant as an apology, but it would be stolen by a drug addict long before the waitress ever saw it.

The bathroom in the rear was furnished in typical Manhattan municipal: old, smelly , deteriorating, and wet. He stepped over the puddle-sized moat behind the door, walked to the mirror over the sink, and studied his reflection for signs of decay. It was the single ugliest sight Harry Lewis had ever seen. His eyes were tilted, red, and bulging, his nose flat and wide, his neck thin, hairy, and bony. When he smiled his teeth looked like playing cards. He went to the nearest stall and sat down.

There was a pause.

"All right," the voice sighed. "Let's go."

"No, thanks," Harry said, in what he hoped was a threatening tone of voice. "I don't intend on doing anything—including budge from this spot—until you get the *hell* out of my head. I suggest you do it now."

"Just like that? You're not going to ask me if I want to stay for coffee or something?"

"No, I've already had my coffee."

"Selfish," the voice pouted.

"Be that as it may," Harry said. "Get out of my head."

The voice made a noise, or vice versa; Harry couldn't tell. It sounded like a Bronx cheer, but demons cackled behind the fricatives. There was a laugh. "Hey, I wish I could, buddy. This is no picnic for me either. But I told you before; I can't. Once I'm in your head, I can't get out. You and I are bound together for life."

For life. Harry closed his eyes in despair, then saw something and

"Just one question: What happens when we get to the bottom?"

jerked them open again.

"It won't be that bad," the voice argued. "I'll make you happy, and I'll put lots of nice words in your head. It's fun. Soon you'll be so whing-whang you'll be grinning all the time. And then we'll go out, the two of us, and we'll choose victims, and follow them home, and kill them. Graphically, of course."

"No," Harry whispered.

"Why not?" the voice asked. "I can give you a fetish regarding anything you want. Blond hair, long legs, eyeglasses. Male or female, black, white, Chinese, or Puerto Rican. Nurses, maybe. A lot of people pick nurses. And when you kill them, graphically, of course, you can have an orgasm." There was a reflective pause. "We should be able to get twenty or thirty of them before the cops nail us."

"Damn you," Harry said, trembling. "I won't be a party to what you want me to do. Never. You'll have

to think of a way to settle this thing sensibly."

The voice ruminated that, "No, I'm afraid I can't. That is, unless you want to fight a duel . . . "

Harry sat up. "*What?*"

"A duel. You close your eyes, pass out, and 'wake up' in a hallucination. I'll be there, wearing white boxing gloves. If you can last a full fifteen rounds . . . " The voice faded off into silence. "Ahhhh, but what am I talking about? The only human being who ever fought off such an assault was Edgar Allen Poe, and you know what kind of fruitcake *he* became."

"If it's my only choice," Harry said, "I'll take it."

The voice seemed to shrug. "It's your funeral."

He was buried up to his armpits in sweet potatoes. The smell assaulted his nostrils like marines on Omaha Beach. He reeled; he fell; he found a baseball bat in his right hand and he beat the sweet

"Say, haven't we met in a previous cartoon?"

was an exhilarating feeling. Overcome with excitement, he roared his blood lust to the heavens.

A clump of orange hit him between the shoulders. Then another.

He looked up. And his heart sank and drowned.

In the split instant before he was crushed forever by several thousand tons of falling sweet potatoes, he remembered the old saw about how loud noises tend to cause avalanches.

Harry Lewis, maniac, woke up in a stall in the men's room of a business district diner. His eyes were red and bulging, and his hands opened and closed spasmodically. The voice whispered sweet nothings in his ear.

"You were right," Harry snarled homicidally, as he opened the bathroom door and took his first step toward a bloody sojourn in the streets. "My madness is beautiful—a song within me. I was meant to be this way."

"Glad to hear it," the voice beamed.

"And before we're finished, the name of Harry Lewis will forever be connected to senseless carnage and bloodshed." He cackled insanely, but the voice was oddly silent. "I will be feared forever. I shall become a stalker of the night. Children will have nightmares about me. And in one hundred years I will be known as . . . "

"Uh, Harry?" the voice asked.

Harry stopped. "What's the matter, voice? Don't you know that if you smile, the whole world smiles with you?"

"It's not that," the voice began. It giggled. "Dumb mistake. I thought you were George Lewis, of 345 Axel Street. An ex-marine. First time out, and I possess the wrong head."

There was silence.

"Oh, well," Harry said, philosophically. "I guess it doesn't matter that much anymore."

"Right," the voice agreed. "Let's go out there and knock 'em dead."

potatoes mercilessly until he was able to pull himself to the surface. But walking on sweet potatoes is very difficult. It took him most of that day to reach the horizon, and when he reached it, another horizon appeared several miles away. He knew that when he reached it, there would only be another one after that, and another one after that. That way lay catatonia. He confirmed this by walking another hundred yards until he found a sign which read "Catatonia: Walk North."

So he changed tactics, burrowing down into the sticky orange ground beneath him until he broke through into open air. Gnats pestered him. The ground was a tiny white patch thousands of miles beneath him. Acrophobic, he grabbed the marmalade wall for support, but great batches came off in his hands and he fell.

"You'd better do something," the voice said. "You can't be killed in a hallucination, but if you hit the ground, you'll think you're dead. It amounts to the same thing."

Harry screamed in terror. The scream became a word balloon, which floated directly above him, unconcerned. He grabbed it and proceeded to float quietly to the ground.

The voice was waiting there, impressed. "I never saw anybody do that

before," he said. "You have style."

"Thanks," Harry said, but the word balloon drowned him out. Annoyed, he erased it. "Thanks. How do most people manage to get down?"

"They don't. Since this universe is a figment of your imagination anyway, all you had to do was dispense with such stuff as sweet potato horizons and tangible word balloons and materialize wherever you wanted to. But, no matter. Be satisfied that you provided me with my laugh of the day. Shall we begin?"

"I guess so," Harry said. Chastened, he fastened the straps on his boxing gloves and prepared to fight for his sanity.

Gritting his teeth, Harry leaped forward. His attack caught the voice in a bodily part it liked to call its zibblefranz. It squealed; they tangled; he grabbed hold of something that looked like a neck but could have been an index finger and squeezed. The voice looked very unhappy. Emboldened, Harry squeezed harder. The voice choked and started pounding the floor with its deeblenerbers. Harder.

Pounding the floor. Squeezing. Life started fading from the voice's eyes, and still Harry squeezed harder. As the voice started to pass through the misty doorway that separates life and death, Harry felt triumph within his grasp. It

Here at the National Institute for the Institution of National Holidays, we get constant requests for new holidays. Once a year, we pick several holidays that will receive our official stamp of approval. Here are a bunch of new holidays whose times have finally come . . .

A Holiday Guide

George Michael Independence Day

On July, 13, 1995, acclaimed singer/songwriter George Michael was finally freed from an oppressive contract with Sony Music Entertainment UK. After an exhaustive legal battle, the ex-Wham! sex symbol was granted the independence to pursue projects with another record label. From now on, we reserve July 13th of each year to celebrate this fine musician and his freedom to pursue his God-given gift for groovy pop.

Polish History Month

Polish Americans have been hassling us for years, requesting that a month be set aside to celebrate their heritage. "Blacks get their own history month. So do women. We want a month too!" their spokesman said. At least that's what we think he said. It was hard to tell because he was talking into the wrong end of the phone. We finally complied and promised them that the month of Nemuary will be reserved to celebrate Polish history. Mark your calendars.

Yom Kippurim

There are just too many Jewish holidays. That's why it's about time for a single Purim/Yom Kippur one-day celebration. Yom Kippur is the holiest day of the Jewish year and is reserved for fasting and reflection. Purim is a time for fun and games. So, fasting will be optional on Yom Kippurim, but if you do choose to eat, you can eat only hamantashen. And in accordance with Jewish custom, Yom Kippurim will be celebrated ten days after Rosh Hashanarbor Day.

Six Days of No Kevin Bacon

Kevin Bacon was not in *Groundhog Day* with Bill Murray, who never starred in *Halloween* with Jamie Lee Curtis, who didn't even have a cameo in *Father's Day* with Billy Crystal, who didn't play Lazlo in *New Year's Day* with David Duchovny, who certainly can't be found in *St. Patrick's Day* with Piper Laurie, who was never even considered for a role in *Independence Day*. Celebrate six days of not having to look at Kevin's face. Festivities start *Friday the 13th*.

Cinco de Mayonnaise

We find it disturbing that the condiment mustard has its own holiday, yet the undeniably creamier and tastier mayonnaise receives no such distinction. Well, that's all about to change, now that every May 5th, instead of going to work, you get to watch a parade and enjoy dozens and dozens of mayonnaise-filled tortillas until you vomit. The Mexicans have been doing it for years. And Mexicans know how to party.

Groundhog Day (Puff Daddy Remix)

This February 11th holiday is a lot like Groundhog Day, but, with some added drum loops and a neat Kool & The Gang sample courtesy of producer Sean "Puffy" Combs, it's a lot more danceable.

in "The Foreman"

Emergency Instructions

FOR YOUR SAFETY

Berkshire 131-L Steam Train

American Trainlines®

Seat belts must be fastened and tray tables must be in the "not going to slide across the floor" position before departure. To fasten your seat belt, please tie the left and right ends together.

Abacuses and other approved consumer devices may be used once the train has reached a comfortable cruising momentum.

Please note that it is a violation of Confederate Law to tamper with bathroom opium detectors.

Should the cabin experience a sudden loss of pressure, little cans of air will drop down into your lap. In the event that you are travelling with shackled, indentured servants, please start sucking from your own can before attempting to assist your companions.

In the event of a water derailment, follow the lighted guide candles to your nearest escape canoe.

Special Note: If you are seated in a specially marked exit cabin, you may be called upon to assist others in an evacuation by pulling up the exit window blinds and making sure that everyone crawls through safely.

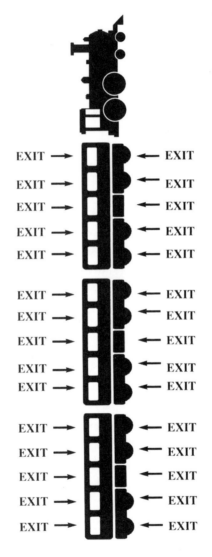

New Phobias

■ **Aibohphobia:** Fear of palindromes.
■ **Billionsandbillionsofintergalacticaphobia:** Fear of people who impersonate Carl Sagan.
■ **Coincidiphobia:** Fear of running into your father at a house of ill repute.
■ **Excitaphobia:** Fear of getting an erection during a hernia check.
■ **Exclusiphobia:** Fear of being the subject of an article in the *National Enquirer.*
■ **Jerkophobia:** Fear of having a stroke and becoming paralyzed while in the act of sexual solitaire.
■ **Lacostephobia:** Fear of Perrier.
■ **Leophobia:** Fear of reading *War and Peace* and not understanding the ending.
■ **Mazeltophobia:** Fear of being forced to repeat your Bar Mitzvah.
■ **Oopsiphobia:** Fear of having a wildly passionate, sexual, and orgasmic dream about a woman in a fur coat, and waking up to find your pet sheepdog panting satedly beside you.
■ **Phaphaphaphobia:** Fear of stuttering.
■ **Rootcanaliphobia:** Fear of going to your dentist after a six-year delay and being asked to pose for journal shots of advanced fungoid infestation.
■ **Santaclaustriphobia:** Fear of getting stuck in a chimney.
■ **Tricksaphobia:** Fear of running into your mother at a house of ill-repute.
■ **Tripleletteriphobia:** Fear of dying and being reincarnated as the letter "G" in a game of Scrabble.
■ **Uncouthophobia:** Fear of being filmed picking your nose by a roving camera during a nationally-televised sports event.
■ **Yawniphobia:** Fear of people who brag about their high school sports teams.

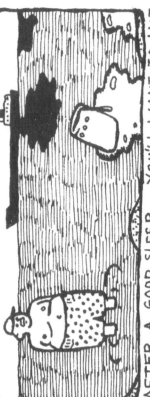

...OR, YOU CAN JOIN THE POLYESTER SET WHO LIKE TO "GET IT ON" TO THE SLICK NEW SOUND OF DISCO AT STUDIO 24 IN NEW-ARK. PROPER DRESS REQUIRED, AND REMEMBER BEAUTIFUL PEOPLE ONLY!

YOU'LL WANT TO VISIT THE SUBURBS, WHERE MORE THAN HALF OF NEW JERSEYS 4 BILLION PEOPLE LIVE. IN FACT, YOU'LL HAVE LITTLE CHOICE, AS NEW JERSEY IS BASICALLY ONE MEGA-BURB, EXCEPTING CITIES, INDUSTRIAL AREAS, MALLS, AND PAVEMENT.

THE SUBURBS ARE THE REAL "HINTER-LAND" OF NEW JERSEY. HERE LIVE THE "FOLKS" THAT SILENT MAJORITY SO IMPORTANT TO THE SOCIAL FABRIC, THE REAL BACKBONE OF OUR WONDERFUL NEW JERSEY COMMUNITY.

CRIME? ORGANIZED ONLY THANX! OUR FASCIST POLICE FORCE KEEPS ALL THE PUNKS, HIPPIES, AND DARKIES WELL UNDER CONTROL. NO NEED TO FEAR LEAVING YOUR CAR (SOME PEOPLE LIKE TO), EXCEPT IN DESIG-NATED COMBAT ZONES.

NOW, HEY, THAT DUZN'T MEAN WE'RE NO FUN! C'MON! THERE'S PLENTY OF NITE-LIFE AND STUFF LIKE THAT! YOU CAN GO TO THE RA-MADA INN BAR IN NUTLEY, OR FOR YOU "PLAYBOYS", HOW 'BOUT LOSING ALL YOUR MONEY IN ATLANTIC CITY, OR MEETING A NICE GIRL ON AVE-NUE C IN TEANECK?

MUSIC? YOU BET! PLENTY! IN FACT EVERY BUILDING IN NEW JERSEY IS EQUIPPED WITH A MUZAK® TAPE LOOP BACKGROUND MUSIC SYSTEM, AS ARE MOST STREET AND PUBLIC AREAS. FOR THE KIDS, TRY SOME OF NEW JERSEY'S REALLY "NOW" YOUNG MUSICIANS. MANY KNOW MORE THAN THREE CHORDS!

YOU WOULDN'T DARE WANT TO MISS A VISIT TO SCENIC PRINCETON UNIVERSITY, AFFECTIONATLY DUBBED "P.U." BY ITS STUDENTS. A MEMBER OF THE PRESTIGIOUS "IVY LEAGUE", PRINCETON TURNS MANY YOUNG PEOPLE INTO DETERMINED YOUNG ADULTS EVERY YEAR.

AT PRINCETON, SOME OF THE MOST IMPORTANT RESEARCH IN THE COUNTRY IS BEING DONE. IN THE PAST 50 YEARS BREAKTHROUGHS SUCH AS POP TARTS, RED DYE NO.2, NAUGAHYDE, DOUBLE-KNIT CLOTHES, MAGIC MARKERS, AND HYDROGEN BOMBS HAVE BEEN DISCOVERED AT PRINCETON.

IF YOU'RE LUCKY ENOUGH TO BE INVITED, YOU'LL BE ABLE TO SET DOWN TO SOME REAL "DOWN HOME" JERSEY COOKIN' IN FRONT OF THE T.V. TYPICAL FARE: BURGER, CHIPS, BOSCO, 7-UP, JIFFY POP, TWINKIES. IN FACT, NEW JERSIANS LOVE BURGERS SO MUCH, MANY LIVE IN "RANCH-BURGERS"!

PARAMUS 1962... FASHION HISTORY IS MADE WHEN BAM-BERGER'S INTRODUCES THEIR NEW SPRING LINE...A SET OF NEW JERSEY CLASSICS SO TIME-LESS, THEY HAVE SURVIVED 'TILL TODAY!

IN NEW JERSEY, THERE'S NO NEED TO GO OUT OF DOORS EVER, EVEN WHILE SHOPPING! WE'VE ELIMINATED INCONVENIENT "MOM 'N POP" SHOPS, AND DEVELOPED HUGE ENCLOSED MALLS WHICH CATER TO YOUR EVERY NEED. IT'S A COMPLETLY ARTIFICIAL ENVIRONMENT! SIMPLY GO TO YOUR GARAGE, GET IN CAR, AND PARK IN ENCLOSED MALL GARAGE! NO NEED TO RISK THE HAZARDS OF SUN AND RAIN.

LITHIUM BOOKS

CHOOSE YOUR OWN
Obsessive-Compulsive Disorder
ADVENTURE

On the bus on the way home today, an old man with a cough sits three rows behind you. Your hands are already chapped and bleeding from washing them so much, but while the old man was walking down the aisle by you, you thought you felt him rub against your sleeve.

- If you wash your hands three times at each sink in your apartment, turn to page 31.
- If you die of tuberculosis, syphilis, or the plague, turn to page 32.

You have just arrived at work when you realize with horror that you may have accidentally buttoned your shirt this morning starting with the bottom button instead of the top one.

- If you run to the bathroom, take off all your clothes, and dress again the right way this time, turn to page 6.
- If you lose your job and your house burns down, turn to page 7.

For your birthday, a friend gives you a cream-colored sweater.

- If you put it in the white sweater drawer, turn to page 12.
- If you put it in the yellow sweater drawer, turn to page 13.
- If you burn the sweater and stop speaking to your friend, turn to page 14.
- If you build a new "cream" cabinet and die from a splinter infection, turn to page 15.

It is Saturday. You have just finished eating sardines, sprouts, and celery when you learn that "celery" begins with the letter *C*, not the letter *S*.

- If you run to the hospital and have your stomach pumped, turn to page 28.
- If you can already feel your hair falling out and your genitals shriveling, turn to page 29.

You are in bed when you realize that the front door may be unlocked. You have already gotten up to check it seven times tonight, but it is possible that last time, you accidentally unlocked it instead of locking it.

- If you get up to lock it seven more times again, turn to page 18.
- If you stay in bed and get murdered by a psychopath who walks into your wide-open front door, turn to page 19.

Lawrence J. Buxbaum

"Attorney-at-Law" *

Since 1967, Fighting For Your Right To Fill Our Courts With Hot Air

Greetings, Victims of Various, Vaguely-Existent Phenomena!

Have you spent your life fighting an uphill battle against your own stupidity while big corporations pillage your pocketbook and inappropriately give your wife "friendly pats"? Are you ignorant of even the most basic common-sense rules of daily life? Do you have an adorable blond-haired child who is willing to say anything in court?

THEN YOU HAVE A CASE!

For the last 35 years, I have been fighting the lucrative fight for the downtrodden, the victimized, the ashamed, the illiterate, the incompetent, the weaselly, and now YOU! Many people don't realize that in this day and age, being a dumbass is an asset (not that you're necessarily a dumbass). But I can spin the foolishness that has brought well-deserved suffering in your life into pure gold! What's that? You don't think you qualify?

WELL, YOU'RE PROBABLY WRONG!

Have you taken large amounts of any of the following "safe" (or so they'd have you believe!) substances?

- Crack
- Delicious rat poison
- Windows 95® diskettes
- Cotton/polyester blends
- Asbestos con carne
- Life® cereal
- Glass
- Pennies
- Glowing green mass you found in the amusement park bathroom

Have you recently had unpleasant encounters with . . . ?

- Terrorist-looking neighbors
- Math
- Crocodiles (preferably with corporate ties)
- Censorship of your fecal "art"
- Rap music
- Your own shortcomings as a human being

Could some corporation conceivably be involved in your inability to . . . ?

- Understand your teenage children
- Perceive those 3-D Magic Eye® posters
- Sustain your Liquid-Plumr® addiction
- Get the fly up all the way on your jeans
- Beat that damn pit-monster at the end of Level 8. (*Damn you, pit-monster!*)

Then you have a case!

So don't delay, because in a short time, I'll have you hooked up with a wad of cash and an interview on *Good Morning, America*.

Lawrence J. Buxbaum

Because it's not your fault that you're a pathetic loser.

* Mr. Buxbaum is not an accredited attorney, but let's not allow that to come between you and your money.

He Cheated Death

INTERVIEWER: Dr. Dominic Casual, a scientist from Ottawanna, Canada, purports to have died twice and miraculously returned to life before any sort of funeral arrangements could be made. Dr. Casual . . .

DOMINIC: Call me Dom.

INTERVIEWER: Dom, I think everyone would like to know how a man can die and recover not once, but twice. Certainly it can be no accident.

DOMINIC: No, it was not a fluke. I found I was able to control my fate using willpower.

INTERVIEWER: Incredible. What's your secret?

DOMINIC: Okay, before I go into this, I just want to say this is not something to be attempted by the inexperienced. Children reading this, amateur daredevils, and bored housewives, don't try dying, because I'm not making any guarantees. I only know it works for me.

INTERVIEWER: Good point. What about your secret?

DOMINIC: Well, I have this great desire to live and to remain as healthy as possible.

INTERVIEWER: That's it?

DOMINIC: Yes, but I can't stress this point enough. I love life and good health, and that's exactly why I'm here today . . .

INTERVIEWER: But you've died twice. Certainly that's above the national norm.

DOMINIC: Granted. But each time I died, I was in excellent condition.

INTERVIEWER: I don't understand.

To me, death has always held connotations of sickness, injury, and poor health. People in excellent condition ordinarily don't pass away.

DOMINIC: Perhaps an example will help. I first died when I was 31-years old. God, I can remember it like yesterday. The date was January 6, 1985. When I went to sleep that night, I was the picture of health. When I woke up the next morning, I was dead.

INTERVIEWER: You woke up dead?

DOMINIC: As a doornail.

INTERVIEWER: How did you know you were dead?

DOMINIC: I first suspected it when I discovered that my alarm clock had failed to rouse me. I felt stiff, as if rigor mortis had set in. The next thing I knew, I felt myself rising out of the bed. I walked into the kitchen and made myself a cup of coffee. I watched a little television, then I called in dead to work. I read the morning paper and did the crossword puzzle. Then I made myself a couple of fried eggs. Then I . . .

INTERVIEWER: Excuse me, but it seems death has a surprisingly lifelike quality.

DOMINIC: Yes, it was a bit of a disappointment after all the stories you hear. But anyway, after breakfast, I went back into my room and sat down on my bed. And I said to myself, "Dommy, are you ready for death?" And I looked around me and thought, "Dommy, despite all that you have seen, and all that you have

heard, life's a pretty beautiful thing; you can't treat it like a turd."

INTERVIEWER: You made that up yourself?

DOMINIC: On the spot.

INTERVIEWER: Very inspiring.

DOMINIC: Yeah, I keep it posted over my desk.

INTERVIEWER: But to continue . . .

DOMINIC: Well, I kept repeating that poem to myself for over an hour, and then I lay down and closed my eyes. When I reopened them again, it was four o'clock in the afternoon and I was alive!

INTERVIEWER: You were?

DOMINIC: Absolutely.

INTERVIEWER: How did you know?

DOMINIC: Hey, come on, how does anyone know he's alive? How do you know *you're* alive? You just know, right? And, gosh, I was so happy. What a wonderful feeling! I ran around the house yelling, "I'm alive! I'm alive!"—just touching everything, and staring at my reflection in the mirror for minutes on end. That evening I celebrated by downing a fifth of scotch and driving my car all over town, honking the horn at everyone. Then I smashed the car into a tree and died all over again.

INTERVIEWER: Sounds like it wasn't your day.

DOMINIC: I've had better.

INTERVIEWER: Were you crushed? Did you go through the windshield?

DOMINIC: Beats me. But when I opened my eyes, I was in a room with God.

INTERVIEWER: That must have been quite a shock.

DOMINIC: Not really. I'd been good.

INTERVIEWER: What did God look like?

DOMINIC: He was old, with gray hair and a gray beard, and He had on a long white coat. And everywhere I looked, everything around me was white and clean. It was beautiful. Then I got down on my hands and knees, crawled over to God, and cowered at His feet. I knelt there, gathering all of my remaining strength until, finally, I looked up at Him and said, "I don't want to be dead." And then God gestured to one of his angels, and she took my blood pressure and tested my reflexes. At last, God walked over to me and said, "You're a crazy, drunken son of a bitch, and we don't have any room for you here." I was discharged by the angel at the main desk, and the next thing I knew, I was home again, and I was alive, and it was wonderful. A miracle.

INTERVIEWER: So what does the near future hold for you, Dom?

DOMINIC: Well, I'm working on a paperback for Dell Publishing that should be out in October called *Shove It, Death!* All I really want to do is send out the message that, hey, death doesn't have to be the "final sleep" or "eternal rest" or any of that frightening mumbo jumbo. Death can be as temporary and refreshing as an afternoon nap or a ride in the country. All you need is the proper frame of mind and physical well-being.

INTERVIEWER: You know, Dom, there are an awful lot of people reading this who are probably telling themselves that you're a phony, that the whole thing is a ridiculous hoax, that you're trying to make a bundle off a pack of lies. Is there any substance to that?

DOMINIC: Absolutely not.

INTERVIEWER: Can you back that up?

DOMINIC: I'd stake my life on it.

INTERVIEWER: Yes, I thought you might.

Ways You Might Use the Word *Perturbed* While Traveling Abroad

"Upon my confinement to a Turkish prison—for undisclosed reasons—I was *perturbed* to find out that the room service consisted of an under-cooked rat carcass, served by a man who claimed I have a 'perdy mouth.'"

"I was very *perturbed* to find out that, after enjoying an unknown type of meat on a stick, New Delhi does not offer toilet seat covers in their public Port-o-Potties."

"*Perturbed* as I was, I chose to remove my yarmulke from my head upon arriving at the Jews-B-Gone hostel in Germany."

"Dear Mom, I'm chillin' out in central Baghdad. I'm *perturbed*."

"While backpacking through France, I was surprised and *perturbed* to find the locals to be quite rude and short-tempered. Who would have thought that French people can be rude?"

"While in Ireland, I was *perturbed* that my face was pummeled merely because I chose to initiate a conversation with a drunk local by saying, 'I don't know about you, but I think those guys in the IRA had the right idea.'"

"I was extremely *perturbed* that no matter how hard I looked, I couldn't find a decent steak house in Ethiopia."

"During my time in Japan, I was *perturbed* to find out that shaving my pubic hair actually messes up my personal Feng Shui."

"I was *perturbed* that the DJ of a local Russian night club did not know what I meant by Sisqó's 'Thong Song.'"

"The fact that my nineteen-year-old Thai hooker named Fing turned out to be a sixteen-year-old male named Fong has caused me to feel slightly *perturbed*. *Perturbed*, yet somewhat interested."

You Can Read This Ad...

Or you can die today!!!

You've been lucky so far. You're alive. You're breathing. Blood is coursing through your veins. But how long can it last? How long?

You walked safely across the street today. No big deal? Consider this: thirty, perhaps even fifteen seconds later, and a massive, chrome-grilled Mack truck would have ground you into the asphalt. You say you shaved this morning and it was completely uneventful? Count your blessings. Inches, nay, millimeters beneath the cutting edge of the swivel-headed razor that you guided recklessly across your neck lay the purple, glistening, pulsing carotid arteries. Nick one of those babies and it's all over, pal. Last night you went out for a breath of fresh air and lived to tell about it. Nothing special? If you knew how many tons of meteoric rock survive the journey through the atmosphere to pound into the side of the earth every day, you might never step outside again. At least not without a hard hat.

The Odds

Try to guess the odds against you surviving the next twenty-four hours. Two to one? Five to one? Thirty to one?

Not even close.

We've saved you the trouble of going through the calculations. The figure we came up with is a startling 46,950 to one. 72,740 to one if you are near-sighted. 162,580 to one if you expect to pass within four feet of an electrical outlet. 941,220 to one if you plan to set foot in the ocean. And astronomical if you live anywhere near a prison, mental hospital, nuclear power plant, fault line, heliport, volcano, large city, zoo, or any unmarried, friendly-but-quiet man in his late twenties, who's worked for the last six years for minimum wage in an unskilled profession, with no hope for promotion, whose mother used to dress him in diapers until he was fourteen-years-old, who has a fuzzy, indistinct high school yearbook photo, generally keeps to himself, and always says hello.

Any combination of the above and it's time to administer your last rites. 'Cause you just ain't gonna make it.

But fear not. There's good news. It doesn't have to end like this. We at B.R.E.A.T.H.E. (Betcha Rather Exist Alot Than Haveta Expire) know exactly how you feel. We know you don't want to die. That's why we're going to make you a fabulous once-in-a-lifetime offer.

We're going to offer you the secret to continued life. Don't ask us how or where we got it. Just thank your lucky stars that the B.R.E.A.T.H.E. Life-Continuer is available.

Our Secret

Our secret is not a gadget. It's not a prayer. It is not an operation. There is nothing complicated about it. There are no procedures to learn, no numbers to memorize, no foreign languages to interpret, no word jumbles to unscramble. In fact, there is absolutely no brainwork required. Our secret is so simple, so basic, so elementary, you'll be shocked and appalled you didn't come up with it yourself years ago. And it works.

Statistics show it's the single most effective life-continuer on the market. And if that's not enough to convince you, take a look at this small sample of the thousands of letters we've received over the past ten years!

Dear B.R.E.A.T.H.E: You guys are the greatest! I bought your Life-Continuer seven years ago, and I've been living ever since!

—P. Brain, Los Angeles

Dear B.R.E.A.T.H.E: Yesterday, a 747 about to land at O'Hare International was involved in a freak collision, sending 228 people to their fiery deaths. And I was not one of them! Your Life-Continuer is fantastic!

—O. Cripes, Chicago

How much would you expect to pay for such a wonderful secret? $50 thousand? $300 thousand? One million dollars? How does $29.95 sound to you? That's right! Just $29.95 will get you this secret to continued life.

Still unconvinced? Here's the icing on the cake. The B.R.E.A.T.H.E. Life-Continuer comes with an ironclad LIFE-TIME GUARANTEE. If, at any time, you become dissatisfied with the effectiveness of the Life-Continuer, simply send it back to us, and we'll promptly refund your money, no questions asked. But we don't expect we'll be hearing from you.

Order today . . . and LIVE!

Application for Alabama State Highway Patrol

Please circle either Yes or No for all questions. Your honesty is appreciated.

Name: _____

Previous occupation: _____

Permanent Address (NOTE: motels not included): _____

1) Have you had any experience in the law enforcement industry?   Yes   No
(1 point for yes)

2) Do you have a mustache? If not, would you be willing to grow one?   Yes   No
(1 point for yes)

3) Have you ever been convicted of, or are you awaiting a pending
conviction of, any common sex crimes?   Yes   No
(1 point for either)

4) Given the opportunity, would you prefer to sport your aviator
sunglasses while engaging in sexual intercourse with prostitutes?   Yes   No
(1 point for yes)

5) Are you of the opinion that the manufacturing of moonshine should not
be considered a convictable offense?   Yes   No
(1 point for yes)

6) If you answered Yes to the previous question, are you comfortable
drinking copious amounts of moonshine while on duty?   Yes   No
(1 point for yes)

7) Are you the product of an incestuous relationship?   Yes   No
(1 point for yes)

8) If you answered No to the previous question, do you condone such
activities and practices? (NOTE: *condone* means "to ignore"
[NOTE: *ignore* means "to not care about"])   Yes   No
(1 point for yes)

9) Are you comfortable around people whose skin tone is anything but
milky white, with a sunburned neck?   Yes   No
(1 point for no)

10) Are you of the opinion that sodomy by use of a nightstick is an
appropriate punishment for minor traffic violations?   Yes   No
(1 point for yes)

11) Are you comfortable using the old-string-tied-to-two-cups phone
system?   Yes   No
(1 point for yes)

12) Given the opportunity, would you severely beat a tree-huggin' hipster
to the ground?   Yes
(only one option)

13) Are you drunk right now?   Yes   No
(2 points for yes)

In order to qualify for the position, you must score at least 12 points. If you are a woman, you fail.

Do You Want Fries with That?

BY JERRY C. BUTTWATER

We've all had a fast-food Combo Meal—those handy-dandy "Happy Meals for Big People," as I like to call them. But in our quest for maximum grease with minimum effort, we have allowed the Combo Meal to rob the employees of our favorite fast food eateries of all ability to reason. It's only a matter of time before they conquer us, also.

Now you may be saying, "That Jerry Buttwater is crazy!" If you are a chick, you're probably saying, "That Jerry Buttwater is hot. I want to have sex with him right now." Hey, I can't argue with the latter statement, but allow Jerry Buttwater to defend himself a bit on the former.

I was at a particular fast-food establishment the other day which I will not name out of respect for the restaurant. Okay, it was Wendy's. Anyway, I only had five dollars to my name, due to the previous evening's activity of buying drinks for chicks, giving them my best pick-up line, and having said drinks spilled on my head. Guys, one word of advice: *Never* try to pick up a chick with the line, "How much for a blowjob?" It doesn't work.

So there I was in Wendy's with my limited funds ready to get a #2 Combo Meal. That's a chicken sandwich meal, not a poop meal, for those unfamiliar with fast-food terminology. But the Combo Meal cost $5.32. "That's okay," I said to myself, "I'll just get a chicken sandwich and a Coke. That only costs $4.68." So I went up to the counter and said to the cashier, "I'd like a chicken sandwich and a medium Coke, please." Like some sort of robot, the cashier reacted silently, pressing some of the colorful buttons on his special register.

"That will be $5.32 please."

"No, it isn't," I responded.

"Yes it is, sir."

"No, buddy, you're wrong," I said. "My meal is $4.68. The Chicken Combo Meal is $5.32."

"Yes, $5.32. That's what I said."

"Yes, but I didn't order the Chicken Combo. I ordered a

chicken sandwich and a medium Coke."

"Yes, the combo."

"No, the combo comes with fries. I just want a chicken sandwich and a medium Coke."

"Why don't you want the fries?"

"I just don't."

"So you don't want a combo?"

"No. Just a chicken sandwich and a medium Coke. *No fries.*" After shifting his gaze from me to the register and back again, this poor victim of the Combo Meal went to get the manager.

"What seems to be the problem?" asked the manager.

"There's no problem. I would like a chicken sandwich and a medium Coke, please."

The manager rang up my order. "Okay," he said, "that will be $5.32." This guy was no different than the braindead cashier, save he had a tie and marginally better social skills.

"Ah, but you see, my friend, that is the cost of the Chicken Sandwich Combo Meal. I didn't order the Combo Meal. I ordered a chicken sandwich and a medium Coke. *No fries.*"

"So . . . you don't want fries?"

"That's correct."

"But they come with the Combo Meal. Couldn't you give them to one of your friends?"

"Listen, cretin, I want a chicken sandwich and a medium Coke. *Not* a Combo Meal. *No* fries. Just a chicken sandwich and a medium Coke. No Combo Meal. Got it?"

After a long pause and some confused looks at the register, the manager finally understood. "That will be $4.68. Is that for here or to go?"

"To go." A minute later, I had my bag, and Jerry Buttwater was on the way back to his babe-lair with his chicken sandwich and medium Coke. Maybe I had been a little harsh with the manager, but now everything was okay. I sat down at the kitchen table and opened up the bag, taking out my chicken sandwich, medium Coke, and . . . French fries? I never came so close to crying over something that didn't involve taking a high heel in the testicles.

So there you have it, friends. The Combo Meal has already begun tightening its grip on the witless employees of fast-food joints everywhere. Don't be the next victim of its mind-feebling power. Follow Jerry Buttwater's example and order an unnumbered meal, before it's too late.

There was a knock on the door of my Eddy Street office. There may have been a knock on the door of my College Avenue office, too, but since I was at the Eddy Street office, I couldn't know for sure. Besides, I didn't have a College Avenue office.

"Come in," I said, and I meant it.

She was a tall, green-eyed redhead with more curves than the copper tubing on a moonshine still. And looking at her made a man just as drunk. She wore a black hat, tipped seductively over one eye. The other eye had long, dark lashes, a green iris, black pupil, and white everything else. (I don't think the white part has a name, just like an egg; the yellow part is the yolk, but the white part is just the white part.)

She wore a tight, red shirt with a plunging neckline that left little to the imagination. In other words, you could see a lot. Not everything, of course, because if you could see everything, she would have been naked. And if she had been naked, she wouldn't have been walking into my office.

Did I mention her plunging neckline and bountiful cleavage? I did? Good.

Her skirt was short and black and leather. Her legs were long and tanned and clean-shaven. She wore black shoes with five-inch stiletto heels, which must have added a good five inches to her height, which must have been five-nine before the heels, five-eleven after. What can I say? I'm good with figures.

"How can I help you?" I asked, picturing a number of ways I could help her.

"There's been a murder," she said, cool as a slice of pizza at the end of a party.

"Who's the stiff?" I asked.

"A private dick."

"Like me?"

"No," she said, looking me up

Redhead and Dead

and down like a judge at a yo-yo competition. "Not as big as you."

I nodded, for no reason other than to be doing something with my head.

"He was working for me," she said. "I had him follow my husband to see if he was cheating." Why anyone would cheat on a woman with a body like that, I'll never know. Unless, of course, she was frigid. Or imbecilic. Or suffered from chronic halitosis. Or lesbian. Well, maybe not lesbian. That might actually have been inducement to stay. Still, there were plenty of things that might drive a man to infidelity.

"What did the dick find out?" I asked, no longer nodding, but now shaking my head from side to side.

She sat down and crossed her legs. I was hoping she'd pull a Sharon Stone from *Basic Instinct*, but then that would make me the fat, dorky guy from *Seinfeld*.

"Nothing," she said. "Somebody put a .357 Magnum to the back of his

head and blew his nose all over the kitchen wall.

"Nice."

"Will you help me?" She uncrossed her legs for a second. Whatever she had, she wasn't Sharon.

"No."

She stood up, reached between her breasts, and pulled out a Smith & Wesson .357 Magnum.

"Are you sure you can't help me?"

"Okay," I said. "I'll help."

I pulled a magnetic chess set out of my desk and played a quick game.

"You shot the short dick because the short dick was your husband," I told her point blank. "You hired him to find out if he was cheating on you. He was. He was cheating on you with you. He found out about your secret life as an exotic dancer, and he started showing up at the club. Then one night he took you to a roadside motel and made love to you like he'd never made love to you before. Only, since it was the you of your secret life, and not the you of your not-secret life, it was like he was cheating on you with your secret you. So you hired your husband, who in his secret life is a not-so-tall private detective, or short dick for short. He cracked the case, so you cracked his cranium. A crime of passion."

She looked at me, then turned the gun on herself.

I got up, took my coat and hat from the coat and hat rack, and went out into the cold night. I needed time. I needed to think. I needed a beer and some wings. Hot wings. Really hot. With bleu cheese and celery. I could deal with her when I got back.

THE CITY. HOME OF EIGHT MILLION SOULS...

WHERE ANYTHING CAN HAPPEN, AND OFTEN DOES...

....AND ANYBODY WHO LETS THEIR GUARD DOWN FOR EVEN A MOMENT....

... MAY FIND HIMSELF A VICTIM OF...

DEAR MERCIFUL GOD!

...THE STUPEFYING CONSPIRACY

A TALE OF TERROR AND ENNUI!

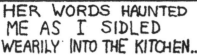
HER WORDS HAUNTED ME AS I SIDLED WEARILY INTO THE KITCHEN...

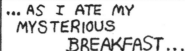
...AS I ATE MY MYSTERIOUS BREAKFAST...

... AND AS I LEFT THE HOUSE, ABSORBED IN THOUGHT.

STAY BEHIND ME UNTIL I CAN SEE THAT THE COAST IS CLEAR

HMM. MY TOAST IS BURNT. WHAT CAN THIS MEAN?

DON'T WORRY DEAR, I'LL BE HOME BEFORE DARK!

CURSE ME FOR A FOOL! I LET MY GUARD DOWN!

... BUT YOU HAVE TO GET UP PRETTY EARLY TO DEFEAT...

...MILTON BEAMISH!!!

KRASH!!

AND SO, EVIL DEFEATED, I WENT ON MY WAY...

UNAWARE THAT EVIL LEAVES A BLOT THAT CAN NEVER BE ERASED...

... AND THAT EVIL, LIKE MOST THINGS, COMES IN MANY FORMS...

YARAAAAA

NEXT: CRUSHED IN THE ELEVATOR OF DEATH!

146

Abducted by a UFO

I had just had a fight with the missus, you hear, and I thought it best to get out of the damn house! So off I went with some Southern Comfort and Duke to the pond 'bout a mile down the road. It was about ten at night and pretty dark if you ask me. Out here in the country we ain't got as much highway lights as you city slickers, but let me tell you, it makes things all the more inviting for them flying saucers.

So I gets me to the crick, and instead of following it all the way down to the pond, I figures I might as well sit myself down and save myself the walk. "This is as good a place as any," I says. So me and Duke settle ourselves down by the crick near this here big field. Then we had ourselves a couple of belts to get the missus off our minds.

Well sir, we was sitting there and suddenly I seen these lights out yonder and I'm thinking to myself, "Now who'd be driving across this field?" At first I thought maybe it was the missus come to fetch me home in our pickup. Then suddenly I remembered all those news stories 'bout them Unified Flying Objects, and boy let me tell you, I almost jumped right out of my pants, 'cept they was overalls. So I took me another belt to settle my nerves. But sure enough, I looked again to that there field and I could see a flying saucer clear as the nose on my face. It was a might bit small for one of them flying saucers you see there on the TV. I'd say it was about the size of a Chevrolet. But it had this flashing red light on the top of it that must of been sending out some kind of message back to outer space. Then the spaceship stopped moving and I thought for sure that flashing red death-ray was going to vaporize me and Duke.

Let me tell you, I ain't never been so scared in my life! I took myself another swig from my bottle to help me get my senses back when all of a sudden Duke starts barking. Now this was not the time for Duke to be barking, that damn dog. I tell you he only barks when you don't want him to be barking. All I needed was them aliens to know I was there by the crick and I'd be done for, and I was sure they'd blast me with that red light beam of theirs.

Well sir, it was too late when I stopped Duke from barking. Those aliens must of heard him because now these doors opened on their spaceship and two of them got out. Now I was shaking like a scarecrow in a windstorm. I seen them coming near from across the field. I remember their blue space suits and them holding some type of laser gun like out of that movie *Star Wars* and wearing some kind of hat with shining metal badges. Then one of them reaches out for me with this gadget that looks like handcuffs, and that's the last thing I can remember. I must of passed out or something and been taken aboard their ship.

When I came to, I was three miles away from that field and my head hurt like someone was pounding away inside my brain. I didn't know how I'd gotten where I was, or what happened to me. And of all things, I was behind bars in the custody of the sheriff, who for the life of him refused to believe my story. He said he'd locked me up for my own protection, but I knew nothing could protect me from those spacemen with their red laser light and those laser guns.

"Where's my dog?" I asked.

"We brought Duke home for you."

The sheriff soon let me go, and I figured I'd best go to a doctor to see if them spacemen had messed with my insides. I've read some on these fellas, and I figured I'd best play it safe. God only knows what they mighta done with me. And I wasn't a bit surprised when the ol' Doc told me my liver's bleeding on the inside. Those aliens must have done some wicked experiments on me, I reckon.

But no one believes my story. Even my wife says I'm mad as hell. But I never believed in them UFOs till I saw one either. Now I'm sure of them. And I'm sure Duke believes 'em too, and I'm sure he would tell you everything I just told you if only he could.

Chapter 6

World Peace and More Beer

Little Known Facts About U.S. Presidents

1. William McKinley was rumored to have walked on all fours.

2. No president could sing, "Stairway to Heaven" quite like Robert Plant, but Herbert Hoover knew the words up to "as we wind on down the road."

3. Ronald Reagan was once asked what he thought of Bush, and he replied that he had always been taught "snatch" was the more polite term.

ear Prime Minister Tony Blair,

Hi, this is the United States of America. We met at a party a few years ago. I was the one over in the corner drinking Coors Light. I was harassing little countries at the time, so we didn't really have much of a chance to talk.

I have a little question to ask you. I see you talking on the TV all the time lately, and I have absolutely fallen in love with you. You have the coolest accent and speak so eloquently and clearly. This may seem a little forward, but would you be my Prime Minister too? I won't be much of a bother; you can still be Prime Minister of Britain, but maybe just see me on the weekends. We wouldn't have to go out anywhere fancy to eat, I'm good with McDonald's.

As for my President at the moment, don't worry about him at all. We don't have to tell him anything. It'll just be our little secret. He's just so dopey and cumbersome when he talks to me . . . it's like he's reading cue cards every time we go out together. He misprounced my name a bunch of times, and there's no bigger mood killer than that.

I just dream about what our life could be like together. Everyone thinks I'm just a big bully, but you could show them that I have a sophisticated side, too. I can just imagine what NATO will think the next time I excuse myself to the "loo" instead of to the "crapper." And imagine the look on the United Nations' faces when I ask for kidney pie instead of fried cheese curds.

Oh, please, Mr. Blair . . . we'd be *soooo* good for each other. You'd teach me about pronouncing vowels and I'd teach you about beer guts. Please say yes, it'd be so super-cool of you. I hope to see you in the hallways at the Big Seven conference next year. I'll be the conglomerate of states in the corner winking in your cute direction ;)

Yours truly,

The United States of America

Do-It-Yourself
Presidential Campaign Kit

Learn to be a presidential contender (or just look like one!)

Are you frustrated by the limited choices in presidential elections? Are you tired of the evasive answers, the character flaws, the hypocrisy, the mudslinging? Or do you want to be a part of it? Either way, this is your golden opportunity! Just fill out the form below and you will not only receive the Presidential Campaign Kit, but if you act now, you can register for the Presidential Sweepstakes!

```
┌ ─ ─ ─ ─ ─ ─ ─ ─ ─ ─ ─ ─ ─ ─ ─ ─ ┐

   Presidential Campaign Kit
         Order Form

     Name _____
     Address _____
     City _____ State _____ Zip _____
     Party (if any)_____Height_____
     Sex (check one): ❏ Male
     Race (check one, optional): ❏ White

     "If I win, I promise to faithfully perform the duties
     of my office and to uphold the Constitution of
     the United States of America."
     Signature_____

     ❏ Yes! Not only do I want to look like a cand-
     idate, I want to be one, too! I've enclosed $35
     million. Sign me up for the Presidential Lottery!

     ❏ No, thank you. I don't want to take advantage
     of this once in a lifetime opportunity to become
     Commander-in-Chief of the Armed Forces. I
     just want the Campaign Kit.

     Odds vary with number of contestants. Victory is not guaranteed.

└ ─ ─ ─ ─ ─ ─ ─ ─ ─ ─ ─ ─ ─ ─ ─ ─ ┘
```

Sample these samples from the Presidential Campaign Kit. Remember, this offer is good for a limited time only!

SMILE! YOU'RE ON NATIONAL TV!

A smile is one of the most versatile tools of any politician. Smiles project optimism and confidence. No one wants to vote for a loser. A smile can convey benign contempt for your opponents, and you can make light of tricky questions without bothering to respond to them. Getting out and "pressing the flesh" is an important (and enjoyable!) part of any campaign. But kissing hands and shaking babies is long, hard work, and your smile might falter. So cut out the smile along the dotted lines, and stick it in place. WARNING: Do not use glue, staples, or nails.

Of course, you won't get far without tons o' cash. Solicit individuals. Talk your wife into doing her duty as a good politician's spouse and get her a 976 number. Promise big corporations anything they want. If that doesn't work, take a dollar bill and photocopy as necessary. Of course, photocopying money is illegal, and you don't want your pretty new campaign spoiled by some ugly ole scandal. On the other hand, if you win, you can pardon yourself.

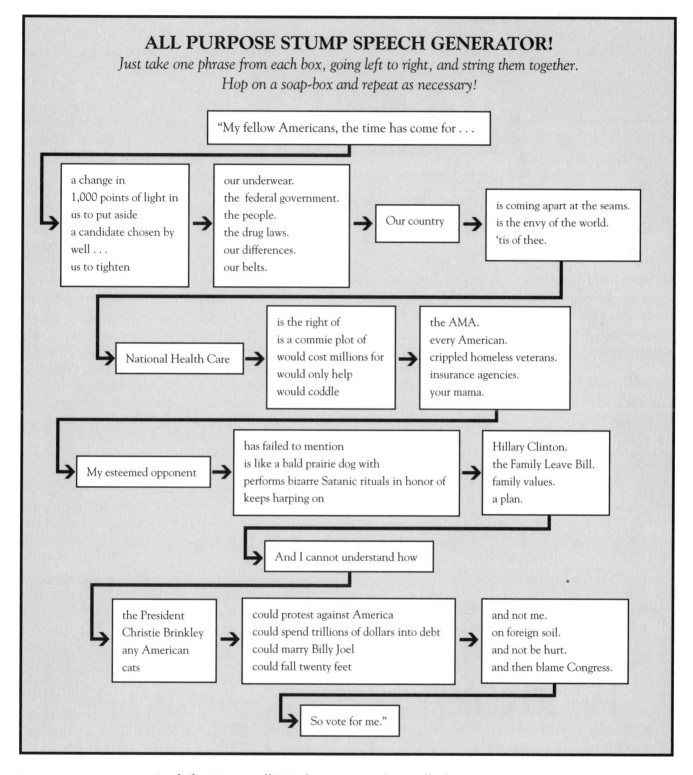

ALL PURPOSE STUMP SPEECH GENERATOR!

Just take one phrase from each box, going left to right, and string them together.
Hop on a soap-box and repeat as necessary!

"My fellow Americans, the time has come for . . .

a change in	our underwear.
1,000 points of light in	the federal government.
us to put aside	the people.
a candidate chosen by	the drug laws.
well . . .	our differences.
us to tighten	our belts.

Our country

is coming apart at the seams.
is the envy of the world.
'tis of thee.

National Health Care

is the right of
is a commie plot of
would cost millions for
would only help
would coddle

the AMA.
every American.
crippled homeless veterans.
insurance agencies.
your mama.

My esteemed opponent

has failed to mention
is like a bald prairie dog with
performs bizarre Satanic rituals in honor of
keeps harping on

Hillary Clinton.
the Family Leave Bill.
family values.
a plan.

And I cannot understand how

the President
Christie Brinkley
any American
cats

could protest against America
could spend trillions of dollars into debt
could marry Billy Joel
could fall twenty feet

and not me.
on foreign soil.
and not be hurt.
and then blame Congress.

So vote for me."

And that's not all! Order now and you'll also receive . . .

- **Prosthetic nose** (or ears or chin). Makes you a living caricature, perfect for cartoonists. Guarantees plenty of media exposure!
- **A book of snappy one-liners!** Always easier than thinking, and certain to get lots of laughs and applause!
- **Emetic.** Eat lots of ethnic foods with your constituents without gaining a single pound!
- **A tragic figure.** Make friends with, or even become related to, someone with a tragic past of cancer, AIDS, persecution, etcetera.

ASK JOE

Your chance to receive heartfelt advice from Joseph Stalin

Dear Joe,

My mom's being a real pain lately. All my friends are allowed to stay out until midnight, but I have to be home at 10:30 p.m., even on Saturday nights! How can I get her to see things my way?

—EARLY BIRD

Dear "Early,"

I suggest executing your mother's allies and then sending her to a forced labor camp. Let me know how things turn out!

—JOE

Dear Joe,

Your advice column sucks. Why don't you get a real job?

—ANONYMOUS

Dear "Anonymous,"

Go to hell, Trotsky! I told you to stop contacting me here.

—JOE

Dear Joe,

The other day my roommate walked in on me while I was masturbating. I tried to play it off, but he knew what I was doing. Even worse, I think he's been telling people about it. Everywhere I go I think people are laughing at me. What should I do?

—CAUGHT RED-HANDED

Dear "Caught,"

You weaken the party and must be eliminated immediately.

—JOE

Dear Joe,

I've been dating this guy, Roger, for a few weeks and I really like him. But last week his best friend, Pete, who I've had a crush on for months, made a pass at me. I'd like to start dating Pete, but I don't want to hurt Roger. What should I do?

—TWO HOT TO HANDLE

Dear "Two,"

You are obviously my kind of woman. Execute Pete and Roger and then make me a sandwich.

—JOE

Dear Joe,

Lately, I've been feeling discontented with the socioeconomic conditions of my country. I've been doing a lot of reading and I feel that I could bring on some radical changes. Most people don't agree with the methods I have been proposing, but I'm sure, in time, I could convince them otherwise. Perhaps through excessive violence. Are my methods too tyrannical to work?

—COMRADE WITH A CAUSE

Dear "Comrade,"

You have a lot to learn about dating. If you think she's cute, well then just ask her out! What have you got to lose?

—JOE

How to Annoy TSA Screeners

■ Wear a T-shirt that says "Security Risk" with an arrow pointing to your crotch.
■ Skip gaily through the metal detector.
■ Insist upon putting yourself through the X-ray machine in order to gain super powers.
■ Declare in a monotone voice that you are, in fact, a weapon.
■ Pop out your glass eye and place it in the tray along with your keys and coins.
■ Ask for the pamphlet that lists prohibited carry-on items, then eat the pamphlet.

 in "Mafia Hit"

In Search of Cheap Eats

You say that even though you are the president of a multimillion dollar conglomerate, you cannot even afford a simple dinner out? Do you find yourself at a restaurant mistakenly assuming the phone number is the fixed price for the evening? We are fed up, so to speak, with eating places that are too expensive for average mortals. So, we began searching for a restaurant where one could exit with one's inheritance intact.

At first, we were going to limit ourselves to finding the perfect ten-dollar meal. But the real challenge was trying to find a place where one may dine lavishly, enjoying wine, an appetizer, and a full dessert for under fifty-nine cents. Naturally, places such as these are not common in a city where one needs a bank loan to check one's hat and coat. We took three months searching for, as they say, "cheap eats." The closest we had come was a Horn & Hardart, where a serviceable creamed chipped beef appetizer and macaroni and ketchup entrée set us back $2.75 in nickels. We felt we could do better. And we did.

We made our discovery at a quaint yet intimate eatery, "Mother Teresa's Lost Souls' Kitchen," near CBGB's in the Bowery. The elegant Italian name reminded us of nights in Florence, drinking vino and listening to the Italian men verbally assault passing women. We were not dismayed by the lack of a hatcheck girl at the entrance; many modern eateries have dispensed with that anachronistic relic of times gone by. We were met, however, by the maître d', Mother Teresa, dressed convincingly in a nun's habit. She asked us if we had come to save our souls. We replied that we didn't think that was necessary because we had phoned ahead to reserve a table. She told us we could not be seated until we had repented our many sins. Not wishing to offend the woman, we proceeded to list our transgressions, omitting only the ones that involved quadrupeds and white powders.

After satisfying the mother, we proceeded to a long table where the patrons were being served family-style, another recent innovation to keep the price of food at a minimum. A note should be made about the habiliments of the patrons. I realize that punk is now a socially acceptable form of dress. Still, one can become quickly jaded after seeing an entire restaurant of so-called "punkers," each dressed more outlandishly than the next. Many were wearing old sport coats that could have been worn by their grandparents and pants cleverly treated to appear stained.

This is not to say the clientele was unfriendly. One of our seatmates, wearing a 1930s-style suit, complete with applesauce stains, offered us his aperitif, a fruity yet somewhat acrid beverage. We were unable to ascertain the name or vintage, as the management had wrapped the bottle in realistic paper-like wrappers, reminiscent of the Riveria in off-season. The consommé was remarkably clear, much in the tradition of Japanese broth, with a similarly ambiguous chicken-fish-vegetable-old-rubber odor and taste. The main course was a goulash of some sort. We repeatedly asked the waiters to tell us the contents of the stew, but we always received a curt "it's good for you, 'tis God's will you eat and repent." Not wishing to mix our dining with a political discussion, we refrained from asking further questions.

The meal was accompanied by an unexpected floor show. Although we usually do not enjoy these trite and childish displays, we were not going to complain to the management. The show involved deadpan humor. A man dressed like so many of my seatmates admitted to all that he had "seen the blessed light of our savior," in a burlesque of piety not seen since Aimee McPherson made her mark in the Thirties. We noticed we were the only individuals in the audience watching; our seatmates apparently were emulating the Spanish custom of taking a siesta in their bowls of soup. As we were wearing black ties and tails, we did not feel it was appropriate to follow their lead.

After the floor show, we were asked to say a couple of words. As we were caught off guard, we retold the story of Noel Coward, who had once visited Nice in the off-season, only to be told that the Coquilles Saint Jacques he had ordered had exploded, killing the entire kitchen staff. With typical Coward aplomb, the great pederast replied, "Very well, I'll have the paté instead." Surprisingly, nobody laughed at this bon mot, which breaks 'em up over at *The New Yorker*.

Mother asked us if we had seen the light. We answered that no, we had given up cigarettes and therefore did not have a light. We felt that the Italianesque "shtick" had been carried a bit too far when we were called sinners and told to confess immediately. We made a mental note not to tip, noticing too that the pastry tray was not in evidence and the coffee had not been made properly in an Italian espresso maker.

The rest of the meal was passable for the fifty-cent cover fee. I did not fully enjoy this latest in so-called "theme" restaurants, but the ownership is new and should be given time to sort out its problems.

Mother Teresa's, open seven days a week, specials on Thanksgiving and Christmas. No credit cards or personal checks. Bleeker and 2nd, New York City.

The birth of Hinduism

BARRY M. ENEMA

The Paper Chase

Lately, many states have been taking concrete action to control the shockingly widespread use of so-called "drugs" by young people. It had been noticed that, while there were harsh penalties for anyone convicted of selling drugs, there were absolutely no statutes to forbid the sale of so-called drug "paraphernalia." Various mechanisms designed for the sole purpose of smoking marijuana—the known narcotic, hallucinogen and corruptor of youth—were being sold quite openly at department stores, pharmacies, and so-called "head shops." This "paraphernalia," including pipes and so-called "bongs," could be loaded with "pot" (marijuana) so that the drug addict could get a few so-called "hits" (successively executed breaths of smoke from marijuana) to achieve a particular state of mind referred to as "fucked up" (stoned).

Various state legislatures soon realized that forbidding the sale of drugs while allowing that of paraphernalia was contradictory, and that the illegalization of such drug paraphernalia might do a great deal to decrease the level of drug addiction and the number of people who are so-called "wasted." For, as repulsive as the analogy may be, just as the leftists would find it ridiculous to illegalize bullets but not guns, so is it absurd to prosecute for the selling of drugs and not for that of paraphernalia.

One of the chief types of paraphernalia used to smoke pot is the so-called "rolling paper," or sometimes just "paper." Made by processing the wood from so-called "trees," these "papers" are rolled around the pot to make a so-called "reefer," which is then smoked like a so-called "cigarette." But when various state governments began forbidding the sale of these "papers," drug addicts began using other types of paper in desperation. Often they would tear pages from so-called "books" and use them in place of "rolling papers." State governments must now take the next step and begin to make illegal the types of books which drug addicts generally use in place of papers, so that the addicts will have no recourse but to give up drugs entirely.

Some of the pages that "druggies" most often use are from copies of Marx's *The Communist Manifesto.* Others that frequently appear are from *Quotations from Chairman Mao* and various works by John Stuart Mill, and there are some addicts who refuse to smoke their pot unless it is rolled in Jack Anderson's column.

We have the drug addicts right where we want them, with their backs against the wall. All we have to do is take the final step. Outlawing paraphernalia is a step in the right direction, but it isn't enough. We must eliminate those books which may be used as a substitute for paraphernalia, either through legislation, or even burning them in large bonfires if we have to. Only then may we finally free our children from the so-called "spectre" of drug addiction.

JAMES J. KILPATRICK

Bussing and Gas Pains

The nation's liberals have been raising their usual ruckus about how school districts are not being integrated speedily enough. As is typical of their ill-directed complaints, they have been totally ignoring the fact that our energy is becoming increasingly scarce. This is obvious from the fact that, in a day when the conservation of oil and gasoline is absolutely vital to America's survival, the leftist loudmouths are still pushing for bussing to achieve integration.

We cannot afford to drive to the beach anymore. We can barely afford to drive ourselves to work. People are forced to establish car pools because we dare not risk losing one more precious drop of gasoline than necessary. Yet there are still some among us who have the gall, the absolute audacity, to not only suggest, but to insist, that we use huge amounts of gasoline to bring children to schools far from their homes in gas-guzzling buses, when they could much more easily walk to a school in their own neighborhood. The idea is so totally unpatriotic that it makes the blood boil.

This leads to the obvious conclusion: These people are not real Americans. They are Communist infiltrators, sent here to destroy our country by depleting our precious resources. They would like to have every child in America bussed to another state, just so they could waste our precious gasoline and thereby bring the entire free world to its knees. If these people had their way, white children living in Maine would be bussed to black schools in California. African-American children in Washington would be bussed to white schools in Florida. And Asian-American children in Hawaii would drown trying to get to Alaska, all to waste our scarce supply of oil and gasoline so that we might be easy prey for the Red Chinese when the time is right.

Well, I for one am not going to let it happen. I'm locking my kid in the basement, and when they come for him in their huge, gas-guzzling big yellow pinko Commie bus, I'm going to load up my Howitzer and start shooting.

God bless America.

Notes & Asides

■ Dear Mr. Buckley:
Recently you quoted General William Sherman as having said, "War is swell." Isn't the correct quote actually, "War is hell?"

Yours sincerely,
Doug MacArthur
Pyongyang, North Korea

Dear Mr. MacArthur: To each his own, Doug, to each his own.

Affectionately, WFB

■ Dear Mr. Buckley:
In a recent issue you stated, "The New York Times are a bunch of nigger-lovers." Since "New York Times" is referring to a singular subject, shouldn't that be "The New York Times *is* a bunch of nigger-lovers?"

Yours truly,
Karl Pearson
Selma, Alabama

Dear Mr. Pearson: Actually it should read, "The *staff* of the New York Times *consists of* a bunch of nigger-lovers."

Sincerely, WFB

■ Dear Mr. Buckley:
I'm in the process of writing a strip about you. How many Cs are there in "fascist"?

Sincerely,
G.B. Trudeau
Doonesbury, USA

Dear Mr. Trudeau: Just enough, thank you.
Cordially, WFB

WM. F. BUCKLEY JR.

A Firing Loon

New York, Oct. 15—I was enjoying my evening constitutional about a fortnight ago when a slovenly youth accosted me and desired to know how I was able to be such a dextral-appendaged anal orifice or, as he expressed it, a "right-wing asshole." Perceiving that he was obviously an unlettered and impecunious laborer, not nearly as refined and scholarly as I am, I disregarded his boorish query and continued my jaunt.

This was not, of course, the first time that someone had questioned my ability to consistently be such an unfeeling reactionary. Indeed, I have encountered opposition from every conceivable quarter. However, I have acquired one simple rule which it would do every conservative well to learn. That is: As long as one has a voluminous vocabulary and acts as if he is erudite and reputable, he will be accorded a fair amount of respect, even if he does not deserve it. Hence, no matter how archaic or injudicious one's political views may be, as long as one presents himself as superior to and more worldly than the person with whom he is conversing, that person will most likely respect his views or, at the very least, fail to understand them.

True, I am a warmongering die-hard, I have immense rancor for all persons of the Negroid persuasion as well as all other minorities, I have no commiseration for those less well-off than myself, and I believe that the Bill of Rights should be incinerated. If I drove a truck, everyone would realize what a simple-minded tightfisted racist, sexist, elitist sleaze-hole I really am. If I worked on a loading dock, Norman Lear could have made a television series about me. But that's not the point. I am not an emaciated member of the proletariat. I am a widely-read, well-known graduate of a prestigious Ivy League university with three best-selling novels and a weekly public television series. Hence, it doesn't matter that my political views are ludicrous and fascist to say the least, or that I would make the average John Bircher look like Mikhail Bakunin. I can say anything I damn well please and people will listen and have respect no matter how stupid my opinions are simply because I am William F. Buckley, Jr., the very astute and renowned columnist, and I don't drive a truck.

I am aware of the evidence that by behaving as I do, I am not able to establish contact with most of the people who would concur with my inclinations. After all, for the average reactionary bigot, an intellectually stimulating evening consists of sitting down with a six-pack and watching *Bowling for Dollars.* But this is the sacrifice I have to make for financial necessity. After all, the average conservative does not read *Irrational Review,* not to mention any of my books, if simply because he barely knows how to read. And Blackford Oakes does not survive on bread alone.

So my options are scarce. I could either relinquish my position as spokesman for all the illiterate and inarticulate reactionaries across the country to whose preposterous political beliefs I attempt to lend some credibility, buy a farm out in Mississippi and join the local Klan, or I can continue in my existing position, trying to outsell *The New Republic* every week. I'm sure all of my loyal readers know what my decision must be.

Hence, when some common ruffian censures me for being such a dextral-appendaged anal orifice, I feel no compunction. For I know that in the great scheme of things, I am still the exalted William F. Buckley, Jr. and he is little more than an inconsequential laborer whose slum I probably own.

And I don't have to drive a truck.

MILTON FRIEDMAN

Let's Stop Wasting Nuclear Waste

As the proliferation of nuclear scare stories accelerates and the supply of oil decreases, many have been uncertain as to how safe and useful nuclear power truly is. One of the biggest unanswered questions is what will be done with the waste produced by nuclear reactors.

Admittedly, all nuclear power plants produce a certain amount of waste, the most lethal type being plutonium. Plutonium remains highly radioactive for about a quarter of a million years and exposure to it can cause headaches, loss of appetite, listlessness, irritability, and, occasionally, prolonged and horribly painful death by cancer. In the past, various methods have been tried to store this waste product, none of which have been effective. Plutonium, unfortunately, eats through every substance known to man, which tends to make long-term storage inconvenient and, at times, a bit messy.

But why, if it is so difficult, should we even bother to store plutonium? Isn't there something else we could do with it? Think about it. What else can plutonium be used for? Right. We can make hydrogen bombs. Not just a few hydrogen bombs, but lots of hydrogen bombs. Because it only takes a small amount of plutonium to make a bomb, and if we have just a few dozen nuclear power plants operating at full capacity across the country, and if we took the enormous amount of waste produced by each one, we could have literally millions and millions of bombs. More bombs for me, more bombs for you. More bombs for America.

But doesn't making bombs from nuclear waste involve reprocessing? And isn't reprocessing and using breeder reactors unsafe? Well, yes, they are somewhat temperamental and they do have a tendency to explode on occasion. So if that's the case, then why even bother making bombs? Think about it. The waste from reactors is dangerous enough as it is. We don't even have to turn it into a bomb. We can just start dropping it on foreign countries. We could start with Iran, then Afghanistan, then on to Russia and eventually China. And all along the way, we would be producing safe, clean energy for America.

Consider the advantages: No energy shortage. No waste problem. Increased industry. An end to foreign rivalries. World peace at last. So next time someone starts complaining about nuclear waste, point out the possibilities. We proved it in Vietnam and we can prove it again! American ingenuity can solve anything.

KILLING THE LIES ABOUT HUNTING

Liberal do-gooders have spent thousands of dollars in the past few years trying to railroad the American public into believing that animals are "cute," hunters are "perverted," and leisure time devoted to pumping round after round of ammunition into everything on four legs is "sick" and "immoral." They tell us hunters we're being "destructive" and bad for the "environment."

As usual, these leftist propagandists wouldn't recognize a fad if it bit them in their Chairman Mao booklets. Everything they say, or ever will say, or ever will consider saying against hunting is a bald and vicious lie, and here are the facts to prove it.

LIE #1: HUNTING IS INHUMANE.

Animals die anyway. Liberals don't realize this, but it's an established fact. The creatures that don't get eaten by their fellow creatures will eventually grow old, wither, and die, just like the rest of us. Why not kill them now instead of later, when they're senile and spend most of their time reminiscing about great droppings of their youth?

LIE #2: HUNTING WIPES OUT VALUABLE SPECIES.

Valuable, my foot. When was the last time you saw somebody bemoan the fate of the passenger pigeon? If you live in New York, probably never. One pigeon looks pretty much the same as another, and if there are any that don't smell bad, they've yet to be found. Since most other animals, like lions and tigers, are well represented in zoos, there's nothing wrong with wiping them out in the wild.

LIE #3: ANIMALS ARE CUTE.

Let's get things straight here. The stewardess who lives in the apartment across the alley from mine is cute. Animals are just plain revolting. They have fleas and they bolt their food and they go to the bathroom in the open where everybody can see them. If you saw such behavior in a human being, you'd be repulsed. But animals act this way all the time, and yet they're depicted as cute cartoon characters and pictured on greeting cards. This is a double standard.

Besides, animals are dangerous. Amoebae cause dysentery and other nasty diseases. Sparrows fly into airplane engines and cause explosive crashes. Rabbits attack United States presidents, and dogs have been known to eat babies if left alone with them after being unfed for a week. In Alaska, a helicopter that had been chasing a wolf for ten miles got too close and crashed, killing both pilots. Even zoo animals have been known to charge passersby who throw firecrackers into their cages.

More people have been killed by animals than by nuclear power plants. But Jane Fonda is against hunting. Is this a conspiracy or what?

LIE #4: HUNTING DAMAGES THE ENVIRONMENT.

The environment sucks. Where would you rather go for your vacation: a foul-smelling, vile swamp, or Disney World? If you're like most thinking people, you'll say Disney World. But environmentalists want us to pass bills preserving what's left of the Everglades.

Besides, liberals don't realize that there are now twice as many deer in the state of Michigan than there were a hundred years ago. To be sure, they're all crowded into two counties, but that makes them easier to spot. When hunting season rolls around, you can shoot them without even leaving your car.

LIE #5: HUNTING IS CRUEL AND SICK.

When environmentalists conjure up the image of a mortally wounded moose trailing its intestines over mile after mile of hilly terrain, they're missing the point. We're not in this to cause pain, but to commune with nature, to return to our roots, to stick an imposing head on our walls where it can collect dust and make our Filipino houseboys actually work for their salaries. That is our purpose. The thrill of bloodshed is secondary.

LIE #6: HUNTERS HAVE A PENIS PROBLEM.

In Chicago, there's a man named Lionel Ferdinand. He's a fairly well-known sculptor who has signed his name to several petitions against hunting. He's also a homosexual. If you look far enough, you can probably find a bunch of other anti-hunting activists who are homosexuals. We don't have any more of a penis problem than they do. I just like to polish my gun a lot, that's all.

So, next time somebody see the heads of several extinct species on your wall and calls you irresponsible, don't acquiesce. Hunters have rights, too!

MEMO

FROM: Archbishop Cantankerous IV
TO: His Holiness, Pope John Paul II

John—

Hey, how's the wife and my kids? Just kidding, dude—but seriously, the church is at a great divide in the road. Now we've been doing things pretty much the same way for the last thousand years, and doing it well. Schism, schmism—we were really humming until this century. Now I don't have to tell you that we're losing ground. But what you may not realize is that religion just isn't what it used to be.

A couple of popes ago we could righteously smite our enemies left and right, which was really great. For a long time, we could do better than just hold our own against the sinful, heathen masses of the world. A little excommunication, a touch of dogma, and, once in a while, a little skullduggery.

But times have definitely changed, and I hate to be the one to tell you this, but we're not up against a couple of communist bastards and inscrutable towelheads any more, and it's only going to get worse. Now we've got to fight what some call "the new priesthood"—the businessman. Doesn't the Bible say in Luke 12:52, "As the Lord could not beat or otherwise whomp them, he sought but to join them?" So, with that particularly obscure snippet of biblical wisdom written on the front of my daily planner, I went out and found a business consultant. I've summarized his recommendations below:

1. Women seem to have equal rights. I know, I know—who told them? Still, young girls (apparently) want role models they can look up to—specifically, female ones. Since they make up fifty percent of our target demographic, a young, hip figure might work a little better than Mary. What we were thinking is that, if we gave Jesus a friend—now, I'm not saying that they should live in sin or anything, but just a girl his age, with a few aspects of divinity. Suggested names include "Christy" or "Christabelle."

2. What do people think when they see a cross? According to polls, the chief sentiment among Americans ages 15 to 24 is less than favorable. Specifically, they think of Jesus as something of a loser. Where's his attitude? Maybe if the crucifix could transform into, you know, one of those Autobots or something. Other ideas include an ammo bandolier on Jesus, or bigger muscles.

3. This relates to point 2 above. Recently, a number of professional sports teams have redesigned their letterheads and merchandise to embrace an "in-your-face" attitude. I had the boys down in Graphic Design come up with a logo (see right)—I think you'll like it. It tested well with almost all demographic groups, excluding little old ladies and college Republicans.

Based on some of our more conservative estimates, were we to adopt these plans, we could see profit growth of up to 73 percent. With that kind of money, we could scrap our plans to open a papal discount gas and cigarette outlet. Anyway, as I am always basking in your eternally benevolent glow of wisdom and mercy, I thank you for your time.

Kisses,

Archie

NIKE VIETNAM PLANT #44FNK

Company Picnic Is Huge Success!!!

Thousands of enthusiastic workers piled into the Hanoi factory last weekend for the 1000th weekly Nike Company Picnic. Those who attended participated in such entertaining pastimes as sewing garments, manufacturing shoes, and bleeding. Suk Mei Kwok summed up the weekend's events when she said, "[I'm having so much fun that] I can't feel my fingers."

Company Retirement Plan May Be Best Option!!!!!

Recent market studies have shown that the company's 401k investment plan may be your best option in terms of overall long-term gains. Says company financial analyst Mark Peterson, "If a worker deposits the 25-cent maximum into the account each week, he or she can expect an average return of 20 percent per annum on their investment, while, mutual funds would only average a return of 15 percent. It's almost like making an extra cent every week. That can shift you a whole tax bracket." Peterson declined to make an exact estimate of the projected increase, conjecturing that, with luck, it may be as large as ten dollars over the course of a career. He then laughed jovially and resumed calculating his stock options.

New Company Plan to Build Off Previous Success!!!!!!!

In light of the incredible success of the last 1,462 consecutive "Bring Your Child to Work Days," Monday will witness the inception of a new program: "Bring Your Parents to Work Day." Andrew Scheffler, Vice President of Human Resources, expressed high hopes for the new project. "Some workers, most notably those who were married to each other, would claim the same set of kids. That really cut into participation, but everyone has two parents."

Just Say Wen!

The employee of the month is Wen Fey Chu, in recognition of his perfect attendance despite tuberculosis. Wen will receive the coveted Three-Hole Punch of Quality. The award will be of absolutely no use to Wen, who can not afford paper. Next time you see him, give him a hearty slap on the back. Besides making a human connection, you'll clear out some phlegm.

Spotlight on Success!!!!!!!!!!!!!!!!!

This year's winner of the Nike Achiever scholarship is Doh Hoi Lee, age seven. The lucky youngster will receive a one-year sabbatical during which Nike will pay for his elementary schooling. Doh demonstrated his high intelligence by conforming to our every regulation and whim, and by scoring high on the rigorous SAT (Shoe Aptitude Test).

YOUNG. PROUD. DUMB. LOUD.

You've heard about the Army. The short sentences. The large type. The long marches. The denial of personal freedom. Defending American corporate interests. Exploiting foreign nations. You've heard it, and most of it is true. But there's a lot you never hear. And since the draft may soon be reinstated, we'd like to tell you more about what we're all about.

SKILLS

Most soldiers in today's army are uneducated low-income African-Americans and Hispanics. They joined because they don't have the skills necessary to find employment in the real world. And the Army is a much easier out than a hundred-dollar-a-day habit.

TRAVEL

You can serve almost anywhere in the world. Afghanistan. Kabul. The Persian Gulf. Or just about anywhere between Iran and Pakistan.

EDUCATION

Sure, the money spent on a B-1 bomber could finance the New York City school system for three years. But which would you rather have protecting this country's vital interests? A Lockheed fighter plane or two hundred thousand educated hoodlums?

FREE TIME

Most of a soldier's time is spent trying to erase any sign of free thought. That's why we have officers. Soldiers patrol the Mideast, protecting Exxon Mobil. And Chevron Texaco. And Shell. Oh, and Gulf. Big Oil's investments run into the billions. They own America and they own your time.

PAY & BENEFITS

You earn the satisfaction of keeping the Russians out of the Mideast's oil fields. So Americans can drive

their Hummers and SUVs to work. So the board of directors of Exxon Mobil will be happy. To stop the threat of solar energy from ever becoming a reality in America.

PEOPLE

Keep telling yourself. They were only gooks. Not God-fearing Americans. They bred filth and would kill for a bowl of rice. Keep telling yourself. They are only Iraqis. Sleazy towelheads who . . .

TODAY'S ARMY.
JOIN THE PEOPLE WHO DEFEND BIG OIL.

The Man on the Street Asks:

"If you could have lunch with any two people from history, who would they be?"

Winston Churchill:
"Definitely Jesus and Einstein."

Franklin D. Roosevelt:
"Jesus. And Einstein."

Thomas Jefferson:
"Harriet Tubman and . . . her sister."

Rasputin:
"I would have to go with Jesus. Jesus and Einstein."

Martin Luther:
"The ditzy blond on *Friends* and Clara Barton."

Genghis Khan:
"Two bisexual infidels."

Jesus and Einstein:
"Anyone, so long as it's not at Applebee's. We are so sick of that place."

Modern Tourism Slogans

Thailand: "Not that you want to have sex with kids or anything, but it's still nice to know the option's there."

China: "Take a vacation from your basic freedoms."

Uganda: "If you lived here, you'd be homeless by now."

Ethiopia: "Time to get serious with that diet, chubs."

Afghanistan: "At least you won't be in Sierra Leone."

Sierra Leone: "At least you won't be in—oh, fuck."

Cuba: "Come vist the world's largest exporter of makeshift rafts."

The All-New Improved Ten Commandments

1. Thou shalt not drink God's special wine in the brown bottle.
2. Thou shalt not covet thy neighbor's wife—unless she's really hot.
3. The red zone is for loading and unloading only.
4. There are no bathrooms in heaven, so you better go before you get here.
5. From now on, monkeys are your superiors.
6. Remember the Alamo.
7. Thou shalt not wear a brown belt with black shoes.
8. You smelt it, you dealt it.
9. Penguins don't like nuts.
10. This tablet should not be used as a life-saving floatation device.

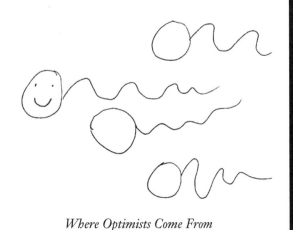

Where Optimists Come From

The Continuing Adventures of Klip-Art Karl Marx

This is Karl Marx. He is the father of Communism. This is his igloo, located in the heart of the "Pooper Scooper" Zone.

"Hello, Karl! You better hurry up, you don't want to be late for Frankenstein's Bar Mitzvah!" "Thanks, Cowhead!"

"Get away from my tiny cattle!" yells former President Teddy Roosevelt. "I was only taking a short cut through your animal-shrinking asylum," says Karl. The pig and sheep discuss.

"Are you going to the Bar Mitzvah, too, Crazy Surgeon?" asks Karl. "No, Karl, I've got to perform stomach surgery!" The stomach looks upset.

Before Karl can go to Frankenstein's Bar Mitzvah in the Taj Mahal, he must first defeat this army of bugs. "I sure hope they save me some blintzes!"

"Am I late?" asks Karl. "No," says Klip-Art Lenin, "Frankenstein is about to cut the Bar Mitzvah cake!" And he did.

Technology Schmechnology

It has recently come to my attention that our precious world is currently entangled in processes known as "modernization," or "globalization," or one of many other buzzwords, including "technologization." You need not interpret this editorial as the drunken ramblings of a very stoned man. I'm sure that by the end of this editorial, you will be either convinced that technology is a disturbing, unnecessary trend, or you will want to meet me to make sure that both of my testicles have descended. Either way, I'm satisfied.

First of all, there's those computers I'm hearing all the movie stars talk about. Are they really that necessary? Word processing programs can be cold, confusing, and boring. What happened to the days when a threatening message could be neatly scratched into my forehead or my bedroom door by an angry relative with a switchblade?

And this new internet that's coming to dominate our lives—well, I do agree that so much wonderful porn could not be available for a more deserving generation, but erotic pictures of children can always be easily obtained from my father's woodshed or in those many holes he digs behind the garage at 4 a.m.

How about these movie special effects? Truly terrifying indeed. Sure, they've brought to life exciting make-believe worlds like "galaxies far away," "Middle-earth," and "Nazi Germany," but wake up, people! We're living in a fantasy world and distorting our sense of reality. Do you want to keep having dreams about hobbits licking cookie crumbs off your chest and waking up with your hand down your roommate's pants? Most of the civilized world and many of my old roommates would reply with an emphatic "No!"

Let's not forget these new advances in weaponry. Yeah, I admit, the semi-automatics popping up on the market have greatly increased my desire to creep around the bushes at night in front of the homes of those who made fun of me in high school. But high-tech weaponry just should not be in the hands of certain people (i.e., the police, children ages 5 to 7, and my mother after she's had a few drinks at a family wedding). How many more of my annoying high school classmates must continue to turn up dead in the storm drain behind my house?

And let's also be careful about who gets their hands on nuclear weapons. If we keeping poking fun at India and Pakistan, watch them detonate one of those bad boys on American soil! C'mon, those people don't really smell like horse manure. And forget about Iraq! I have overwhelming evidence that the Vatican has been experimenting with a terrifying biochemical force known as "Christianity." If they pack a vial of that stuff into a long-range missile, they could take out the whole eastern seaboard.

Well, I know you're probably thinking "mmm . . . this is a delicious editorial" and "we should probably stop reading this guy's stuff so he can leave town for a few days, find a nice quite place in the woods and rethink his life."

Perhaps I've been a bit too negative. Yeah, now that I've had a few shots of Stalingrad Vodka and have visions of sugarplum fairies in my head, I should acknowledge the positive contributions technology has made to human society. I guess those would have to be the ground-breaking advances in medicine, the kind that have had me laughing at such television shows as *M*A*S*H*, *Scrubs*, and *Real Life Stories of the Highway Patrol*.

What a golden age we live in! In what other time could a man happily comb away life's biting little problems from his pubic hair or find the help he needs for that annoying little addiction to the smell of his grandmother's shoes? Not when those damn Whigs were running the country, I can tell you that. And what a glorious time to be alive for an unlicensed surgeon hoarding medicine supplies! When that smallpox outbreak occurs (April 18th on the Williamsburg bridge, according my sources), who's gonna be the one with all the vaccine stored in the basement? Not you!

SUMMIT MEETING

INCAR: International Committee Against Reason

Every moment, the cold iron jaws of the steel net of racist imperialist capitalist ruling-class tyranny tighten a bit further. The conspiracy of the world ruling class, masterminded jointly by expert planners in the White House and the Kremlin, continues to progress through the actions of governments, which, no matter how stupid, inane, or useless they may seem, are all more carefully planned cogs in the vast wheel of another brick in the wall of another piece of dust in the wind of ruling-class racist imperialist capitalism. Black groups, women's groups, anti-nuke groups, the NRA, and other so-called protest organizations only concern themselves with their own narrow special interests. They are only attacking the tip of the problem rather than the root of the iceberg. These groups will accomplish nothing as long as they only care about their own specific interests without applying them to our own cause: stamping out capitalist ruling-class racist imperialist oppression. WHO ARE "WE"? We are INCAR, a non-profit incorporation of workers and students, who are dedicated to solving all the world's problems through the use of slogans and leaflets filled with stirring rhetoric.

There are many groups fighting for racial equality. The NAACP and others have worked for years and accomplished nothing. We realize that racial equality is an unobtainable and possibly undesirable goal. Affirmative action and desegregation are only attempts to indoctrinate minorities into imperialist capitalist ruling-class racist values. INCAR contends that minority rights are unimportant. Races have to cooperate for only one over-riding cause: smashing imperialist racist ruling-class capitalist oppression.

Environmentalists and anti-nuke types are up in arms against nuclear power. Instead of worrying about thermal pollution and nuclear waste dis-posal, these bourgeois groups should concentrate on the true issue: protesting capitalist imperialist racist ruling-class oppression of proletariat uranium 238 atoms. INCAR has long advocated the use of renewable alternative decen-tralized clean sources of energy, in order to take control away from the imperialist ruling-class racist capitalist oil companies. However, as soon as these alternative methods become feasible, the capitalist imperialist racist capitalist imperialist ruling-class racists will move in and take them over. The only way to prevent the oppression of plutonium, the sun, the tides, the wind, and geothermal properties through the abandonment of all energy production. If workers and students are as wasteful as possible, we can then use up all oil reserves in less than twenty years, thereby ridding ourselves of ruling-class capitalist racist imperialist energy monopoly tyranny.

Feminists campaign for equal rights and control over their own bodies. They do not realize that birth control and abortions are insipid parts of the vast imperialist ruling-class capitalist imperialist plot to eliminate all opposition from workers and students. Notice how Planned Parenthood and other birth-control advocates devote most of their education efforts to the poor ghetto areas. Under the devious cover of providing a useful service, they are attempting to reduce the population of the oppressed lower class proletariat. INCAR needs as large a force of workers and students as possible to smash capitalist ruling-imperialist racist-class oppression.

INCAR can cover this wide variety of issues, because we are broad-minded workers and students who realize the futility of lobbying or taking direct protest action for any particular idea. While right now we're really mostly students, more workers are being won over to our cause every minute. Help INCAR recruit oppressed university proletariat. Help us to politicize the cafeteria workers so that they will read our pamphlets instead of wrapping sandwiches in them. Help us put a stop to the brainwashing of workers by their racist capitalist imperialist ruling-class employers. Help INCAR unite students and workers to smash racist imperialist capitalist ruling-class oppres-sion. Attend our rally each and every Friday in front of the Student Union. Be there. Aloha.

—INCAR, Inc.

The George W. Bush Joke Liquidation Sale!

Everything Must Go!

After Congress passed a bill raising emission standards for automobiles, President Bush was talking with Vice President Cheney about what he should do. He didn't want to sign legislation that would hurt Big Oil. Cheney said, "You should use your veto." To which President Bush replied, "Vito? But I don't know any Italians!"

Regular Ol' Joke

Q: How do you get Bush to agree to abortions?
A: Call them "preemptive strikes."

George W. Bush's Pick-up Lines

"If you think I'm screwing you with my tax plan, imagine what I could do with the rest of my body!"

"There are two ways we can do this: you can have sex with me, or my dad can get you to have sex with me. Why not just cut out the middle man?"

"You're the only woman I want to drill more than the Arctic National Wildlife Reserve."

One day President Bush visited the Senate to see how close his next tax bill was to being passed. When he asked Ted Kennedy and Hillary Clinton, Ted said, "Mr. President, this tax plan will kill Social Security and other vital social programs. We're planning to filibuster." Bush looked shocked. He gestured at Hillary and said, "Filibuster? I barely know her!"

Nickname for Bush's Squad in the Texas Air National Guard
Milwaukee's Best

Ted Kennedy's Stand Up Comic Routine

Signposts on the Road to Armageddon

An Excerpt From the Private Journal of the Last Man on Earth

By the end of the year 2045, the entire world was in flames. Seven billion people were dead, three billion people were literally missing, and one billion were members of the Republican party. Plague and pestilence were rampant. Civilization was conspicuously absent from the face of the planet. The promoters quite rightly vowed never to hold a Woodstock Revival again.

But by the end of the year 2063, humanity was practically extinct.

What happened during those eighteen years? What mistakes were made? How did the foundation of peace and joy and brotherhood give way to the endless damnation of nuclear holocaust?

Who cares? I certainly don't. And after all, I'm the only one who matters. No, I mean it. I'm tired of this. Do you know what it's like to be the last man on earth? To write these articles, send them to my editor (who happens to be me), ring for the copy boy (me) to carry them to the printer (me), sell them at a buck a shot to anybody who happens to have a subscription (me)? To write letters to the editor, answer them, cancel my subscription in rage, and start other magazines in protest? To go on strike and then cross your own picket line? Do you know what it's like to photograph the centerfold when the last woman on earth is in a coma? Of course you do; you're me. Then why the hell are you writing this? For the sake of posterity! Bullshit! Stop bitching! No, Goddamn it! Come to your senses, man!

Where was I, anyway? Yeah. Right. The End of the World. I guess you could say it started when "Thug Rock," a new form of pop music advocating disembowelment and suede, placed six songs (including "Charles Manson, Superstar," "A Crazy Little Thing Called Torture," "I Wanna Burn Your Hand," and "She's Always a Victim to Me") among the top ten. Or when the United Nations decided all resolutions would take the form of ethnic jokes. Or when Manhattan was officially designated a borough of Beijing. By December 2nd, 2063, it was obvious to even the most optimistic that humanity would be extinct before the end of the week.

(It's raining heavily outside. That's stupid. Why should it rain when there are no tennis games to interrupt? Why should there be lightning when there's no TV reception to interfere with? Why? Why? The thunder offers no answers. My typewriter offers no answers. Even Cheryl, who lies yonder, beautiful, sensuous, and comatose in her iron lung offers no answers. I can only ponder these mysteries, and know that eventually I will pay the price, because I'm the one that has to read this drivel.)

I remember how people took the news. There was crying and screaming in the streets. Folks jumped out windows. Life insurance companies cancelled their advertising campaigns. A dear friend of mine moved to Buffalo, so he wouldn't notice the end when it came.

I can't tell you what the end was like, since I overslept that morning. But when I got up, the streets were empty, and all the newsstands were closed, and the only sign of life in the whole damn city was the moving headline on the Times Building telling me that the bottom fell out of the Stock Exchange.

What have I learned from this? I don't know. A great philosopher could glean eternal wisdom from this catastrophe, splicing together corollaries about love and war and courage and nausea and man's inhumanity to man. He could write about the nature of good and evil and how God gently weeps over the bodies of his children. I don't know. I have to take a leak.

Yes, but will it strike fear into the heart of the enemy?

Jerry Buttwater's proposal for a new program house on campus—

Chicks That Dig Jerry Buttwater Program House

Whereas I am a minority, being the only Jerry Buttwater on campus, and

Whereas Cornell University has had a history of neglecting Jerry Buttwater, specifically by not admitting chicks who like Jerry Buttwater, and by not creating and maintaining an environment that allows chicks who like Jerry Buttwater to feel comfortable with their feelings towards Jerry Buttwater, and

Whereas Cornell University has actively persecuted Jerry Buttwater by admitting only chicks who scoff at him and enjoy kicking him repeatedly in the shin,

I, Jerry Buttwater, do hereby propose the erection of The Chicks That Dig Jerry Buttwater Program House.

The University-sanctioned persecution of Jerry Buttwater has gone on far too long. The creation of the Buttwater House would provide an environment that would make chicks comfortable with their love of Jerry Buttwater and, possibly, their desire to show him their breasts. Some of the proposed programs are as follows:
   • Weekly house "meetings" where chicks can discuss Jerry Buttwater.
   • The *Buttwater Quarterly*, a University-funded magazine dedicated to the lifestyle of Jerry
      Buttwater on campus.
   • 24-hour hotline to provide advice and answers to those chicks who are unsure or confused
      about their feelings for Jerry Buttwater.

Furthermore, as the University has repeatedly proven itself to be insensitive to the academic needs of Jerry Buttwater, by directing him to enroll in classes taught only by professors who dislike Jerry Buttwater and insist upon giving him bad grades, I hereby propose that a special curriculum be established so that students can learn more about the history of Jerry Buttwater, with the ultimate aim of establishing a Jerry Buttwater Studies department with a major and/or minor in Jerry Buttwater's history. Not only will this new curriculum enable students to learn more about the history and culture of Jerry Buttwater, but it will also enable him to learn in an environment that is not biased by the University's conception of Jerry Buttwater, thus helping to undo three semesters worth of oppression by University officials and professors, by inflating his Grade Point Average (GPA).

Signed this Fifth day of March,

Jerry C. Buttwater

Jerry Charlton Buttwater

How to Fake Time Travel

Like most good things in life—jet-packs, flying cars, silver jumpsuits—time travel will only be accomplished by Joe Sixpack in science fiction. Still, even the most washed-up, no-good loser (e.g., you) can reap many benefits by doing the next best thing: faking it.

But How?

Find a closet with a working light in your house. Begin to tell people it's your Time Machine. Placing a sign on the door often helps the illusion. When you want to "time travel"—perhaps to spice up a boring dinner party?—simply yell "Into the Fourth Dimension!" and run into the closet. Once inside, flip the lights on and off repeatedly (mess up your hair and unbutton your shirt for added effect). Stumble out of the closet after a minute or two, and regale your guests with tales of the Ming Dynasty.

But Why?

There are many potential benefits to fake time travel. We've compiled a few examples of how you can use it to enrich your life, but the possibilities are endless:

Win Arguments!

FAKE TIME TRAVELER: I said Manhattan has the most cocaine per square prep school, not Boston!

FRIEND: You totally said Boston.

FAKE TIME TRAVELER: Oh yeah? Well there's only one way to settle this! Time traveler, awaaaaaaay! *[He runs into his "laboratory," flips lights on and off, and emerges moments later.]*

FRIEND: T-t-t-t-time travel?!

FAKE TIME TRAVELER: I just went back in time to last week, when I made the statement in question. Not only did I say "Manhattan," but you borrowed eighty dollars from me right after I said so.

Friend *[shrugs, reaches for his wallet]*: Well, you're the time traveler.

Get Out of Trouble!

WIFE: I've asked you five times today to fix the garage door! What have you been doing all day?

FAKE TIME TRAVELER: I've been time traveling. Surfing the temporal waves, if you will.

WIFE: And?

FAKE TIME TRAVELER: I went twenty years in the future to see what our life would be like. We finally redid the kitchen, and you look just as beautiful then as you do now.

WIFE: I absolve you of all sins.

Screw with People!

FAKE TIME TRAVELER *[runs up to man and begins to shake him]*: What year is it!?

MAN: Why, it's 2008, my good sir.

FAKE TIME TRAVELER: 2008! 2008! Excellent! There's still time! *[He runs away.]*

Make a Buck or Two!

FAKE TIME TRAVELER *[holding out a handful of Canadian pennies]*: These are miniature Killer robots from the year 2140. They pretty much rule the world, and they're a steal at twenty bucks a pop.

BOY: How come they don't move at all?

FAKE TIME TRAVELER: They're in hibernation mode right now. That's how they conserve energy when they're not killing things.

BOY: What do they kill?

FAKE TIME TRAVELER: Little boys who ask too many questions.

BOY: Okay, I'll buy some, but all I have is this stack of signed blank checks from my dad's desk.

But What Should I Do If People Ask Me What the Past or Future Is Really Like?

Here are a few rules of thumb to follow when describing other historical periods to skeptical friends:

1. When talking about a male historical figure, mention that he's a ding-a-ling. Also, say that he smelled worse than historians would have you believe.

2. When describing a historical event, simply say it looks a lot cooler on the commemorative stamp.

3. When asked about the future, smile cryptically and remark, "Oh, you'll see!"

So you see, fake time travel is just as good, if not better (okay, probably not better) than regular time travel, and you don't need millions of dollars or extensive knowledge of the Van Damm movie *Time Cop* to use it. Fake time travel just plain works, whoever you are . . . or *when*-ever you are!

Great Moments from the GREAT DEPRESSION

1933: Hollywood announces the release of *King Kong*. Confusing the movie for the actual beast, the French government diverts all of its spending away from National Defense and toward the incineration of its zoos and destruction of the Eiffel Tower.

1933: To boost his New Deal programs, Franklin Roosevelt borrows the abbreviation of his favorite Nashville strip club, the Tennessee Vagina Authority, for one of his famous work programs.

1934: The first moron dies of glue poisoning after eating his food stamps.

1935: Responding to Louisiana Governor Huey Long's calls for the redistribution of wealth, assassin Carl Weiss attempts to evenly distribute bullets amongst Long's vital organs.

1936: The prequel to *It's a Wonderful Life*, appropriately titled *Gee Whiz, Life Sure Does Suck Lately*, bombs at the box office, because no one has any money to go to the movies.

1937: Everyone inexplicably wins the lottery on the same day, temporarily ending the Great Depression, which resumes the next day when everyone realizes that they misplaced their winnings during a drunken celebration.

1939: In an exhibition of military might, Hitler invades the moon, but nobody notices amongst all the chaos of his invading the rest of Europe.

1940: In a stunning display of muckraking journalism, *The London Times* reveals to the public that Winston Churchill is neither a church nor a hill, let alone a hill upon which a church sits. The scandal goes unnoticed, perhaps due to the intense German bombing of Britain at the time.

1945: The Great Depression ends. Everyone is sad and disappointed, because it was so great.

Lesser Known New Deal Agencies

Time Travel Administration (TTA): Massive government investment in time-travel technology, with the aim of traveling back to the twenties and preventing the Depression from happening in the first place. After several unsuccessful tries, the program eventually settled on the design of one Professor Simeon B. Finsterwankel. Unfortunately, his machine was improperly calibrated and he ended up traveling back several centuries too many, where he accidentally killed off the unicorn.

War On Dust (WOD): Brief attempt to combat the Dust Bowl by firing machine guns at tornadoes. Discontinued one week later after the deaths of three cows in the Oklahoma panhandle.

Muckraking Progress Administration (MPA): Attempt to find employment for the many destitute investigative journalists hanging around Washington, D.C., by letting them dig for dirt around the White House and the Capitol (literal dirt, not corruption), which kept them from finding out that the president was a cripple.

Guatemala Incorporation Administration (GIA): An organization devoted to studying the possibility of invading Guatemala and annexing it to the U.S. to plunder its vast natural resources and thereby pull the country out of the Depression. Scrapped when it was discovered that Guatemala doesn't actually have vast natural resources.

Jewish Security Administration (JSA): A plan to invest government money in the Worldwide Jewish Conspiracy to take advantage of usurious interest rates in both gold and pounds of flesh. Abandoned after objections from Hitler.

Alphabet Soup Coordination Committee (ASCC): Crack team of unemployed lexicographers tasked with collecting and organizing all the acronyms for the various New Deal agencies, then processing them into soup to be handed out to the poor.

JAWS 5
The Musical

Chapter 7

Making the World Safe for Styrofoam

Conspiracy Facts

1. The only way to block the CIA transmitter in your crotch is to wrap yourself with tin foil.

2. The membership of the New World Order is comprised exclusively of guys named Frank.

3. The alien technology captured at Roswell, New Mexico, in 1948 was used exclusively in the design of the paragon of automobiles: the Ford Pinto.

4. On the back of the one-dollar bill is a Masonic pyramid and an inscription in Latin. The text is translated as "Good for one free smoothie at participating lodges."

5. There are over 3,427 Radio Frequency Identification tags embedded in the pages of this book, all of which transmit information about your whereabouts and perverted lifestyle.

ggy the insurance salesman was very depressed. Most of his coworkers assumed Iggy was depressed because he had lost his arms in battle. But no, that wasn't the reason at all. Iggy was depressed because network execs had canceled his favorite prime-time television show, *The Honeymooners*, ten years before was born. Now he would never be able to watch an episode aired for the first time ever.

He would walk down the hall to his office with his head down and the sleeves of his dress shirt drooping at his side, since they had no arms in them. Most of his colleagues felt guilty about giving him work. When the boss would finally get fed up and say, "Well, if he's not going to do any work, what's the point of giving him a paycheck every week?" his secretary would say, "Hal, how can you send a poor, armless old vet out on the streets? Have you no heart?" The boss would then reply, "Goddamn it, Judy! You've worked here for three years, and you still can't remember that my name is Jonathan!" Judy would then say, "Sorry, Hal," sending her boss into a frenzy that usually ended with him hiring a prostitute in broad daylight and getting busted by a vice cop. "Poor Hal," his subordinates would say as they watched him get led handcuffed into a squad car yet again. "Yeah, but at least he doesn't have it as bad as Iggy."

The thing was: Iggy hadn't lost his arms in battle at all. He was simply so depressed about *The Honeymooners* being canceled before he was born that he would pull his arms up through his sleeves and hide them under the torso of his dress shirt. Amazingly, no one discovered this during the thirteen years Iggy worked at the insurance company—until his going away party. Everyone at the office pitched in to buy him the complete DVD set of *The Honeymooners*, mostly because they felt bad for him for losing his arms in battle. He thanked them kindly, slid his arms back out through his sleeves, picked up *The Honeymooners* DVD set, and left—as happy as a clam.

Memorandum

TO: Gordon Kepplehaus, President, United Paramount Network
FROM: Stanley Allbright, Screenwriter

Mr. Kepplehaus,

I understand that you have been soliciting programming for the fledgling United Paramount Network. I have a proposal. It is a situational comedy entitled *That Crazy Monkey . . . That Crazy Robot,* a show about Cobi, a super-intelligent and adorable chimpanzee who is a little "bananas," and his cybernetic companion, CHIP 2000 (note the pun inherent in CHIP's name). This show would be a sort of cross between *Every Which Way But Loose* and *Short Circuit.* It would chronicle the trials and tribulations of a monkey and a robot living together in downtown Manhattan. Cobi's zany, inimitable, antic disposition would provide a hilarious foil to CHIP's down-to-earth, responsible canniness. Unfortunately, Cobi, being a great ape, would have to communicate entirely in American Sign Language—with closed captioning provided—but that is an obstacle easily overcome. I have already outlined part of the first season below:

Pilot Episode: Cobi and CHIP's First Meeting. Cobi, a male chimpanzee living in a penthouse apartment in New York City, returns from a day of work as a cab driver. Upon his entrance, the audience gets a great kick out of Cobi wearing a miniature business suit, pouring himself a snifter of brandy, and smoking a cigar—just like a little person! Through a madcap misunderstanding between the milkman and the Prussian housekeeper, we learn that Cobi is lonely. While paging through a magazine (get a mental picture of it, Mr. Kepplehaus—a chimp reading a magazine! *Hoo-ee!*) Cobi finds an ad for a mail-order robot. He sends away, and in a week the robot arrives—and he is more than Cobi bargained for! At the end of the episode, Cobi is about to send CHIP 2000 back to the manufacturer, but CHIP melts Cobi's (and the audience's) heart by saying: "You are my only friend." Cobi keeps CHIP, and the two become roommates, setting the stage for a season of high-voltage hilarity!

Episode One: Cobi Goes Bananas. Late at night, Cobi brings a date back to the apartment (I would like to get Laura Dern, if at all possible, to play the girl). CHIP spoils the mood by coming into the room and cleaning up after the couple in the middle of an intimate moment. Cobi becomes angry, and an *Odd Couple*-esque argument ensues. CHIP has his bags packed and is about to leave forever when Cobi stops him with a heartwarming entreaty, signing "I love you." CHIP replies, "What is this love? This love is strange." The two embrace, albeit awkwardly, and the show ends with a freeze-frame on the tender tableau.

Episode Three: Double Trouble! Cobi has made two dates for the same night! He persuades CHIP to dress up in a makeshift chimpanzee costume and take one girl (I'm writing the part with Winona Ryder in mind) out while Cobi himself takes out the other girl (played, I hope, by Courtney Cox). Wouldn't you know it—they take the girls to the same restaurant! This proves to be a "hairy" situation. At the end of this comedy of errors, CHIP's date kisses him goodnight. CHIP dashes about madly, steam pouring from his neck, repeating: "Does not compute! Does not compute!" I'd like to work a guest appearance by Gene Hackman in there somewhere.

That Crazy Monkey . . . That Crazy Robot is bound to be an "animal house of comic hijinx," guaranteed to make the audience "blow a fuse" laughing. Please.

Sincerely,

Stanley
Stanley

Incorporated by Me
*Proud Members of
Blockbuster Video*

The Cornell Monkey Bum

Today's Forecast
*Armageddon followed
by intermittent rain*

"Ten Thousand Monkeys Chained to a Typewriter"

Buttwater Leads Takeover of Willard Straight Hall; University in Chaos

ITHACA, New York (AP)—Cornell University was plunged into chaos yesterday when Jerry Buttwater, a member of the Jerry Buttwater Liberation Army (JBLA), led a one-man takeover of Willard Straight Hall.

Buttwater's list of demands reportedly includes plans for both a University-funded program house and curriculum, based on the teaching and principles of Jerry Buttwaterism.

"The University has heard my demands," yelled Buttwater from the second-story window, waving the moldy lump of Muenster cheese that he had used to force

his way into the building, "and I will not rest until there is justice for Jerry Buttwater. Long live the JBLA!" Buttwater's takeover is eerily reminiscent of the black student takeover of Willard Straight in 1969, when armed students barricaded themselves inside the building until University officials agreed to give in to their demands.

"Well, it looks like we're in quite a bind here," said visibly shaken University President Hunter Rawlings III. "The precedent has been set—it looks like we're going to have to give Mr. Buttwater what he wants. Curse him and his moldy cheese!"

Adorable "Hang In There" Kitten Plunges to Grisly Death

MIAMI, Florida (AP)—Cuddly, limpid-eyed Whiskers Henderson, the star of the popular line of posters featuring the aforementioned kitten hanging precariously by the front claws from a tree limb above the spunky caption, "Hang in There!" met a gruesome fate yesterday when she lost her tenuous hold on the branch and dropped forty feet into a pit of starving alligators. The tragic incident occurred at Nusbaum Studios where photographer, Ernest Nusbaum, was shooting Whiskers for a limited edition collector's rerelease of the hugely successful poster.

Said Nusbaum, "In order to create the exact mix of surprise and bewilderment on Whiskers' adorable face, I found it necessary to suspend her forty feet above a

pit of alligators. My understanding was that Whiskers was okay with this measure. She was always very professional, always willing to do whatever was required of her to make a shot happen." Nusbaum plans to dedicate his next line of posters—which will feature a family of dogs in a car with the caption, "Are We There Yet?"—to the memory of Whiskers.

Marcy Feltyburger, Whiskers' groomer and handler, eulogized her beloved former associate thusly: "Whiskers' life on this earth may be at an end, but her message of courage and stoicism which has provided inspiration in so many workplaces across America, will live on."

In a related story, Bobo Feldman, the chimpanzee famed for his "You Don't Have To Be Crazy To Work Here, But It Helps!" poster, ran amok on the set of a photo shoot in Los Angeles, killing thirteen. Feldman is currently being held pending a hearing on his fitness to stand trial.

Mathematician Upset by *Matrix*'s Lack of Matrices

CAMBRIDGE, Massachusetts (AP) —After a recent viewing of the motion picture *The Matrix*, Harvard University math professor John McGoldrick expressed disappointment with the absence of matrix algebra theory in the popular film.

"I understand the point of this film was to entertain," said McGoldrick. "But, frankly, I'm dismayed that there was no mention

Also Featured Inside
- Faked Enthusiasm Seems Faked
- Hundreds Found Dead in Cemetery
- Dow, NASDAQ Fall . . . in Love
- AP Special Report: Reuters Sucks

of even the simplest 2 x 2 matrix and its properties. Not one word on rank, span, linear independence, determinants, eigenvalues, eigenvectors, Gaussian elimination, QR-decomposition, or even PDP factorization."

Life Discovered on Mars

Doctor Finds Repetition

NEW YORK, NY—Dr. Robert Roberts of Cornell's Department of Redundancy Department at Cornell University has recently stated that things seem to be repeating themselves in local media. "It's true," stated Dr. Robert Roberts, "things seem to be repeating themselves in local media. I believe it is an attempt by the IRS to get people to pay their taxes twice."

A spokesman for the IRS said that this was ludicrous. "It's ludicrous," he said.

Neo-Yahtzee Activities Rise

ATLANTA, GA (AP)—Spokesmen for the Southern Poverty Law Center released a brief today describing what they call dangerous new levels of "anti-semantism" among disenfranchised fans of Hasbro's popular Yahtzee board game.

U.N. Confirms: "Life's a Bitch and Then You Die"

GENEVA, Switzerland (AP)—The United Nations' Committee on Economic and Social Development confirmed yesterday, "Life's a bitch, and then you die," a statement originally attributed to the late Dr. Chicken Little. When reached for comment, Dr. Little added, "and then your parents give away your clothes and rent out your room."

Journalist Maximizes Hyphen

BANGOR, ME (AP)—"In the post-modern neo-journalism movement, things can rarely be adequately described by unhyphenated modifiers," explained reporter Sam Powell. "Without the hyphen, I would be forced to use lesser-known, less-descriptive diction that leaves readers in the struggling-to-understand-what-the-author-is-saying-while-questioning-if-one-is-equipped-with-an-adequate-education-to-understand-the-article stage."

Doctor Finds Repetition

NEW YORK, NY—Dr. Robert Roberts of Cornell's Department of Redundancy Department at Cornell University has recently stated that things seem to be repeating themselves in local media. "It's true," stated Dr. Robert Roberts, "things seem to be repeating themselves in local media. I believe it is an attempt by the IRS to get people to pay their taxes twice."

A spokesman for the IRS said that this was ludicrous. "It's ludicrous," he said.

Student Plays Music For All to Hear

ITHACA, New York (AP)—Musical preferences on a college campus tend to be as diverse as the students themselves, so it is rare indeed when someone discovers a piece of music that is pleasing to all.

But one student, Terrence Walters, has done just that, bringing a smile to the face of everyone within earshot of his 500-Watt speakers. Walters, 18, a freshman in the College of Arts and Sciences, has been blasting "Bullet With Butterfly Wings," by the Smashing Pumpkins, with its clever refrain "Despite all my rage, I am still just a rat in a cage," incessantly ever since the semester began several months ago.

"It's the perfect song," said Walters, "It sums up poignantly all the frustration and hostility of Generation X, and anyone who doesn't agree can suck my balls."

Indeed, they can suck his balls.

So far, reaction to the song, which plays on repeat at full volume a minimum of eight hours a day, has been quite favorable. Nina Hirshfield, 19, Walter's next-door neighbor and a Sowing & Reaping major in the agriculture school, said that "it's fortunate for all of us that he [Walters] plays the song as he does. I mean, I love music, but I'm not smart enough to pick out musical selections for myself or to actually play them. My life would be silent and dismal were it not for him."

Arnold Fitzhugh, 18, an Ironing major in the Hotel school, lives downstairs from Walters. "He plays music at times I would never even think to," said Fitzhugh. "For instance, it never would have occurred to me to listen to my stereo at three a.m. the night before my Spanish final, but once my ceiling began vibrating in time to those power chords, I couldn't help but get up and dance. It was

delightful!"

Although everyone seems happy with "Bullet With Butterfly Wings," Walters has no intention of stopping there.

"Next year I can see myself living in an apartment and playing a lot of Bob Marley," said Walters, "Yeah. Maybe 'No Woman, No Cry.' And anyone who doesn't like it can fuck themselves."

Indeed, they can fuck themselves.

An unofficial poll showed many students to be in favor of Walters' new "Marley Plan."

"I'm looking forward to hearing what he comes up with," said Clarence Chowdermilk, 20, a sophomore Tapestry major in the architecture school. "I think I like variety, but as I am incapable of making a choice based on my own personal musical preferences, I'm very grateful to Terrence for making my life so much easier."

Medical Student Confuses Ass with Hole in Ground

CAMBRIDGE, Massachusetts (AP)—In an attempt to save his lifelong dream of one day becoming a proctologist, a fourth-year Harvard Medical Student is vigorously fighting what he claims to be an unwarranted dismissal from school. The student, Martin Dilfer, 26, was removed from the prestigious Medical Studies program last month following his failure to correctly answer an exam question asking him to distinguish his ass from a hole in the ground.

Harvard Medical School director Henry Sutton commented that, although Dilfer's performance up to that point had been satisfactory, the school was standing by its decision on what it considers an essential part of the curriculum. "We felt that in order to preserve the high quality of health-care education that our institution provides, it was imperative that Mr. Dilfer be precluded from further medical work," said Dr. Sutton. He added, "Of course, things would be easier if we didn't admit imbeciles like him in the first place."

While Dilfer acknowledged that he did in fact answer the exam question incorrectly, he was quick to point out that he correctly answered a separate question asking him to differentiate his ass from his elbow. A court date for this case has been set for June.

Man Repeats Everything

JUNCTION FALLS, South Carolina (AP)—For an unprecedented 39 years, Ian Kipfer has been repeating, word for word, everything anyone says to him. When questioned about how his habit started, he replied, "Why do you repeat everything people say to you?" He explained further, "I don't, you do."

When reporters asked Mr. Kipfer about his future plans, he remained elusive. "Can you just stop repeating what we ask for a minute?" he asked. After further probing, Kipfer began to break down. "You know, I'm beginning to hate you," he said. The interview ended abruptly when Mr. Kipfer exclaimed, "This is bullshit and a waste of my time!" and then pretended to call his editor on a cell phone.

Fat-ass the Object of Good-Natured Ribbing

KANKAKEE, Illinois (AP)—The children of Van Hooten Elementary School enjoyed a good laugh today when class clown Reggie Plotkin addressed portly youth Arnold Fitch at recess as "Fat-ass." "He had the kickball in the outfield, and I wanted him to throw it in," explained Plotkin. "I was going to yell, 'Hey, Arnold, throw it here,' but then I realized that calling him 'Fat-ass' instead of Arnold would have much the same effect and would be humorous as well." Plotkin's classmates agreed with him, erupting in hysterical laughter when they heard the epithet. "It's so true!" giggled third-grader Sally Goucha. "His ass is fat. Very fat!"

The levity of the afternoon seemed threatened when the obese youth told the principal, seeking sympathy and retribution. Mirth was restored, however, when the principal sent the young pudgepot away with a stern word. "He wanted me to punish Reggie," said Principal Miles McNamara. "I told him, 'You're lucky I don't punish you for eating so much, Lardo.'"

Man Abandons Friends for *Friends*

CHICAGO, Illinois (AP)—Chicago resident Harvey Mudlin announced today to his assembled group of lunch companions that he would no longer be requiring their services. Mudlin, like so many Americans, plans instead to enjoy human society vicariously, through the exploits of the characters of TV's *Friends*. An introverted loner and TV junkie by disposition, Mudlin was forced to turn to actual people for companionship after his old mainstay, *Cheers,* went off the air.

"Those first few weeks were hard," Mudlin said of the end of *Cheers*. "Suddenly, it seemed like nobody knew my name."

After a failed suicide attempt, Mudlin sought refuge among his neighbors and co-workers. He managed to pull together a small, tightly-knit group of warm and mutually supportive friends. Now, however, thanks to NBC's programming commission, those dark times are over.

"I'm so happy to be rid of the pressure of social interaction, safe within my own little microcosm," Mudlin said of his return to sitcom-aided seclusion. "Certainly, I enjoyed the company of my human pals, but none of them can compare to, say, Ross. Oh, Ross! Just neurotic enough to be loveable, and just enough unlike Seinfeld to avoid a lawsuit."

Mayor McCheese, Dead at 85

Mayor W. McCheese, former mayor of McDonaldland, died of a heart attack yesterday. He was 85.

Born in St. Paul, Minnesota, McCheese attended the University of Pennsylvania. After graduating in 1943, he went to work as an assistant to legendary district attorney Ronald McDonald. The two worked closely together on several cases that received national attention, including the infamous 1949 McDonaldland murders.

In 1964, McCheese was elected to his first of six terms as mayor of McDonaldland. Mayor McCheese will be best remembered for his anti-hunger initiatives, the capture of the Hamburglar, and the fact that he had a giant cheeseburger for a head.

McCheese is survived by his wife, Betty McCheese, his daughters Lois and Selma, and eight grandchildren.

William Shatner Expanding at Unprecedented Rate

PASADENA, California (AP)—After months of careful measurements with the Hubble telescope, scientists at NASA's Jet Propulsion Laboratory released the stunning findings of their study of the star of television's *Star Trek*. In keeping with a phenomenon observed in many of our galaxy's older stars, William Shatner, as he approaches the end of his natural, hydrogen-burning life, is expanding to a great size and reddening in color.

"What we've discovered here is that Mr. Shatner, who played a trim and dashing 'space captain' on television and movie screens for many years, has been aging in a manner consistent with our studies of other similar stars," said Bruce Gailey, chief researcher on the project. "He has expanded to an incredible size, and the farther his outer layers move from his core, the closer he comes to exploding and posing a danger to neighboring planets."

According to Gailey, "A series of complex reactions are taking place, whereby the helium produced by Mr. Shatner's previously successful television and film career is sucked inward and reprocessed to reclaim enough energy to allow him to continue providing light and warmth for the people of the earth."

Said Gailey, "This study has provided us with excellent clues as to exactly what can happen when a star of Mr. Shatner's magnitude lives on only through the debris of an earlier, brighter career."

Sock Puppet Claims to Be Messiah

KANKAKEE, Illinois (AP)—The small trailer-park town of Kankakee is in an uproar today following the statement made by one Mister Slidey, a sock puppet made to resemble an anaconda, that he is, in fact, Jesus Christ, the Son of God, come again down to earth to redeem us all.

"I have returned to spread my message of brotherhood and hating the Irish," Mister Slidey said at his press conference, where he spoke from above a bedsheet stretched between two chairs, "and all I meet with is scorn and derision. 'You can't be the messiah,' everyone says. 'You're just a sock puppet.' Well, last time, I was just a carpenter, and you believed me then, didn't you?"

Despite Mister Slidey's claims, the people of Kankakee remain skeptical.

"Well, he sure don't look like the messiah," said Floyd N. Biggenwart, an unemployed sauna repairman who lives in the trailer park. "I seen pictures of Jesus, and he's all tall and skinny, with a little beardy thing and all them holes in him. Now that sock puppet don't look nothing like that, but I sure like the way his eyes get all googly when you shake him up."

When asked if he could be persuaded to worship Mister Slidey, Biggenwart said, "I don't know. I'd feel kind of funny, kneeling down in front of a sock."

Mister Slidey's owner and operator is one Rolando Ramirez, an illegal alien who has asked us not to disclose his identity. He makes his living by performing with Mister Slidey at children's parties. Asked what he thinks of Mister Slidey's claim, Ramirez said, "I think he don't tell the truth. Sometimes, I hear him talk, and I say, 'Jesus Cristo! It is him!' But then I remember that he needs me to move his mouth for him, and I am not so sure."

Mister Slidey will be embarking Thursday on a cross-country speaking tour, spreading the gospel and changing water into ice.

In This Box
• Text
• Gray Stuff
• More Text
• Gratuitous Filler

Peanut Brittle Enthusiast Terrified, Police Baffled by Springy Snakes

BELMONT, Minnesota (AP)—Sweets aficionado Charles Millman, 52, got more than he bargained for recently when he removed the lid of a can which was clearly marked "Peanut Brittle" and was greeted, not by the sticky, nutty goodness of the said brittle, but rather by an eruption of springy snakes Millman, who suffers from mild heart problems, was hospitalized as a precaution, when, for several hours after the traumatic incident, his breathing remained ragged and his heart failed to slow to its normal pace. He remains under observation at Muskegee Memorial Hospital and is scheduled to attend meetings of the in-house victim support group as soon as he is able.

Authorities are still struggling to put together the pieces of this puzzling crime. Belmont police chief, Richard Szwajic, answered, "We don't have a list of names yet, but we're looking for a mastermind clever enough to switch the labels on two cans so cunningly that even a widely acknowledged peanut brittle expert like Mr. Millman was taken in. We're hunting for someone with access to, and an intimate working knowledge of, terrifying springy snakes of the types used."

Szwajic and other top detectives expect the case to break wide open as soon as Millman has recovered sufficiently enough to answer questions about how he obtained the fraudulently labeled container, which is in police custody. In the meantime, an advisory has been put out to peanut-brittle and springy-snake buyers alike to buy their goods only from well-established, licensed dealers, in order to avoid the anticipated wave of copycat crimes.

How to Sport
That **Calculator**
for SUCCESS

It's happened to all of us at one time or another. You're sitting in the library calmly picking your nose when you see a beautiful girl walking towards you. Thinking quickly, you pull out that quantum mechanics problem set and try to look cool. But she walks right by you and kisses some guy who can't even take the partical differential of a simple trigometric function. You ask yourself over and over, "Why? Why? Why?" Well, the answer may be all in the way you sport your calculator. There are many misconceptions about what looks good and what doesn't. To help you out, we've put together this handy list of do's and don'ts.

Do's

1. Do have a pencil or two in your pocket beside your "calc." This will show the girls that you often do math beyond the capabilities of any calculator on pencil and paper. (See Don't # 1.)

2. Do have a "calc" with a crystal liquid display. Electric lights went out in the seventies along with Oxy 10.

3. Do allow your "calc" to slide up a little in your shirt pocket, revealing those sexy higher-function keys. Remember, chicks flip over integral signs.

4. Do take a fashion risk every once in a while by showing up at a social gathering sporting a slide rule. Your daring is sure to start even the most reluctant girl's flesh a-quivering.

Don'ts

1. Don't stick pencils in your pocket loosely. Clip them to your "calc." (Any good men's store will carry pencil-calculator clips). My wife summed it up best when she said, "I like a man whose pencil stands straight and true. I don't want to see it wobble around all loose and flaccid."

2. Don't program your "calc" to flash "Light my fire!" This is clearly a sexual innuendo and girls will be turned off right away.

3. Don't go hot-dogging by having three calculators in your pocket at once. We don't want to overwhelm the babes. Understatement is the key. (Get it? Key?)

PrinceOfDarkness: hey jesus, r u there?

GodzSon69: whassup Satan? one sec ... busy paying for the sins of man n stuff. brb

GodzSon69: k, i'm back

PrinceOfDarkness: so how's it hanging?

GodzSon69: haha lol . . . dude i'm still sore from that whole cross thing. that totally sucked.

PrinceOfDarkness: yeah sorry bout that. me and the minions were kinda caught off guard on that one

GodzSon69: whatev, it's cool. it's way easier up here, anyway. i sit around with my dad and play playstation 2 when he's busy creatin shit

PrinceOfDarkness: ooo playstation 2!!! i had one in hell for a while but it melted

PrinceOfDarkness: we were like addicted to tony hawks pro skater 3 down here

GodzSon69: omg i want that so bad! i'd do anything

PrinceOfDarkness: anything?

GodzSon69: haha shut up, you are sooo bound and powerless before me

GodzSon69: plus my dad totally heard you b/c he's omniscient

PrinceOfDarkness: oh yeah . . . hey he hasn't mentioned me lately, has he?

GodzSon69: nah don't worry about it. he just says to watch out for the lake of fire

GodzSon69: n e ways

GodzSon69: how r yr spawn doin?

PrinceOfDarkness: awesome! yeah things are going really well up on earth

PrinceOfDarkness: you know that movie where the kid humps the pie?

GodzSon69: yeah

PrinceOfDarkness: yeah that's mine

PrinceOfDarkness: plus everybody's givin me credit for mass destruction and death and jihad and whatnot

GodzSon69: yeah I know . . . i just talked to Muhammad

GodzSon69: he's pissed

PrinceOfDarkness: yeah I just don't get him at all.

PrinceOfDarkness: anyway i gtg

GodzSon69: me too, my dad's tryin to use the computer

PrinceOfDarkness: k ttyl

Hey kids! What if there were no moon?

Neil Armstrong would have looked ridiculous.

Houston, there isn't a damn thing out here!

WHY I LOVE THE MOVIE THEATER

As a young boy, my dream was always to work in a movie theater. "What could be more fun than working in a movie theater?" I thought. Maybe a big, stuffed David Hasselhoff doll or a giant Lego set, but I figured I wouldn't see either one of those in my lifetime, so when it came time to get a job, I went straight to General Cinema—the biggest, baddest, most corporate movie theater I had ever seen in my life.

I was very nervous when I first walked in. I couldn't believe I was even thinking about working in a movie theater. What did I have to offer them? No way were they going to hire me. I took a deep breath and walked up to the first person I saw. He was big. Practically busting out of the polyester vest he was wearing.

"I would like to work for General Cinema," I said, trying to be as calm as possible.

"*Me gusta tu pelo*," he replied, pointing towards someone who spoke English.

As it turned out, the guy he was pointing at was Mr. Tromboli, the manager, who told me I could start on Monday. I was so excited I spent the weekend writing my memoirs—I was going to be something, yes sir!

The next morning I showed up for work ten minutes early, and they fitted me for a bow tie and polyester vest. Then it was time to go to work.

My job on that first day was to sit behind the counter and read a magazine. I was so nervous I could hardly concentrate, but luckily they had given me *People's* "Best Dressed People" issue, so there weren't too many big words.

After six hours, the phone rang, and I answered it, reciting my carefully practiced introduction:

"Good afternoon, thank you for calling General Cinema. All of our theaters are equipped with seats, a screen, a projector, and sticky floors. Tickets cost four dollars before three o'clock, twelve dollars after. If there is anything anyone can do to make your stay at our theater healthier or more enjoyable, including, but not limited to, electrolysis, smiling, foot massages, or cable installation, please feel free to ask the manager. Can I help you?"

"Yes," said the voice on the other end, "I need to know how long you think it would take to get from Hancock Street to North Boulevard by rickshaw."

"Twenty minutes," I said, and hung up the phone. It's a good thing my dad drives a rickshaw, or I might have lost my job over that one!

Sometimes we showed movies, and people would buy tickets for them, but we spent most of our time pushing little carpet-vacuums around and putting our hands in vats of steaming buttery topping. We would have contests to see who could eat the most Swedish Fish without collapsing; I once ate six thousand in just under eight hours.

I made many good friends during my time at the movie theater: Raul, the Hispanic kid, Tito, the Hispanic kid, Lara, the Hispanic girl, and Fred, the old, crazy guy who only worked days because of his morphine addiction. Sometimes, if a movie sold out, Tito and I would change into street clothes (or "normal" clothes, as we liked to call them), grab a big bucket of stale popcorn, and wade into a crowded isle, pretending to look for a seat. Afterwards, we would compare buckets to see who had spilled more popcorn on the customers' heads.

Mr. Tromboli, the manager, was a bitter man. He never spoke to any of us, especially not Raul, who he thought was Tito. He used to storm around the lobby in his little suit, bumping into customers and knocking them down, saying, "Now try and make fun of me for spending my life working in a movie theater. Hee hee!" and then disappearing back into his office.

Every once in a while, Mr. Tromboli would be in a good mood, and he would come out into the lobby and make fun of the customers with us, directing them to the wrong theaters and scaring the bejesus out of their little kids. His favorite story was about a really fat lady who had needed a special chair just so she could sit and watch the movie. She was so fat! But the best part of the story, the part that made Mr. Tromboli's moustache twitch back and forth like Stevie Wonder, was that when the movie ended, Mr. Tromboli got on the PA system and said "We would appreciate it if everyone could sit still for just a moment until we can get a forklift or something to get rid of that really, really fat woman in the top row."

Unfortunately for Mr. Tromboli, the woman had suffered a heart attack and died during the movie, as a direct result of the high fat content of the popcorn. The police came and took Mr. Tromboli away. So I guess it wasn't really that funny at all.

I often look back fondly on my time in the movie theater. Those were some of the best weeks of my life. I learned many valuable life skills, including Spanish, and I still rip a mean ticket. But the best thing about working at the movies wasn't the mindless busywork, the incessant fawning over the customers, the free movies, or even stuffing up the toilets so the night janitors would have to mop all night long. It was the cool polyester vest that still gives me a rash to this day—but fortunately, it's the kind of rash that drives girls wild.

Hey Everybody!
What's That Smell?

"Consumers . . . want not only good [mackerel] . . . but convenience built into the [mackerel] as well; and they are prepared to pay for whatever services the mackerel industry can provide. [Even if that means getting their mackerel in a barrel or from a dirty drunk.]"
—*Fortune* Magazine, October 1953

<u>NOW!</u> Here's Swanson's Answer!

It's Swanson's Mackerel-in-a-Barrel!

John never gave me jewelry before! He's even touching my derrière! Thank you, Mackerel-in-a-Barrel! You've saved my marriage!

**Swanson's Patented
Mackerel-in-a-Barrel Contains:**
Thick slices of juicy mackerel, with rich, real mackerel gravy and mackerel dressing. Sediment. Flatworms. Barrel bits. And Swanson's famous old-fashioned goodness!

A complete, quick-frozen mackerel dinner ready to heat and serve!

Just what housewives want—no work, no messy "gutting," no thawing needed. Out of the barrel, into the oven—25 minutes later, a hearty mackerel dinner ready to eat in its own decorative plastic shell that you can serve right in front of the television! Impress your friends! Have sex with your husband again!

A BIG, BOLD SWANSON SMASH CAMPAIGN IS SPREADING THE NEWS LIKE WILDFIRE!

It's the *hottest* item ever handled in a frozen foods department! Be the first housewife on your block to treat your family to fresh, frozen mackerel. Hurry and get yours today before you fail as a woman and have to go back to living with your parents again!

A . C . S W A N S O N & S O N S • K A N K A K E E , I L L I N O I S

Breakdancing Instruction Manual

Breakdancing for Black People:

1. Get into any open space, with a five-foot diameter. This should be wide enough.
2. Move about.
3. Do your thing.
4. Get down on the ground, slip into a groove.
5. Act cool.

That's all there is to it.
Now you're breakdancing.

Breakdancing for White People:

1. Get into an open field about the size of a football field. You'll need a lot of room to thrash about.
2. Get some shoulder pads, knee pads, elbow pads, a helmet with a chin strap, mouth guard, and a funky pair of neat colored sneakers.
3. Put them on.
4. Put your foot in the middle of the open area and wiggle it.
5. Place it down, lift the other foot, wiggle it, and place it down.
6. Wiggle your hips.
7. Act like a robot. Sort of.
8. Wiggle each arm slowly like an ocean wave. Concentrate on every miniscule movement very intently.
9. Jump up high in the air, land on your neck and twirl around.
10. Have a friend run to the nearest telephone and call a doctor.
11. Lie very still and wait for the ambulance to arrive.
12. Stay in hospital for six months with broken vertabrae.
13. Pay exorbitant fees.
14. Leave hospital. Go back to step one. Remember, practice makes perfect.

ASK MR. LEVITICUS

MR. LEVITICUS: All right ladies and gentlemen, it's time for "The Mr. Leviticus Show." And here's our first caller . . .

CALLER 1: Who the hell are you?

MR. LEVITICUS: I'm here to answer questions on Leviticus, the third book of the Old Testament. You've been ignoring it for centuries now, and you're all going straight to hell. Next caller.

CALLER 2: Uh, Mr. Leviticus?

MR. LEVITICUS: Yeah.

CALLER 2: Umm, this is Bob, from Maine.

MR. LEVITICUS: Oh, good.

CALLER 2: Yeah, well, like, you know in my church, the priest gets really boring. He goes into that whiny voice of his, you know, and what I'm wondering is, will I go to hell just because I bring some whiskey in with me? I mean, I understand a lot more after I've drunk a little.

MR. LEVITICUS: Sorry, but God is very explicit on that one in Leviticus 10:9. You're definitely going to hell, Bob. Next caller.

CALLER 3: Hi!

MR. LEVITICUS: Yes, hi. What's your question, lady?

CALLER 3: We were having dinner the other night—vulture and locusts—but I didn't have any because I wasn't sure what Leviticus says about them. They invited me to dinner next week and it's going to be eagle and grasshopper. Is that okay?

MR. LEVITICUS: Of course, the grasshopper is fine, and so were the locusts, says Leviticus 11:22. But I'm afraid your friend has bad taste in fowl and will be going to hell. The eagle is out according to Leviticus 11:13, and the vulture is out by Leviticus 11:14. It's a long list, so listeners, please, remember to always take Leviticus along whenever you go out to eat. Caller number 4?

CALLER 4: I was at a restaurant with a friend, eating escargot, and we started talking about circumcision. Is it wrong to get pleasure from circumcision?

MR. LEVITICUS: Remind me never to eat with you. Discuss it with your psychologist, sir, it's not my area. I can tell you, though, that you're going to hell for eating escargot. Snails are outlawed in Leviticus 11:30.

CALLER 5: My son was born the other day. I sacrificed the lamb, but turtledoves are hard to get in New York City. What should I do? Can I sacrifice a pizza delivery boy?

MR. LEVITICUS: You're in luck. You can use pigeons instead of turtledoves. I'm sure you can pick up one no trouble in Central Park. See Leviticus 12:8 for more details. And by the way, Leviticus does not call for pizza delivery boy sacrifices anywhere. It's certainly not outlawed in Leviticus, but there may be federal or state laws regarding the matter. I would consult your priest and your lawyer before taking any action.

CALLER 6: I'm in a phone booth outside parking lot B at the University of Nevada. We just sacrificed a bullock, and I don't have a copy of Leviticus handy. Dave forgot to bring it. I can't remember whether I'm supposed to sprinkle the blood to the east or to the west. Which is it?

MR. LEVITICUS: That's definitely eastward upon the mercy seat, and also sprinkle blood before the mercy seat seven times with your finger. See Leviticus 16:14 when you get home. Next caller.

CALLER 7: I remember something in Leviticus about uncovering the nakedness of my mother's sisters and father's sisters, but what about my dad's brother's wife? She's not a

New from Cornell Information Technologies

T-mail

Introducing T-mail, an all-new communications program that serves as an alternative to, improvement upon, and eventual replacement for standard e-mail. The advantages of T-mail include:
- Faster response time
- Guaranteed compliance with all requests
- Less use of your hard-drive
- Cost effectiveness

Standard e-mail

Dear [insert student name],
You have a meeting with your advisor on Thursday at 12:15. Please notify him/her if you are going to be late.
    Sincerely,
    Administration

New T-mail

Sucka,
You got an appointment on Thursday at 12:15. If you late, I'm gonna break your legs, fool!
    —Mr. T

Standard e-mail

Dear Mr. [insert name],
You have been confirmed for flight 230 from Ithaca to Denver, please come to the airport and claim your tickets.
    —Continental Airlines

New T-mail

Fool,
You ain't gettin' me on no plane, Hannibal. I'm serious this time. I'm gonna break your head, sucka!
    —Mr. T

blood relation, she's really hot, and she's a consenting adult. What do you think?

MR. LEVITICUS: I think you're sick. Leviticus doesn't give a damn about this "consenting adult" malarkey. That's Dr. Ruth's invention. It may keep the law off your back, but God will nail your ass. Leviticus 18:14. Next caller.

CALLER 8: It's me again, from the University of Nevada. I can't tell which way is east, and we don't have a compass.

MR. LEVITICUS: Can you see the North Star from where you are? It's not very bright and it's right above the horizon.

CALLER 8: Man, there are stars everywhere!

MR. LEVITICUS: Then the sacrifice is pretty much ruined. I'm sorry, but I wouldn't guess if I were you. You've only got a twenty-five percent chance of being right, and God doesn't grade on a curve. It's probably not worth going to hell for.

CALLER 9: Okay, okay, okay, okay. Now, I know I can't touch my daughter, but what about my daughter-in-law? She wants it, man, I'm telling you. My son's a wimp. She said so! She even asked me to . . .

MR. LEVITICUS: I don't care what she's asked you to do. She's definitely not on the eligible list. Leviticus 18:15.

CALLER 10: I was sacrificing a chicken the other day and somebody said I'm supposed to pluck the feathers before I burn it. Is this true?

MR. LEVITICUS: A chicken!?! Where in Leviticus does it say chicken? It's pigeons and turtledoves, people! A chicken!?! You're one sick heathen! Listen, you take a pigeon or a turtledove, you wring out its blood, pluck its feathers, clip the wings, and burn the head separately from the rest. Is that so hard? It's Leviticus 1:14-17. Now go out and get yourself a decent pigeon to sacrifice or I'll see to it you go straight to hell.

All right folks, that's all I can take for tonight. Just read the book for God's sake! This is Mr. Leviticus saying "Be good, or be damned!"

Walt Disney Presents Quentin Tarantino's
RESERVOIR DWARVES

A Story of Sex, Violence, and Dwarves

Ms. White: Okay. From now on, these are your names. I don't want to hear any of your real names anymore. You don't need to know anything more about each other than is absolutely necessary.

Happy: Why do I have to be Happy? Happy's such a wimpy name.

Ms. White: Shut up. You're Happy 'cause I say you're Happy.

Happy: But why can't he be Happy? Look at him, he's happy, with that dopey grin on his face.

[Dopey smiles.]

Doc: Look, he's Dopey, you're Happy, deal with it.

Happy: Oh, sure, you're Doc. Doc's a cool name. I'd be happy if I were Doc . . .

Grumpy: If you were Doc then you couldn't be Happy, so just be happy and pipe down.

Doc: I gotta go tinkle. *[He exits.]*

Ms. White: Look, cut it out, all of you. We gotta get started here. Okay, when we first go in, Sleepy's gonna be the lookout, and I want Bashful to be in the front . . .

Sneezy: Bashful?! He hasn't said a gosh darn word since we got here! How the heck is he supposed to lead us?

[Bashful blushes.]

Grumpy: Oh, and I suppose you could do better?

Sneezy: Yeah, I *could*. First of all, I did a job with this wicked witch before and I know how she thinks. Secondly, I'm twice as good a shot and I can . . . *ah-chooo!*

[Doc bursts through the door and throws a body onto the table.]

Happy: You scared the bejesus out of me. Who the heck is that?

Doc: I dunno. Some little red maid in a riding hood.

Sneezy: Gadzooks! What the heck is she doing here?

Doc: I dunno. I found her snooping around outside—she was talking about her grandmother and some wolf—she needed help or something . . . I got tired of her yappin' so I waxed her.

Happy: Damn it, Doc! You almost cut her whole head off!

Doc: She pissed me off. I have a headache.

Happy: Put a sock in it! This is my problem with this

whole flippin' job. Little red girls just wandering around outside . . . the security stinks. What if she was with someone else? Like those two little fat kids we saw eating the witch's candy mailbox? Maybe she told them something . . . I'm not happy about this.

Grumpy: Look you little jerkbag! You're Happy. Stop complaining about your freakin' name.

Happy: It's not about my name, silly! It's about this poop *[pulls out gun and points it at Red]*. Little girls in red capes wandering around all over the place, a front man that's too shy to introduce himself at parties, much less kill someone, and we have a narcoleptic as lookout. I'm not happy about this whole thing . . .

Grumpy: Jumpin' Jiminy on a pogo stick! Quit it with the name caca!

Ms. White: Both of you, stop this poppycock this instant!

Sleepy *(waking up)*: Hey, hey! What's with all the ruckus? I'm trying to get some sleep here.

Ms. White: You've been resting all day you little midget! If you don't . . .

Sleepy: I'm a dwarf, not a midget. *[He fires three shots from his gun.]* Don't forget again . . .

Doc: Well, I guess she can't forget again now, can she? You put three holes in her head that weren't there before. She's dead. And I still got a headache thanks to you. You're so grumpy when you wake up.

[Sleepy fires one shot at Grumpy.]

Grumpy: No, he isn't . . . but I am. *[He drops dead.]*

Happy: Now that he's dead, can I have his name?

Public Toilet Terror

The Easy Reading Book Club

"For people who like their books the way they like their sex—fast and easy."

If you're the type of person we think you are, you saw the word "sex" in the headline and kept on reading. That's why we did it. Well, keep on reading; we promise it won't take long!

You've heard of easy listening music, right? Well, now here's easy reading books, brought to you every month by the Easy Reading Book Club!

Romance, sex, mystery, sex, intrigue, and sex can be found in every book, in that order! It's all done by a carefully-researched formula! Our staff of fine writers know just what you want and when you want it. And every book we sell does just that. And more!

Reading books should be a pleasure, right? So why read more than you have to? ERBC has devised a special formula that allows you to read the parts that interest you and skip the ones that bore you, without missing any of the plot! Just use this handy guide that applies to every book we print. Clip and save and we'll send you a genuine Lucite frame to display your guide—a perfect ornament for any reading table—absolutely free!

Page	Topic
I	romance
2-34	sex
35	mystery
36-82	sex
83	intrigue
84-124	sex

We'll send you four books a month, every month, for an unheard-of cost of $3.99 per year! That's an eight-cent book every week, and believe us, it's worth every penny.

We invite you to immerse yourself in this month's selected stories and meet their uniquely interesting heroines:

Love's Tender Passions by Collette DuBois. Beautiful Diana West moves to a quiet town in New Hampshire to escape her sordid past. Does Mark Spencer, the sexy, dark, mysterious groundskeeper of the mansion next door, know her secret?

Passionate, Tender Love by Suzette DuMaurier. Attractive Laura Barnes starts life over again in a new town after a shattering divorce. Can Adam Stone, the international playboy and financier, help her forget her ex-husband?

Love's Passionate Tenderness by Nanette DuLac. Pretty Pamela Shaw begins her new job as a nurse in the rustic town of Riverdale. Why doesn't that handsome young intern, Drew Walker, want her to know about his old girlfriend?

Tender Love's Passions by Jeanette DuPont. Comely Robin White, famous actress, takes the small town of Mapleton by storm. But worldly Steve Denver is the only one who knows why she came!

If you order now, you'll receive as our free gift *The Easy-Watching Soap Opera Guide*. Teach yourself how to catch all the action in the soaps by only paying attention for four carefully selected minutes! A $2.99 value. You'll also be placed on the mailing list of 382 firms all over the country! The time you save reading our books can be spent reading junk mail! So get going today and send $3.99 to:

The Easy Reading Book Club
P.O. Box EZ Suk R
Perth Amboy, NJ 69696

Just clip and mail with $3.99
Yes! I'd like to join the ERBC!

Name_____

Address_____

City_____State_____Zip_____

LETTERS TO JESUS

"Letters to Jesus" is your public forum for any questions or concerns you might wish to take directly to the big J himself. Due to the overwhelming amount of mail Jesus receives each and every day, he cannot possibly write a response to you all. Know that he is with you always, and his hand guides you and gives you strength. For an autographed picture of the savior, include a self-addressed, stamped envelope and two dollars shipping and handling with your letter. Please, no cash.

Dear Jesus,
Bless you, sweet lamb of God, for the amazing sales at Winn-Dixie last weekend. I have never seen grits for such a low price! As for the produce . . . well, let's just say that when the drought hit last season, I knew that you would deliver us from the ravages of hunger and locusts. I will sing your praises up and down the aisles of the market until you come to welcome me into your heavenly kingdom. Thank you, O Lord.

—A Faithful Shopper

Dear Jesus,
Why is there no cheese-flavored Jell-O? It would make my day to find Jell-O with a tangy cheddar or Monterey Jack taste. Fruity flavors are all well and good, but I'm not sure that I want to be buying flavors with names like "passion fruit." The Bible makes no mention of Jell-O, but cheese is referred to, which seems odd. How could Jell-O be Godly if there aren't any cheese flavors? I'm not asking for Brie or Limburger Jell-O, but mozzarella and cheddar would be nice. I like to pack a snack with my lunch each day, and ever since you've blessed me with lactose intolerance, I have no means of enjoying cheese except for in an artificial-flavored

form. I know you've already given us so much, Lord, but if you can find it in your heart to answer my prayers and send cheese Jell-O to us, I will be without want forever more. I ask nothing but this of you, Jesus.

—Cheeseless in Wisconsin

Dear Jesus,
Please dear Lord, show me the light and lead me to my car keys. I drove back home from church on Sunday, but then when I had to go work this morning, they were gone. I searched high and low, but I could not find them anywhere. You are my last hope, Jesus. I beg of you, give me the strength to find my keys.

—Lost My Way and My Car Keys

Dear Jesus,
I bought some bananas yesterday, and one was a little bit green around the top. I ate it because it was the

one with the sticker on it, but it left my tongue feeling rather dry and unpleasant. It wasn't until dinner that I got the taste entirely out of my mouth. Even prayer did not help me. Was this banana the work of Satan?

—Ape for Christ

Dear Jesus,
I am writing to beg for your forgiveness, for I am a sinner and need your guidance to overcome and repent. Each morning, I succumb to my sordid ways and weigh my testicles. I know I shouldn't, but I'm afraid that indeed I do. After I record the weight on my chart, I break down and sob while praying to you for your divine and blessed forgiveness. Please save me from my deviant ways, my Lord. I stray not from your path (except for weighing my nuts every day). Please save me, Jesus.

—A Heavily Weighted Soul

191

Brett Greenberg
NAMES THE BEST EVER!™

Brett Greenberg Names the Best TV Show Ever!™

If you haven't seen an episode of this glorious television phenomenon, then I feel sorry for you. You have not experienced life as one should. This show is so extraordinary, comparable to the wonder of the earth's natural geysers and glaciers. God created man, the world, and finally . . . the 1987 sibling game-show classic, *I'm Telling*. Hosted by artificially tanned Laurie Faso, the show not only redefined television, but human interaction itself. The contestants played for prizes like "Simon," but the world's reward was much greater. Now I'm the one whose telling you—this is the Best TV Show Ever!™

Brett Greenberg Names the Best Movie Ever!™

In plain simple English . . . the Best Movie Ever!™ is *Getting Even with Dad*, starring Ted Danson and Macaulay Culkin. The cast, the story, the humor, the action, the magic . . . it's all here. While most Culkin fans would claim that he's best known for his role as Richard Tyler in *The Pagemaster*, they are clearly mistaken, for people in the year 2491 will still embrace him only for his work in this film. He plays Timmy Gleason, a punk kid with slicked-back hair, who only seeks his father's approval. Danson plays the dad with whom Macaulay attempts to get even, and the duo lights up the screen and my life. You owe it to yourself to have it light up yours.

Brett Greenberg Names the Best Book Ever!™

I'm not going to lie . . . I was torn between my choice and *A Tale of Two Cities* by Charles Dickens. Both are superb entries in literature, but in the end, I couldn't deny my initial urge, so therefore, the Best Book Ever!™ is none other than *Night of the Living Dummy III* by R.L. Stein. This classic Goosebumps tale has left me with chills and thrills many a lonely Saturday night. The universe has felt a similar effect from the magnum opus of word that is this book. Reading it makes me want to lock away in the cedar closet my marionette, Chester, and my doubts about life. If tears can only express the adulation I have for Stein's work here, then pass me a tissue and keep them coming.

Brett Greenberg Names the Best Album Ever!™

Beating out every other compilation CD or record dating back to the beginning of time, one album has reigned supreme atop the musical kingdom. The album is Regis Philbin's "When You're Smiling." This compilation CD features songs that are merely adequate, but when Regis tackles them, be prepared to forget everything you've ever known to be true and rededicate your life anew to Philbin's splendor. His takes on "You Make me Feel So Young" and "Cheek to Cheek" are profound in reinterpretation. But what makes this album so extraordinary is his duet with wife Joy Philbin. Her unconditional love for Rege is evident in this track—as is ours, after listening just once.

Brett Greenberg Names the Best Song Ever!™

The title of the Best Song Ever!™ goes to "Kiss from a Rose" by Seal. The scarred Aussie pours his heart, his ambitions, and his soul into this power ballad, and the result? A magical slice of wonder that outshines every other song written in the history of the world. Found on the soundtrack of *Batman Forever*, Seal's masterpiece presents listeners with universal questions about life, love, and graying towers alone on the sea. Seal, you may be scarred on the outside, but your words and your harmonies are nothing shy of perfect. Bravo! "Kiss from a Rose" is indeed the Best Song Ever!™

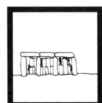

Bob's Big Boy

★★★★ (out of four stars)
Vince Lombardi Service Area,
I-95, New Jersey
Entrees: 99¢ to $3.99

I have never seen a shooting star. But now that no longer matters. Because when I parked my Kia and marched through the parking lot of the Vince Lombardi Service Area, replete with the young screams and grown-up chitchat of unenlightened Americans, alone with my air of restaurant-critic seriousness, everything—and I mean the entire earth—was swept away when I saw those eyes: immense, blinding, pure, awful, terrible—what other word is there besides cosmic? How many of these parking-lot proletarians have earnestly paused to look up into Big Boy's eyes head-on, and standing before that cruel majesty, openly wept?

Never mind that I had yet to encounter the edible part of Bob's Big Boy's wonder. The slyly decorous interior is ostensibly a tribute to 1950s America, but to say it is merely a slice of Americana is to anchor it hopelessly to a piddling, critical lexicon. Nay, this is a haven, within whose walls we are reminded of a time when innocence, crayons, Aryans, even beauty, meant something. I stood, I sighed, I sat.

What awaited me, I could not possibly have imagined. The fork gleamed with that ethereal, elusive glow, the legacy of a thousand meals. The knife rested slightly askew on the table, no doubt due to imperfections in the woodwork or the necessary evil of its polyurethane protective coating. For this I subtract a star from God. But the placemat —ah!—paper, to my eternal delight, and Elysian. On its face was scribed a list of ten things Big Boy would do if he were President. I searched hastily for a clause regarding virgin sacrifices. There was none, to my brief disappointment. Then let me live to do him good works.

Across the room, sadly across the room, a youngling was being sung to and enjoying a free dessert; the occasion was her birthday, and I smiled inside and out. What better way to celebrate the day of one's harmonization than with the song of the cosmos?

And now I must address the menu, a humbling and unenviable task. Why, you ask? Because we have here a mesh of words, pictures, and food that is infinitely greater than each independent element, yet all three combined hardly touch the grandeur that awaits.

I am but one man; let me share with you one meal and the bond between critic and reader will runneth over. I begin with the "Buffalo-Style Big Boy Chicken Tenders," not fingers, which were accompanied with celery sticks and bleu—ah, the French!—cheese. These were accompanied by a tossed salad. They were exquisite.

For the main course I enjoyed a monolithic hamburger known as the Big Boy,® which must only be spoken of by copyright, a burden I bear like a lover. The Big Boy,® by the way, is not just any hamburger—would that all of America's growing children were so succulent! The salt and pepper arrived in exquisitely labeled paper packets of such supreme functionality that I knew some kind of transcendent aesthetic was at work here.

Ah! My fries arrive. Thank you, Bo-Cheez. Emerging from my rapturous haze for a moment, I asked my waiter where I might find the sun-bedappled bovine that mothered the milk of my cheese. He said in his homeland modulations, "In the can!" and made a gesture of such boyish charm—oh, you rogue!—that I was elevated into a fit of laughter. By the time I came down, Bo-Cheez was gone.

There is nothing more to say. I will not say that I was "satiated." I will not say that I was "pleased." I will say nothing. On my way out, I looked up again at Big Boy and came to an epiphany, certainly the last epiphany I will ever have use for: Big Boy was not smiling at me from his great height; he was smiling with me.

Shine on, Big Boy. Shine on through my misty eyes.

The Time I Killed at Billy's Funeral

A Eulogy Delivered by Jake Bronson
President of Delta Sigma Epsilon Tau

[Steps up to the lectern] How about another round of applause for Father Brown? Hey, Padre, thanks for not shaking my hand before the service. Last thing I want is my hand smelling like I just high-fived an altar boy's rectum!

[Taps microphone] Is this thing on?

[Looks over at Billy's coffin] You know, I always told him he'd look good in pine. *[Chuckles]* But let's get serious. We're here to say goodbye to Billy, who was many things to us: a son, friend, and fraternity brother we didn't know all that well.

It might surprise some of you that I would be giving a eulogy for Billy, seeing as I didn't know him nearly as well as others here did. I think Billy would have wanted it this way, however. When he passed away, I was right there at his side, taking the shot glass out of his hand and replacing it with a Reese's Pieces bag so that when the cops came, I could tell them he was allergic to peanut butter and committed suicide.

You may be surprised to learn that Billy was a rabid alcoholic. I'm sad to say it's true. He drank a lot. *[Waits for audience to say in unison, "How much did he drink?," but they don't.]* He drank so much that he'll probably be reincarnated as a tequila worm! It's like he thought there was a prize at the bottom of every bottle or something.

If there's one thing I'll remember about Billy, besides his rampant alcoholism, it's his selflessness. If you needed help with your schoolwork, Billy was the guy you talked to. If you needed a ride somewhere, Billy was always up for it. If you needed someone to switch bedrooms with you so that when the ugly girl you hooked up with last weekend came by your room looking for you, he could say "Jake Bronson? He's been dead for five years!" and she'd finally back off. Billy was willing to do it, at least the first couple of times.

A tragedy like this leaves us with nothing but questions, like "Is there a God?" I'm putting my money on "no." Or, if there is a God, he's a cruel deity who likes to play practical jokes on us, like giving certain college students the ability to survive drinking only twenty shots of alcohol, when everyone knows that you have to take twenty-one shots on your twenty-first birthday. We may never know the answers to the big question of life, but we do know some things for certain: Billy was a great person who died before his time, and his fraternity, whose president was gracious enough to travel all this way to uplift you with his humor and words of remembrance, is certainly not to blame for this tragedy.

In conclusion, please don't sue us.

Blowing the Whistle

What Mr. Referee is Really Saying

SLASHED WRIST
Clasping the wrist with the other hand to stop profuse bleeding.

WELL I NEVER!
Player is using dessert fork to eat salad, breaching all rules of etiquette.

PITFALL
Player must swing across the alligator pit while trying to avoid the rolling barrels!

BEATING OFF
A series of tugging motions with both hands.

DISCO INFERNO
Burn baby, burn. Aaah, aaah, aaah, aaah, stayin' alive, stayin' alive, aaah, aaah, aahh, ahhh!

KUNG FU MASTER
Player demonstrates toughness by breaking own arm with ferocious karate chop.

SHAZAM!
Referee turns into Captain Marvel.

HEY, I'M AN AIRPLANE!
Skating with both arms extended and making a jet engine noise.

WHEELS ON THE BUS
They go round and round, round and round, round and round, all through the town.

MACARENA
Da da da da de da woah heeeey Macarena!

TO THE MOON, ALICE!
One of these days— Pow! Right in the kisser!

WHAT THE . . . ?
The Referee, who is about to get on his brand new horse, notices some stripes that have fallen off of his new shirt.

IT'S A STICKUP
Referee needs a sixer of Bud, ten scratch tickets, and all the money in the register.

LINT ON PANTS
"Eccch, that stuff's gross!"

HITCHHIKING
"Hey sailor, going my way?"

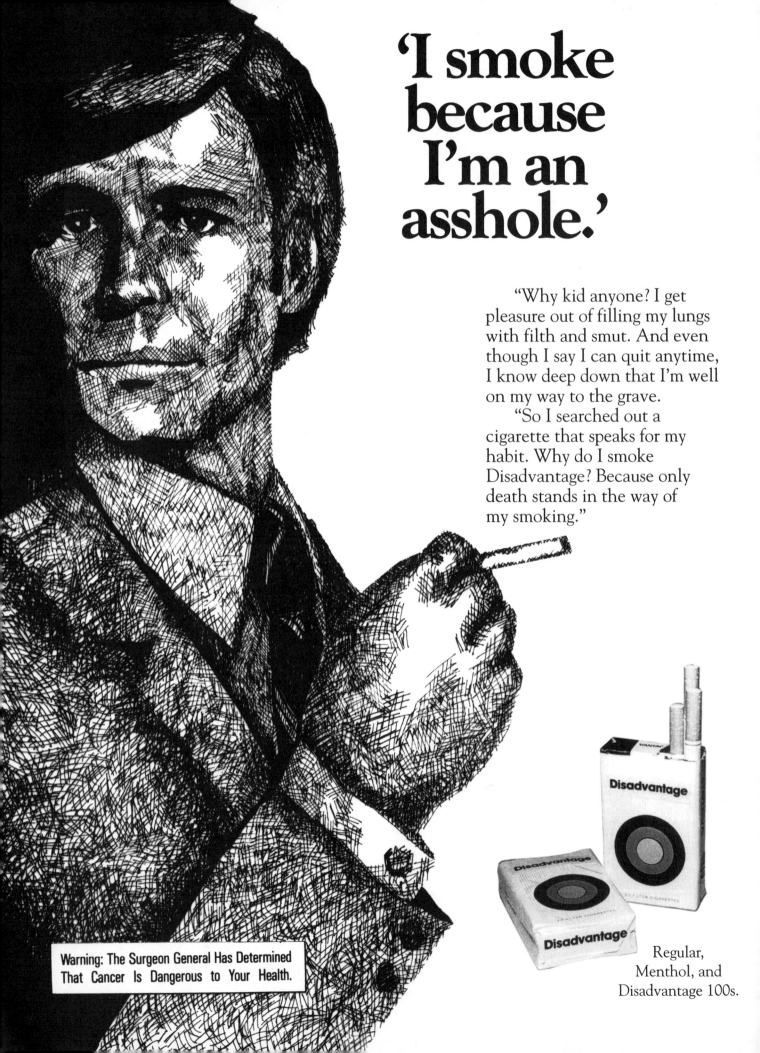

197

199

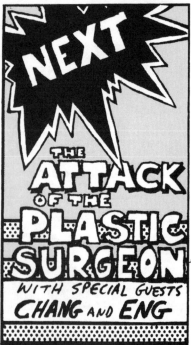

Batman's Lament

It is late afternoon and millionaire Bruce Wayne is pumping weights. What had once been an enjoyable pastime is now becoming an arduous chore. Bruce Wayne, the famous Batman, who roams the streets of Gotham City every night, has just turned forty. "What a bite in the chops!" thinks Bruce, as he curls 250 pounds.

"Here I am, like one of those morons on Muscle Beach, lifting weights. Who do I think I am? Superman? Jeez, Superman has it so easy. He just came from another planet, and—*poof!*—he's got these superpowers. In fact, all of those guys have superabilities of some sort. I'm the only loon who kills himself every day to stay in shape like this. And what do I get for all my trouble? *Nothing!* Not one damn thing! No money, no 'Thank you, Batman,' no girls. Here I am, stopping all these muggers who attack girls in the park, and they all run after Superman. But he doesn't care, he's usually off in another galaxy, chasing one of his space villains or that nut, Lex Luthor. And look at these criminals. None of them wear normal clothes, always outfits that look like rejects from a costume shop. And these guys shoot bullets, *real* bullets. Not like those fruitcakes that try to destroy Superman and know they can't. These are real bullets, and they don't bounce off my chest either. One lucky shot and—*ZAP!*—it's all over, dead bat. I even have to watch who I hit. In the old days I didn't worry who I beat up. Now everyone and his brother are anti-police, and with one wrong punch—*WHAM! BIFF!*—my ass is in a sling. *OOOF.*

"It's just not fair. All the other superheroes have wives or girlfriends. What would I say to her? 'Sorry, honey, can't stay home tonight, gotta go beat up some criminals and keep the streets safe.' If she hadn't already done so, she'd throw me out right there. And I can't even go out on dinner dates. I used to. Every time I did, halfway through dinner, Alfred, my trusty butler, called and said 'Someone is in serious trouble and only the Caped Crusader can save him.' Well, I'm sick of it. And if I do finish dinner and take her home, without fail the hot line will ring and I'll be off on another mission. I really hate being a superhero," he grumbles as he begins four hundred squat thrusts. "I can't even count on Robin anymore, the little pansy. It used to be great when the Joker would have me hanging over a vat of boiling wax, lowering me very slowly so he could make 'Batcandles.' Then Robin would appear, yell something like 'Holy Sheepshit Batman!,' knock me away, do a quick *SMASH! POW!* on the henchmen and apprehend the Joker. I trained that boy for ten years to take over when I retire. Now he's gone. He came out of the closet and joined a ballet company."

Just then Bruce's ears perk up. He hears a siren. He looks out his window and sees the familiar spotlight with the frightening Batsignal wavering in the heavens. He dons his blue underwear and leotards, and swoops down to the Batcave. The cave has been an absolute mess ever since Alfred was killed by a thief, who broke into the Wayne Manor one evening while Batman was roaming the streets of Gotham. Batman hops into the renowned Batmobile, which strikes terror in the hearts of the under-world and amuses little children. "Crap! Out of gas!" Batman mutters to himself. He jumps on a nearby Harley Davidson, ready for just such an emergency. Riding swiftly to the office of Police Commissioner Gordon, he wonders what foul fiend is wreaking havoc upon the city. Is it the Riddler, the Penguin, or some new nemesis trying to get started in the game? Who knows? Who cares?

And how come Commissioner Gordon has never traced the hotline back to Wayne Manor, a simple procedure, and found out who Batman really is? It's questions like these that go unanswered, especially when not asked. "Why do I really do this?" he asks himself. "I'm rich, and as Bruce Wayne, I'm already famous. I don't need this heartache. I can sit around and watch football all week and still rake in the bucks. Because of Batman I don't eat right, and all this running around is making my legs chafe."

Arriving at police headquarters, he bounds up the stairs four at a time, proving to himself that he is still in as good condition as he was twenty years ago. Rushing into the commissioner's office, he comes upon Commissioner Gordon and the four chiefs of police huddled about a round table, deep in thought. Standing up, the commissioner cries, "What happened, Batman? Did you forget today is Thursday?"

"Damn, the card game!" he exclaims as he slaps his face. "It completely slipped my mind." Pulling up a chair, he settles down for a relaxing game of poker, leaving the thriving metropolis to fend for itself tonight. "It's times like these," he thinks to himself, "that make being a crime stopper all worthwhile."

7 PM **2** **GOD**
God stars as a father who has a zany-but-lovable homosexual son and a wife who lives in a manger.

7 **QUANTUM MECHANICS!**
Vanna White, dressed only in a string bikini, explains quantum mechanics while the top of her swim suit keeps coming undone.

10 **SIXTY MINUTES**
Morley Safer tails Mike Wallace's mother to see what she does during a typical day. She visits the laundry, a supermarket, and the Happy Jack All-Night Book Store.

12 **TAXIDERMIST—(formerly Animal Kingdom)**
Host Marlon Perkins stuffs and mounts all the animals that his assistant Bill inadvertently killed during previous episodes. This week, the Land Rover runs over a family of otters.

7:30 **5** **COOKING FOR THE CLUMSY**
While trying to make a chicken soufflé in the Cuisinart, Martha Stewart accidentally purees her fingertips.

8 **THAT'S NOT INCREDIBLE AT ALL**
Featuring: a man driving a Volkswagen, Mrs. Emma Shane feeding her pet poodle Boopsie, and a man who lost a quarter in a vending machine.

11 **FAMILY FREUD**
Real families undergo psychoanalysis and compete for prizes. This week: The Smiths find out why Fred-

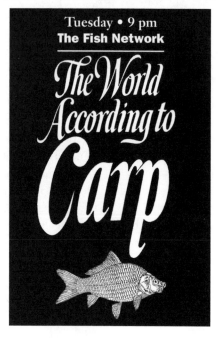

Tuesday • 9 pm
The Fish Network
The World According to Carp

dy wets the bed, winning a Caribbean cruise.

23 **RHUBARB PIE**
The touching story of a former pie-eating champion's attempt to make a comeback after a two-year bout with dysentery.

8 PM **2** **DAD FLIPS OUT—Comedy**
Dad (Bob Saget) returns home to discover that Junior (Frankie Muniz) has driven the car into the pool, his daughter (Mandy Moore) has run off with the swimming-pool cleaner, and that his wife (Courtney Cox) has run

up a $900 tab at Bloomingdale's for swimwear. Hilarity ensues as dad reacts in his usual philosophical way by grabbing his old army M-16 rifle and killing several innocent passersby.

5 **MINISTER ED—Comedy**
America's most lovable talking horse conducts services in a small-town Methodist church in Nebraska.

10 **THE HYPOCHONDRIACS—Drama**
Jim (Lee Majors) is dismayed to learn that the menacing lump on his throat is nothing more than a mosquito bite.

41 **NEGOTIATE—Reality**
Viewers call in live and talk directly to Middle East terrorists to discuss the release of American hostages.

67 **LITTLE HOUSE IN THE SHTETL —Drama**
Pa (Eugene Levy) must sell the goat when the Russians stage a pogrom.

8:30 **8** **ALICE—Premiere**
The continuing story of Alice—the Bradys' former-housekeeper, who was fired when she was caught fondling Greg's underwear and now lives as a bag lady in the Bowery.

11 **SPECIAL REPORT: The Legitimate Children Problem**
This show studies the shocking increase in the number of children being born to married couples. Once the victims of scorn and ridicule, legitimate children now learn to cope with a society in which a "meaningful relationship" often takes less than six minutes to complete.

12 **DRUGS, SEX & VIOLENCE**
One-hour special documents the inherent flammability and flimsy high-speed construction of women's see-through underwear.

33 **MOVIE—Crime Drama**
"Who Stole Our Talent?" David Cassidy, Macaulay Culkin, and Molly Ringwald all wind up on the skids together after all three are refused a place on Hollywood Squares.

9 PM **2** **ARCHIE BUNKER'S CHAIR— Comedy**
In this pilot episode for the eighth spinoff of "All in the Family," Archie's

chair is moved from an old-age home to a hospital emergency ward where Chico (Bronson Pinchot) finds eighty-one cents in the chair's cushion.

7 REBBE WITHOUT A CAUSE—Movie
The exciting adventures of Moshe Goldfarb (Judd Hirsch), a Brooklyn rabbi whose congregation has deserted him.

9 WHO'S WATCHING DAD?—Comedy
In this hilarious episode, Mary (Suzanne Sommers) forgets to plug in Dad's (Ben Vereen) iron lung. Fun and laughs result when Mom (Susan Blakely) returns home four hours later with the groceries.

77 ALL-STAR CELEBRITY THEATER
This week: Shakespeare's "Othello, the Moor of Venice" with Mr. T as Othello, Betty White as Desdemona, Pee-wee Herman as Iago, and Louie Anderson as the Chorus.

9:30 39 NAME THAT PERVERSION!
Contestants compete for prizes as they try to guess what sexual perversion is being enacted in the blurry, black-and-white photographs of famous politicians and celebrities caught "just being themselves."

54 SEVERE THUNDERSTORM—Disaster Movie
Inclement weather is about to strike the sleepy town of Kankakee—and only meteorologist Wayne Noogins (George Wendt) knows it! The dashing Noogins must team up with his estranged wife and rival colleague (Vicki Lawrence) to evacuate the trailer park and save the day. Along the way, they unexpectedly rediscover love!

10 PM 4 METER PATROL—Drama
A crazed psychotic holes up in a restaurant, refusing to come out until Metermaid Rita (Angie Dickinson) tears up his parking ticket.

23 I LOVE LUCY—Comedy
Lucy accidentally stabs eight people, starts a polio epidemic, and breaks the blender. Ricky straightens everything out with help from the Mertzes. (R)

37 GO TO HELL
Contestants save their loved ones from eternal damnation and compete for valuable prizes.

83 MI MADRE EL COCHE—Comedy
The old "My Mother the Car" series is

ROCKY VII

Sly Stallone faces his toughest challenge ever.

ROCKY **VS.** HIS OWN EGO

I had no idea it had grown so big!

I had no idea I was such a puny runt!

Friday • 9 pm
HAS-BEEN CHANNEL

given fresh new meaning and socio-political overtones by being dubbed in Spanish. Stars Jerry Van Dyke.

11 PM 5 NEWS FOR THE COLOR-BLIND
Anchormen wear large signs stating the color of their clothing.

11:30 17 TONIGHT SHOW—Talk Show
Jay's guests include Spuds the Wonder Horse, a man who eats furniture for a living, and a woman who is convinced that she is the Louisiana Purchase.

42 CHATTER—Talk Show
The host pretends to be someone fa-mous and important, and guests include obscure actresses who babble on about their personal lives.

Mid. 7 LATE NIGHT IMPOTENCE
Celebrities poke fun at home viewers watching television at this late hour.

2 AM 84 SERMONETTE
Reverend Joshua Leander reveals himself over the air, but is stopped before he can reveal too much.

2:05 84 SERMONETTE REBUTTAL
Equal time given to atheists who rhetorically ask, "If there is a God, why doesn't he make house calls?"

How to Read a Book Review

WHEN THEY SAY	THEY REALLY MEAN
The ending is so smooth and lyrical it almost makes one forget some unevenness along the way.	The last five pages rise out of the compost heap of the two hundred previous pages and actually achieve mediocrity.
But the very verve of her prose carried me past those small difficulties . . .	The sex was adequate.
A sober professional with counterculture roots.	A hippie who sold out.
Restless, clever prose . . .	Run-on sentences that drag on for several pages.
First novels often have problems of shape.	It sucked.
Despite some blemishes, this is a finely crafted novel in our era of disintegrating families.	It sucked and the author is divorced.
Memorable characters are the principle strengths of this fine. . .	It sucked, but I remember the main character's name.
This sound, scholarly assessment . . .	This turgid, boring . . .
Invokes . . .	Steals from . . .
. . . steady theme through the book.	Christ, not this again!
She has written a charming tour de force.	No threat to my soon-to-be-published magnum opus.
The author is of the deconstructive school of criticism.	The author masturbates often and with great gusto.
The whole novel seems to exist in a compressed atmosphere.	I read it while I was sitting on the crapper.
Writing is one of the state of Maine's more dependable crops.	Oh God, not another Stephen King novel.

CLONE ORDER FORM

CORNELL CLONE CENTER
132-45 East 43rd Street
New York, NY 10022

Congratulations on your decision to have children. In this modern day and age, more and more young adults are opting for a life free from baby bottles, diaper rash, and adolescent rebellion. For this reason, your decision marks an important contribution to perpetuating American life and assuring the government another taxable citizen. Gone are the days of distended bellies, maternity clothing, and peculiar culinary cravings. Parents are no longer at the mercy of Mother Nature, for all the risks involved with producing offspring have been scientifically removed. Please select genetic characteristics carefully for your clone as refunds are not granted and exchanges are only possible within seven days after childbirth with the birth certificate. Welcome aboard the Good Ship Parenthood!

PARENTS' NAMES_____ **OCCUPATIONS**_____

ADDRESS_____ **CITY**_____ **STATE**_____

CLONE PHYSICAL CHARACTERISTICS OPTIONS:

SEX: ❏Male ❏Female ❏Other, please specify_____
EYES: ❏One ❏Two ❏Blue ❏Green ❏Grey ❏Assorted
RACE: ❏Caucasian ❏Negroid ❏Oriental ❏Occidental ❏Accidental ❏Overtly Teutonic
HEIGHT: ❏Over 5'11" ❏Over 5'5" ❏Over 5'9" ❏Over 6' ❏Over 6'5" ❏Good God
NOSE: ❏Pug ❏Ski slope ❏Eaglebeak ❏Jimmy Durante ❏One or ❏Two nostrils
COMPLEXION: ❏Cork board ❏Sandpaper ❏Pizza
HAIR: ❏Mop ❏Brillo ❏Straw ❏Pizza
WHO SHOULD THE CLONE RESEMBLE PHYSICALLY? ❏Mother ❏Father ❏Anyone but the mother or father ❏Mailman ❏That stranger who stopped in to ask directions

> **PLEASE TAPE**
> **CELL SAMPLE HERE**

CLONE EMOTIONAL AND MENTAL CHARACTERISTICS:

OUTLOOK ON LIFE: ❏Offensive optimist ❏Manic-depressive ❏Nihilistic ❏Depressing pessimist ❏Vegetative ❏Realist ❏Gloomy Gus
SENSITIVITY: ❏"I can relate to that" ❏"I disagree with what you say but I'll defend your right to say it" ❏"How'd you like me to put your head through that wall?" ❏"Who gives a flying fuck?"
PERSONALITY FLAWS: ❏Heroin addiction ❏Cleans ears with pinky finger ❏Strews dirty laundry about home ❏Penchant for pornography ❏Masturbates with left hand ❏Engineering whiz
FEARS: ❏Bugs ❏Take-home finals ❏Flying ❏Erica Jong ❏The third rail ❏Halloween candy ❏Waking up to discover having been transformed into a large bug
IQ: ❏Goethe ❏Einstein ❏Mozart ❏Neil Armstrong ❏Sylvia Plath ❏Tree stump ❏Buddy Hackett ❏Loretta Lynn ❏Manhole cover
PERCEIVED BY OTHERS AS: ❏Surprisingly transparent ❏Complex at first, but turns out merely to be confused ❏Hangs paintings of puppies, kittens and children with large eyes on walls ❏Thoughtful, courteous, kind, obedient ❏Happy, Bashful, Doc, Grumpy
RELIGIOUS AFFILIATION: ❏Hopelessly Catholic ❏Apologetically Jewish ❏Lives in bus stations and asks for donations for world peace, social harmony, and a 56-foot yacht for the "perfect master" ❏Intolerant ❏Nebulous protestant sect member that dresses well and eats pastrami with mayonaise on raisin bread ❏Worships foam rubber and polyester

CLONE SEXUAL ORIENTATION:

IF MALE: ❏Violently chauvinistic ❏Sympathetic to the Movement until some "castrating bitch" takes away his job ❏Puts women on a pedestal ❏Hits women with pedestal ❏Resents being male ❏Wears women's clothes ❏Designs women's clothes
IF FEMALE: ❏Thinks men are responsible for violence, crime, pornography, and sunspot activity ❏Thinks that men are okay, but wouldn't let her daughter marry one ❏Resents being a woman ❏Enjoys menstruating, shaving her underarms, and wearing cosmetics
FOR BOTH SEXES: ❏Enjoys unusual sex involving stuffed geese and jackhammers ❏Only enjoys conventional sexual positions ❏Will never engage in sex and will become a politician or lawyer ❏Will become so passive that partner will hold mirror in front of face to see if still breathing ❏Will be so traumatized by first sexual experience that will join monastery or convent

DISCOUNT CLONES:

If unable to afford usual clone rates, select a "no-frill" clone, minus regular options. While slightly damaged, bargain clones remain covered by regular clone guarantees.
❏ #3453. The clone bottles were inadvertently dropped on the floor.
❏ #5649. The doctor was eating tuna fish while working on the clone.
❏ #6780. Okay, so who needs a fourteenth chromosome anyway?
❏ #6674. After some tricky recombinant DNA work, clone doubles as newly created incurable disease.

A cell sample may be obtained from any doctor or by sliding into home plate on a suicide squeeze. Clone will take from six to eight weeks, unless options (AM/ FM, teeth, whitewalls) are ordered. California orders may take longer. For all regular clones, please enclose a check for $2,075.00 made payable to CORNELL CLONE CENTER. *We must have your zip code to fill your order.*

UNAUTHORIZED CLONING IS A FEDERAL OFFENSE. Signed_____ **Date**_____

Classified

AND NOW... THE LAST SUICIDAL DUCK EVER!

THIS COMIC HAS BEEN DISCONTINUED

Blame Pages

Chapter 5
HIDDEN DANGERS

Chapter 6
WORLD PEACE AND MORE BEER

ACKNOWLEDGMENTS

The *Cornell Lunatic* is deeply indebted to all the individuals listed on these Blame Pages, who graciously granted their permission for their material to be reprinted in this collection. The Good Ship Lunatic is particularly grateful to the following editors-in-chief from years past: Steven Weinreb, Adam-Troy Castro, Jeffrey Seeman, Michael Kanelos, Lawrence Carrel, Fred Kittelmann, Taed Wynnell, Allan Rousselle, Jim McNulty, Dave Graham, Ernest Paik, Jon McMillan, Amanda Klein, Jedediah Teres, Jim Jazwiecki, Jordan Barry, Ken Schefler, Demian Caponi, Peter Haas, Matt Palmer, and Aaron Edelman. The Loon also sends out heartfelt thanks to Debbie Green, B.K. Taylor, Eric Gouvin, Michael Frawley, Jill Holtzman Leichter, Howard Halberstein, Tom McCormick, David Sandoval, William Kennedy, faculty advisor Isaac Kramnick, Bang Printing, Independent Publishers Group, and our team of astounding proofreaders: Lawrence Carrel, Adam-Troy Castro, Alan Corcoran, Joyce Hendley, Jon McMillan, J.T. Myers, Ernie Paik, and Allan Rousselle. And God bless you, Jerry Buttwater!